INERRANT
the WIND

INERRANT
the WIND

The Evangelical Crisis of Biblical Authority

Robert M. Price

Prometheus Books

59 John Glenn Drive
Amherst, New York 14228-2119

Published 2009 by Prometheus Books

Inquiries should be addressed to
Prometheus Books
59 John Glenn Drive
Amherst, New York 14228–2119
VOICE: 716–691–0133, ext. 210
FAX: 716–691–0137
WWW.PROMETHEUSBOOKS.COM

13 12 11 10 09   5 4 3 2 1

Library of Congress Cataloging-in-Publication Data

Price, Robert M., 1954–
    Inerrant the wind : the evangelical crisis of biblical authority / Robert M. Price.
        p. cm.
    Rev. of: The crisis of biblical authority. 1981 doctoral dissertation at Drew University.
    Includes bibliographical references and indexes.
    ISBN 978–1–59102–676–1 (hardcover)
    1. Bible—Evidences, authority, etc.—History of doctrines—20th century.
2. Bible—Inspiration—History of doctrines—20th century. 3. Evangelicalism—United States—History—20th century. I. Price, Robert M., 1954– Crisis of biblical authority. II. Title.

BS480.P757 2008
220.1—dc22

                                                                        2008030718

Printed in the United States on acid-free paper

CONTENTS

PREFACE

$\mathcal{T}$his book is dated. Except for slight modifications, it represents my 1981 doctoral dissertation (at Drew University), "The Crisis of Biblical Authority: The Setting and Range of the Current Evangelical Controversy." I have more than once looked it over to see what updating might be required. I was surprised to find that very little seemed to be in order. That is not because nothing new has happened since. Rather, it is because evangelical scholars who have not continued fighting the same old battles I describe here have moved on to other interesting questions (such as "Open Theism") or have launched out on the adventure of recreating evangelicalism on a whole new basis. More power to them. Dave Tomlinson's *The Post-Evangelical* (Triangle/S.P.C.K., 1995) and Gary Dorrien's *The Remaking of Evangelical Theology* (Westminster John Knox Press, 1998) are particularly interesting. But I have decided not to extend my analysis to include these developments, mainly because the book deals with a self-contained topic and period, a time of ferment and innovation that has led to some of these latter-day developments, some of which I predicted. But the book is not merely a period piece, because the books and thinkers I discussed still deserve and widely receive attention. People are still working their way through the same issues, and I hope this old book of mine may serve to aid them in their deliberations.

As I studied the work of the thinkers involved in the biblical authority debate, I discovered the obvious: many of them were equally engaged in adjacent discussions among evangelicals (old and new) on topics including the verifiability of supernatural involvement, not in ancient miracle stories, but in modern Christian conversions. Apologetics has similarly been inseparable from questions of inerrancy and

7

infallibility: Should these beliefs be put on the shelf while arguing from the gospels as (merely) more or less reliable sources for the historical Jesus? Is it possible to argue sincerely in such a fashion while committed to belief in the inerrant accuracy of such texts on prior dogmatic grounds? And then why not focus on the evangelical scholar who has pursued all these questions the most rigorously and in unpredictable directions? I mean Clark H. Pinnock, who figures so largely in the inerrancy debate. He has much more to say, and I felt it would enrich my readers' grasp of the issues, as well as of the evangelical theological agenda, if I were to append three other studies I undertook during the same period I was putting together the main portion of the book. I hope the main work and the appendices will shed light on each other; I am pretty sure they will, no matter in which order one chances to read them! One final note: those who kindly supplied blurbs for this book did not know about the appendices. I do not think they would object to anything in them, but, for the record, I shouldn't give the impression that they meant to endorse the appendices, too.

Robert M. Price
January 23, 2007

INTRODUCTION

THE SURPRISING RANGE OF OPTIONS

*C*onservative Protestantism in America has always wrestled with doctrinal controversies over issues ranging from predestination to the mode of baptism, from charismatic gifts to biblical prophecy. But probably none has threatened the American evangelical movement as much as the recent "battle for the Bible." It began, to all intents and purposes, with the 1976 publication of Southern Baptist Harold Lindsell's gossipy *The Battle for the Bible* and continued for years in the systematic purge of moderate seminary professors and administrators in the Southern Baptist Convention. And though the controversy began in Southern Baptist circles and has perhaps achieved its most violent eruption there in recent years, the struggle over the Bible has affected evangelical Christians and institutions of every stripe.

At stake in the recent crisis of biblical authority is the very epistemology that formed the basis for all the previous evangelical debates: Can the Bible be held as authoritative in such a way that the citation of any text (in context) will settle a question? "For up to the present time any text from any part of the Bible was accepted as a proof-text for the establishment of Christian teaching, and a statement from the Bible was considered an end to the controversy."[1] Now some evangelicals have doubted (loudly and publicly) that biblical authority operates in precisely this way. This issue, besides being exceptionally thorny in a conceptual way, is perceived as particularly volatile since it raises the ghost of the "fundamentalist-modernist controversy" of an earlier generation. Those who believe in biblical inerrancy fear that the non-inerrantists are, potentially or actually, following in the footsteps of the old modernists. Non-inerrantists repudiate this claim, yet they must take it seriously for fear that the evangelical movement at large will believe it. If they do, the non-inerrantists will find themselves alienated from the evangelical mainstream, or even forced out altogether.

The difference of opinion here is commonly represented as if one side believed in "inerrancy" and the other did not. The latter either, negatively, believed in "errancy" (as the inerrantists charge), or, positively, protested that "inerrancy" was simply an inappropriate category, or that it needed to be "nuanced" or "limited." But in fact there is much more diversity here than is usually recognized by either side in the debate. The main body of the present study will sort out the various non-inerrantist approaches to biblical authority, inspiration, and hermeneutics. There are at least five distinct viewpoints, or at least distinct emphases, each of which, pursued consistently, would compel a different redefinition of biblical authority. In each case, there are surprising parallels to various mainstream Protestant or even Catholic views previously found to be unacceptable by evangelicals. The study will begin with chapter 1's discussion of the claims of Harold Lindsell, Francis A. Schaeffer, and other inerrantists, that a new fundamentalist-modernist controversy was on the horizon, if not already breaking. Contemporary developments on the evangelical scene will be reviewed in order to evaluate the inerrantists' claims. Do such developments parallel those of the original "controversy"? Chapter 2 offers a survey of doctrinal developments in the neo-evangelical period (late 1940s through 1960s), vis-à-vis biblical inspiration and inerrancy. This should help fill in the background for a consideration of the ongoing crisis. Chapter 3 commences a more detailed summary and analysis of the several non-inerrancy viewpoints. These will be shown to lead logically into one another. Chapter 3 deals with attempts to "limit inerrancy" only to certain kinds of matters, or only to "assertions," so as to allow for simple factual inaccuracies. Chapter 4 goes on to describe the "partial infallibility" position of those who recognize not only factual errors, but also theological contradictions in scripture. They respond by taking as normative a "central message," or lowest common denominator, in the Bible. Chapter 5 concerns those exegetes who find very little agreement among the biblical writers. They find any common denominator of biblical teaching to be *so* low, that they try to locate normativeness precisely in the main, pluriform, body of the text. Chapter 6 analyzes the position of those who apply the biblical text, in all its own variety, to a wide variety of cultures and worldviews today, an effort that comes to involve greater relativization of biblical thought-models than has been traditional among evangelicals. Chapter 7 addresses itself to those evangelicals who fear the theological relativity and/or pluralism implied by the previous two approaches. To escape the effects of both criticism and hermeneutical pluralism, these evangelicals have sought asylum in ecclesiastical authority, rather than in *sola Scriptura*. The conclusion will present some suggestions as to the ultimate direction of noninerrantist thinking.

The present work will attempt, in short, to mediate (or at least referee!) the recent evangelical debate over the authority of the Bible. Because of the polemical, one might even say propagandistic, nature of most of the relevant literature, it is often far from clear to the antagonists themselves just where the various parties stand. Inerrantists try to portray non-inerrantists as prodigals headed down the path to perdition, so it is to their interest to paint non-inerrantists with a single broad stroke. Whatever variety there may be seems irrelevant. After all, what does it matter whether it was strychnine or arsenic that the suicide drank? On the other hand, non-inerrantists would dearly love to persuade the evangelical public that there is little real disagreement at stake, so as to avert suspicion. As a matter of fact, however, the changes being navigated in the non-inerrantists' understanding of the Bible are much more complex and farther-reaching than anyone in the discussion seems to realize, including the non-inerrantists themselves.

NOTE

1. Dyson Hague, "The History of the Higher Criticism," in *The Fundamentals*, 4 vols., ed. R. A. Torrey and A. C. Dixon (Grand Rapids: Baker Book House, 1980), 1:32–33.

Chapter 1

TROUBLING THE HOUSE

A New Fundamentalist-Modernist Controversy?

THE BATTLE LINES

$\mathcal{E}$vangelical Christians have never stopped waging a "battle for the Bible" against some enemy or other. Anyone familiar with the vast polemical and apologetical literature of the evangelical or fundamentalist movement will recall endless rehearsals of how the Bible is to be defended against the attacks of the infidel. The identity of the villain might change with the times. The apologist might find him- or herself squaring off in the ring of faith against Liberal "Higher Critics," or militant out-and-out agnostics (often, one suspects, disenchanted fundamentalists themselves), or well-meaning but confused doubters whom one hoped to win for Christ, or even the ghosts of eighteenth-century Rationalists like Paulus, Venturini, and Reimarus. But in every case, it was clear who was wearing the black trunks. The defenders of the faith, conversely, could almost always be spotted by their swift punches of rhetoric and the fancy footwork of their biblical harmonization.

But in recent years, it has become a little more difficult for most Bible-believing, born-again Christians to determine just whom to root for. Both contestants in the latest round of the "bout for the Bible"[1] seem to be wearing white trunks! Both parties to the contest sincerely claim to be evangelicals. Tensions had been brewing for quite a while among evangelical biblical scholars and theologians over the question of biblical inerrancy. In June of 1966, Harold John Ockenga convened a conference on this issue at Gordon College in Wenham, Massachusetts, hoping to iron out the differences between those who believed that the inspiration of the Bible implied its "total inerrancy," and those who did not. Apparently, Ockenga hoped to iron things out in the direction of inerrancy, but no unanimity of any kind was forthcoming. The papers presented at the Wenham Conference were never published, and no public controversy ensued until 1976, with the publication of Harold Lindsell's *The Battle for the Bible*. Neither the arguments for inerrancy nor the catchy title phrase were original. The former represented the stock polemics and harmonizations of old-time fundamentalism, while the latter had cropped up already in Clark H. Pinnock's 1971 volume *Biblical Revelation: The Foundation of Christian Theology* ("The battle for the plenary inspiration of the Bible is part of the larger struggle for authentic biblical religion.")[2] But whereas Pinnock's work was an articulate critique of mainstream Liberal theologians, Lindsell's book was a frontal attack on scholars and institutions that most people would have placed squarely in the evangelical camp. And therein lay the explosive quality of the book. Fuller Theological Seminary and other defendants did not take kindly to such accusations. Soon, professors at Lindsell's own school, Gordon-Conwell Theological Seminary (where he was chairman of the board), came under suspicion for dangerously nuancing their doctrine of inerrancy.

In the war thus declared by Harold Lindsell, ink flew at least as thickly as prayers among the divided hosts of evangelicalism. Inerrantists charged their opponents with affirming biblical "errancy." Harold Lindsell claimed they were "embracing a doctrine of an errant scripture" and admitted condescendingly, "No doubt a case for errancy can be made in such a way that the unlearned and unsophisticated will fall for it."[3] Similarly, in "the inerrancy/errancy controversy," Carl F. H.

Henry assumed that his opponents actually "affirm[ed] biblical errancy."[4] Charles Caldwell Ryrie of Dallas Theological Seminary asked rhetorically, "But why say 'limited inerrancy'? Why not 'limited errancy'? If the Bible has limitations on its inerrancy, then obviously it is errant, though not completely so. So limited inerrancy and limited errancy amount to the same thing. But why do the proponents of limited inerrancy not want to use the equivalent label 'limited errancy'? . . . Intentional or not, it is a semantic game played to help cover up a dangerously deceptive view."[5]

The objects of these attacks denied that they were proposing a "doctrine of errancy," claiming instead that "inerrancy" as defined by the conservatives was simply not an appropriate category to apply to the biblical text. J. Ramsey Michaels of Gordon-Conwell Theological Seminary pleaded, "The point is that the term *inerrancy* (or *errancy* for that matter) is simply not applicable to much that is in scripture."[6] Sidney Greidanus agreed: "It is illegitimate . . . to impose on these writings standards which proceed from a modern, western mentality, whether that be the positivistic ideal or an unbiblically defined concept of inerrancy."[7] "Infallibility" might be a better term, they pleaded. But inerrantists were not convinced (not "fooled," they might say). After all, mustn't we imagine that some of the trickier Ephraimites hastily suggested a different password at the ford of the Jordan, when required to pronounce "Shibboleth"?

Doubtless the most painful accusation (both to make and to take) arising from the new dispute was that non-inerrantists or revisionist inerrantists were, however slowly, surely slipping down the slope to apostasy (or to Liberal theology, which was perceived as the same thing). In fact, the analogy was explicitly drawn with the famous "fundamentalist-modernist controversy" of the 1880s and 1930s. The inerrantists painted their foes as insidious wolves-in-sheep's-clothing, as they had mythologized modernists like Harry Emerson Fosdick and Charles Francis Potter. Lindsell minced no words concerning the significance of the new controversy as he saw it:

> In the United States . . . the real struggle [for biblical inerrancy] was
> fought in three periods of recent history. The first real battle started
> in the 1880's and the chief protagonists were Warfield, Hodge,
> Briggs, and Smith. The second battle was fought during the 1930's
> and the name that stands above all others is that of J. Gresham
> Machen. The third battle is the one being fought right now.[8]

This, of course, is the "battle for the Bible" in which Lindsell himself
is a principal combatant. Of his opponents, he remarks: "It is among
this new group of evangelicals that an incursion of disbelief in
inerrancy has come just as in [Charles Augustus] Briggs' day. . . . All
they are doing is repeating history."[9]

How did the non-inerrantists react to such charges? It will come as
no surprise to learn that responses varied. In general, one receives the
impression that non-inerrantists objected to being cast in the role of
the villains in a replay of that primordial theological struggle, the saga
of which was part of their own lore. Clark H. Pinnock writes with dis-
cernible discomfort:

> What seems so unfortunate about the "inerrancy debate" today . . . is
> that it has to be taking place between evangelical scholars, pitting [them-
> selves] against one another, rather than between the whole evangelical
> coalition and those who are *bona fide* opponents of biblical authority
> such as Barr, Nineham or Evans. . . . What sense is there in leveling our
> critical guns at our allies when so many worthy targets exist?[10]

Along the same lines, Ben Patterson, in his *Wittenburg Door* editorial "The Battle for the Tent," compared inquisitor Lindsell with a
young camper waking up in the tent, needing to "go," but afraid of the
imaginary terrors outside the tent. Pain finally overcame fear, and the
boy stumbled over his tentmates in the dark until (he thought) he
found the tent flap. He didn't, however, and merely wound up
relieving himself all over his tent mates' sleeping bags.

The tent is evangelicalism, and the monster lurking outside in the shadows is Liberalism. Threatened and confused, [strict inerrantists] are anxious to conduct a purge of the tent, lest this monster have any confederates among them. The problem is, all they seem to be doing is clearing the tent of everyone but themselves. . . . It's dark outside and Lindsell has to go.[11]

Most seemed to discount the validity of the charges, but they had to take them seriously for fear that the evangelical community at large might be persuaded. In this case, the non-inerrantists might find themselves in need of a new ecclesiastical home.

On the one hand, Stephen T. Davis represented those repudiating the idea of a new fundamentalist-modernist controversy:

I believe that [Lindsell's] divisive inerrancy [view] is a doctrine that is being pushed on us by an older generation of evangelicals. Inerrancy is a doctrine whose attractiveness we can perhaps understand in the context of the battles these people [for example, Lindsell, Carl F. H. Henry, Ockenga] once had to fight against modernism, but I feel no need to fight these battles again.[12]

On the other hand, Richard J. Coleman seems to accept the historical parallel:

Surprisingly enough the discussion of Biblical inerrancy swirls around us with almost the same ferocity as in the 1880's and the 1930's. . . . Well fought issues do not die easily and such is the case with the inter-relationship between scriptural inerrancy and its inspiration. The difficulties faced by Warfield and Machen in defending a strict view of inerrancy are still with us, if not more intensely, and thus the proponents of some kind of limited inspiration are still with us.[13]

Coleman himself falls into the latter category. However, as he goes on in the same article to show, he appears to hope that his attempt to reconcile the issues he mentions can avert a new fundamentalist-modernist battle.

Finally, Clark H. Pinnock (who has modified his theological position, as well as his polemical stance, since his *Biblical Revelation* mentioned above) is most worried about the destructive potential of Lindsell's analysis as a self-fulfilling prophecy. "The evangelical movement could easily divide into two camps over this question: a defensive fundamentalism armed with a slogan and a neo-liberalism stumbling ahead into more and more biblical denial."[14] Pinnock hopes that there may yet be time for a peaceful settlement of differences before mere "rumors of war" escalate into the real thing.

PREPARING FOR BATTLE

The inerrantists' perception of a new fundamentalist-modernist controversy has not been restricted in expression to mere verbal polemics. Lindsell and company have moved quickly to back up their words with action. And their actions, whether wittingly or not, turn out to recapitulate almost exactly those of the original controversy. This interesting parallel appears to have gone largely unnoticed in recent studies of the "battle for the Bible," so it will be worthwhile briefly to survey these developments here. The first of a number of striking parallels presents itself in the founding in 1977 of the International Council on Biblical Inerrancy (ICBI) by Lindsell, Francis A. Schaeffer, Ockenga, J. I. Packer, Bill Bright of Campus Crusade for Christ, James Montgomery Boice, Norman L. Geisler, Jay Grimstead, and several other prominent inerrantists representing the leadership of various segments of the evangelical/fundamentalist community. A mimeographed paper prepared for one of the early organizational and planning conferences set forth ICBI's purpose in these terms: "To take a united stand in elucidating, vindicating and applying the doctrine of Biblical inerrancy as an essential element for the authority of scripture and a necessity for the health of the Church of God, and to attempt to win the Church back to this historic position."[15] In a subsequent publicity pamphlet the purpose is repeated in almost identical words, with the following addition:

"This will be done in both academic theology and practical Christian instruction and it will require a sustained effort over an initial period of ten years."[16]

Students of the history of fundamentalism will instantly recognize what looks like the "second coming" of the old "World's Christian Fundamentals Association" (WCFA), a quasi-denominational structure founded by fundamentalists in 1919 to combine their disparate forces and facilitate the crusade against modernism. The latter-day ICBI parallels its forebear not only in general purpose, but also in several specifics. The members of the WCFA sought to "purge their denominations of heretics."[17] Sentiment for such action surfaced early in the planning of the ICBI, when J. Barton Payne urged "alerting evangelical organizations that hold to inerrancy, of the deviations of some of their members" and "alerting those that do not, of the need to include such in their ordination vows or employment contracts."[18] The WCFA "encouraged conservatives to apply pressure upon educational institutions to produce theologically safe graduates."[19] The strategy here was to organize a group of Bible schools with a mandatory creed of adherence to inerrancy and other "fundamentals." Ernest R. Sandeen compares the envisioned result to an "agency of Christian accreditation."[20] Similarly, in 1978, the ICBI sent out feelers to a number of seminary professors concerning the feasibility of a proposed "Coalition of Inerrancy Seminaries," all of which would adopt a mandatory inerrancy loyalty oath, thus separating the wheat from the tares. (No such framework ever emerged.)

But not everyone attends seminary or Bible school, even among evangelicals. So the need was felt to spread the inerrancy gospel to the masses of lay folk lest they be abandoned and blown about by every wind of doctrine. Accordingly, the WCFA undertook one hundred local conferences on "Christian fundamentals" in both the United States and Canada.[21] Again echoing its predecessor, the new ICBI planned a series of traveling, standardized seminars to educate laypeople as to the truth of inerrancy and the dangers of compromise. Many were eventually conducted around the country. Incidentally, an interesting irony may occur to the reader, and one can only wonder if it ever occurred to the ICBI strategists: Might not such an operation actually be counter-productive, informing isolated and hitherto blissfully ignorant evangel-icals that there are other available options besides strict inerrancy? It's hard enough keeping 'em down on the farm after they've seen Paree; is it wise to try to warn 'em not to stray in the first place by giving 'em a slide show depicting the sinful amusements to be found in Paree? Per-haps the best-remembered stratagem of the WCFA was its remarkably ambitious publishing program, which sought to supplement the educa-tion of the masses by better educating their Sunday School teachers and pastors. This plan saw its fulfillment in the production and distribution of the many volumes of *The Fundamentals*, edited by A.C. Dixon, Louis Meyer, and R.A. Torrey, paid for by Lyman and Milton Stewart. These volumes were admittedly partisan propaganda, though this did not prevent the contributors from manifesting a high caliber of scholar-ship (or, in some cases, at least articulateness). These works remain one of the principle sources for any historical understanding of the funda-mentalist movement. They cover nearly the whole range of controver-sial issues, including Christ's virgin birth and divine nature, the atone-ment, biblical inerrancy, and the impropriety of higher criticism. Despite various differences, Princeton Calvinists, Dispensational Mil-lenarians, and other inerrantists realized the necessity of a united front against modernism.

Less impressive, and in the long run less significant, is the parallel publishing program of the ICBI. They expressed their concern to indoctrinate the laity by preparing volumes including *The Foundation of Biblical Authority* (edited by James Montgomery Boice), *Can We Trust the Bible?* (edited by Earl Radmacher), *Does Inerrancy Matter?* (written by Boice), and *Inerrancy* (edited by Norman Geisler). On the whole, these books are disappointing in their monotonous rehashing of standard inerrancy apologetics. Since the only possible readership for the books was the usual group of seminarians and pastors already steeped in these arguments, it is hard to see the point of publishing them. Better just to reprint Warfield. In fact, the prime significance of these books would seem to be the parallel they help to complete between the 1970s scenario and that of the original fundamentalist-modernist controversy.

To finish this sketch of the parallels between the WCFA and the ICBI, brief attention should be paid to the attempts of both organizations to produce a creedal affirmation as a battle standard to rally inerrantists. Though debate rages on among Ernest Sandeen, George M. Marsden, and others over the official status and origin of the famous "Five Points of Fundamentalism," it is at least clear that the World's Christian Fundamentals Association formulated an official nine-point creed affirming many of the familiar "fundamentals," including of course the verbal inspiration and inerrancy of the Bible. Likewise, the International Council on Biblical Inerrancy called a summit conference in October 1978, which issued the "Chicago Statement on Biblical Inerrancy." The principle result of this document was to provide a target for non-inerrantists who had little difficulty in pinpointing certain fatal ambiguities and contradictions in it. The manifesto may have lacked an impact broader than this because of the pitfall Paul had (inerrantly) warned of long before: "If the trumpet does not sound a clear call, who will get ready for battle?" The clarity of the Chicago Statement is blurred by the startling juxtaposition of two seemingly contradictory viewpoints. Article XII of the document says, "We deny that Biblical infallibility and inerrancy are limited to spiritual, religious, or redemptive themes, exclusive of assertions in the fields of history and science." This seems clear enough, yet what is the hopeful reader to understand when he or she comes to the very next article? In Article XIII (and in interpretative paragraphs 5 and 6 under the heading "Infallibility, Inerrancy, Interpretation") the signatories announce that we ought to expect in the Bible "non-chronological narration and imprecise citation" of Old Testament texts by New Testament writers, "phenomenal descriptions of nature," "lack of modern technical precision," "the use of hyperbole and round numbers," "variant selections of material in parallel accounts" of the same events, and so on. Instead, "inerrancy" is supposed to concern only the "focused truth at which [the] authors aimed." Obviously, Article XIII sounds remarkably like the non-inerrantist (or limited inerrantist) position it purports to challenge. Clark Pinnock has noted that such confusing ambiguity occurs in so much inerrantist literature that inerrantist polemicists often wind up condemning non-inerrantists who hold virtually their own position minus the slogan.[22]

What accounts for the curious ambivalence whereby "inerrantists" Francis A. Schaeffer and J. I. Packer can stand shoulder-to-shoulder even though Packer allows that inerrancy need not forbid the interpreter to take Adam and Eve as allegorical ciphers, and Schaeffer demands that Genesis chapters 1–11 be taken literally lest biblical authority collapse?[23] Catholic historical theologian James T. Burtchaell noticed the same sort of apparent double standard in the polemical works of Catholic inerrantists and "content-inspirationists" in the nineteenth century. Under the same rubric, Joannes Baptista Franzelin (*Tractatus de Divina Traditione et Scriptura*, 1875) had taken a more conservative position, while Joannes Perrone (*Praelectiones Theologiae*, 1835–42) had been more adventurous in clearing room for biblical errors.[24]

Why would the strict inerrantist condemn a less conservative opponent while making most of the same factual concessions? The answer is that the inconsistency appears only in the perspective of theological belief, whereas there is no problem at all if one's focus is on apologetical strategy. For the fact is that while some of the same concessions are made by inerrantists and non-inerrantists, the former make them in order to appease and satisfy biblical criticism at an early, comparatively "safe" stage; the latter use them as wedges to open the theological door ever wider to criticism. Inerrantists seek to persuade the doubter that he can deny the literal factuality of Adam and Eve if he will but refrain from touching the ark again, as if the two were compatible. The non-inerrantist means it to be understood that if Adam and Eve must be taken other than literally, then so must a good deal else. Incidentally, the WCFA did not hesitate to include Darwin's theory of evolution among its targets, and neither does today's ICBI. Though this issue has not loomed as a major issue (at least not in explicit terms) on the agenda of the ICBI, neither has it been ignored. For instance, the *ICBI Update* newsletter for Fall 1979 announces a "Lay Seminar" scheduled for San Diego. On the schedule is Duane T. Gish, associate director of the Institute for Creation Research, who is slated to speak on "The Bible and Science." Actually Gish is a traveling debater and lecturer opposing Darwinism in behalf of Six-Day Creationism and the Flood of Noah.

These observations lead us to pass from the more general warnings and preparations for war by the inerrantist party, to the more specific dimensions of the new fundamentalist-modernist controversy they anticipate. So far, the reader might find himself wondering if the gathering storm is not after all a product of the inerrantists' own fears. Is this new controversy merely a self-fulfilling prophecy, like the Salem witch craze, generated out of thin air by the fears of zealots? Or is there really something out there to fear? The answer will become clearer with a survey of the major questions debated in the fundamentalist-modernist battle. Just what was at issue in the dispute of the 1880s and 1930s? Isolating specific points of division, it will become possible to determine whether today's crusading inerrantists are merely shadow boxing, or if they are really facing challengers, that is, evangelicals who actually hold positions analogous to those taken by the old modernists. The issues of the fundamentalist-modernist controversy, at least in the contemporary fundamentalist mind, fall into three basic categories: the theory of evolution, the Social Gospel, and higher criticism. Obviously, all three are related, yet they represent distinct emphases. The present discussion will deal only briefly with the first two questions, reserving the bulk of attention for the third, which bears most directly on the subject of biblical inerrancy.

To anticipate the discussion, and to make clear its direction, let it be noted at the outset that a reduplication of these three modernist emphases would indicate that Lindsell's claim is justified. If there became evident among evangelicals a movement toward the left in these three directions (evolution, the Social Gospel, biblical criticism), it would be fair to say that the fundamentalist-modernist controversy had been "born again" in the present day. This conclusion would be strengthened all the more if it became apparent that yesterday's controversy had been, like the present one, an "in-house" struggle between fellow evangelicals.

THE THEORY OF EVOLUTION

To the American public at large, probably the central image of the fundamentalist-modernist controversy was (and still is) the courtroom battle between fundamentalist politician William Jennings Bryan and agnostic lawyer Clarence Darrow, technically over the fate of nondescript high school teacher John Scopes, but actually over the validity and legality of Darwinism. In fact, one suspects that most people would have forgotten even this incident had it not been immortalized by being embalmed in celluloid, in the movie version of Jerome Lawrence and Robert E. Lee's *Inherit the Wind*, which surfaces now and again in television syndication. So, many Americans (scientists more than anyone else) were shocked to learn of a new legal offensive by "Scientific Creationists."

In Bryan's day, the legal and political goal of fundamentalist opponents of evolution was to keep the teaching of Darwin's theory out of public schools. The taxes of Bible-believing parents went to support the public schools, so shouldn't they have the right to protect their impressionable children from having to learn this God-denying propaganda? Bryan wrote, in a pamphlet called *The Modern Arena*: "Why should Christian taxpayers permit the Bible to be attacked by their hired servants where defense is not permitted? Why should the children be taught that it is more important to know the age of rocks than to trust in the 'Rock of Ages'?"[25] As everyone knows, this battle was lost; every single anti-Darwin law was repealed, declared unconstitutional. So today, the tactics of creationists must be different, but basically the goal and the presuppositions are the same. Now creationists demand "equal time" for their belief, which is dressed up as an alternative scientific theory of origins deserving of (compulsory) inclusion in any (in fact, every) biology curriculum. Bills to this effect have thus far been defeated in at least fourteen state legislatures.[26] In the first round of the fight against Darwin, fundamentalists organized themselves into several groups, some of which posed as pure research agencies. They had names like "The Anti-Evolution League of America," "The Bryan Bible League," "The Research Science Bureau," and "The American Science Foundation."[27] Their counterparts bear the names "The Creation-Research Society," "The Institute for Creation-Research," and "The Bible Science Association."

Just why have fundamentalists so vehemently opposed evolution? Besides the obvious fact that the inerrant creation account in Genesis left no room for a gradual evolution of life-forms, there seem to have been two important reasons. First, there is the fear that acceptance of the theory will destroy public morality. If people become convinced that they are no more than animals, they can be expected to act like animals. For this reason, William Jennings Bryan branded Darwin's theory "a menace to . . . society and to civilization."[28] Contemporary creationists Boardman, Koontz, and Morris agree. "As far as individual relationships are concerned, since man is really only a highly evolved animal [or so say evolutionists], it is psychologically healthy for men to live like animals." Again, "It is important to recognize the fact that racism in its virulent forms is mainly a product of evolutionary thinking."[29] The second reason for antipathy toward evolution lies in the theological compromise thought to be implied in a favorable estimation of the theory. George McCready Price, the Seventh-Day Adventist who formulated fundamentalist "flood geology," warned believers not to tamper with the literalist understanding of Genesis: "No Adam, no fall; no fall, no atonement; no atonement, no Savior. Accepting Evolution, how can we believe in a fall?"[30] Bryan echoed the warning: "Evolution, theistic and atheistic, carried to its logical conclusion, robs Christ of the glory of a virgin birth, of the majesty of His deity, and of the triumph of His resurrection."[31]

Actually, this distinctly theological disdain for evolution tended to place fundamentalists like Price and Bryan in a logically embarrassing position. What they feared such biblical and doctrinal compromise would lead to was the modernist theology of their day, with its overoptimistic dream of building God's Kingdom on earth by human effort. Thus by espousing both the general moral argument *and* the specifically theological argument, the polemicists were simultaneously claiming that evolution must result in both an overly low *and* an overly high estimate of human potential, that is, as a depraved beast *and* as a utopian godling. Among modern creationists and inerrantists, there may be heard the same sort of warnings not to compromise biblical authority by accommodating it to evolutionary biology. The statements of Price and Bryan quoted above are frequently paralleled by Duane T. Gish, Francis A. Schaeffer, and others. Gish warns ominously:

> The direction in which one's thinking is influenced by his views of the early chapters of Genesis also strongly influences one's views of other scriptures. Those who reinterpret Genesis in order to reconcile it with evolutionary doctrine, often reinterpret other portions of scripture dealing with natural phenomena. Belief in the virgin birth of Christ is readily abandoned, and certain supernatural events, such as Christ's changing water into wine and his raising Lazarus from the dead, may be no longer considered literal events. . . . This logical chain of events in the interpretation of scripture culminates in the abandonment of the blood atonement of Christ. There remains no real Christian gospel.[32]

Francis A. Schaeffer agrees, and in almost the same words:

> Consequently, what is involved here . . . is not just the first chapters of Genesis but the authoritativeness of the New Testament as well, and especially the writings of Paul. If Paul is wrong in [his] factual statement about Eve's coming from Adam [1 Corinthians 11:8], there is no reason to have certainty in the authority of any New Testament factual statement, including the factual statement that Christ

rose physically from the dead. If we say this factual statement about Eve was culturally oriented, then every factual statement of the New Testament can be said to be culturally oriented; and any or all the factual statements of the New Testament can be dealt with arbitrarily and subjectively.[33]

But in today's anti-Darwin crusade, despite these warnings, there really do not seem to be any particularly modernist villains in view. Instead, the usual target is "Humanism," characterized as a conspiratorial and ubiquitous atheistic antireligion. Sometimes, it is true, "Liberal theology" is implicated here, but so far evolutionist evangelicals have borne relatively little of the brunt. And there are plenty of them, easily enough to make a manageable target if inerrantists were so inclined. The American Scientific Affiliation is composed largely of theistic evolutionists in the evangelical ranks. Perhaps such evangelical scholars (e.g., Bernard Ramm, David S. Willis) receive comparatively lenient treatment because their manner of relating evolution and the Genesis creation accounts is neither uniform nor clearly opposed to literalism. At least some evangelical evolutionists claim that Six-Day Creationism is to be challenged precisely on the basis of a literalistic exegesis of the text! They may argue that the words translated as "day" and "create" are unclear as to precise meaning, and may well allow for "day" periods of innumerable years and for the operation of secondary causes.[34] It is hard for Six-Day Creationists to respond to this, since they claim precisely the same latitude in interpreting the word "kinds" (of animals) to allow for microevolution within species, which even they can no longer deny.

By and large, creationists seem to limit their attack on evolutionist evangelicals to impugning their scholarly integrity vis-à-vis science, not the Bible. This they must do in order to explain away the disturbing anomaly of Bible-believing evolutionists. These latter seemingly should not exist if evolution is, as creationists claim, only accepted in defiance of scientific evidence as a last ditch expedient by atheists and humanists who must evade repentance at any cost. Theistic evolutionists would not seem to have such an antireligious axe to grind. Instead, creationists charge, they are, like Joseph of Arimathea, disciples of Jesus in secret, for fear of their colleagues. They love the praise of men more than that of God and so bow the knee to Darwin. But it is seldom claimed that they have bowed the knee to Bultmann or Schleiermacher. So the parallel between the antievolution crusades of yesterday and today, though strikingly close, is not completely exact. It would have to be admitted that, yes, the fundamentalist-modernist controversy vis-à-vis evolution *is* being largely reenacted in the present day, but not in the precise sense implied by Lindsell's claims. The unbelievers involved here are "secular humanists" but not (or at least seldom) non-inerrantist evangelicals.

THE SOCIAL GOSPEL

Biblical inerrancy did come into play in the controversy over evolution but it was not as obviously important in the second major issue at stake in the fundamentalist-modernist controversy, namely, the Social Gospel. Here, a repetition of the original movement toward modernism will denote not primarily "declension" from biblical inerrancy. Rather, it will simply fill out the picture of a general leftward shift (paralleling that of the original fundamentalist-modernist controversy) of which the Social Gospel and the denial of inerrancy are alike symptomatic. As will become evident shortly, the parallel does hold good, since there were indeed some rather obvious and important targets among contemporary evangelicals if Lindsell and the inerrantists had only looked for them. But oddly, they did not.

As is only too well known, the original fundamentalists loudly repudiated the Social Gospel. Writing in volume 3 of *The Fundamentals*, George W. Lasher makes his objections plain:

The most glaring and fatal mistake in the religious world today is the effort to reform men and reform society by making reformation a substitute for regeneration. . . . [In fact] a fatal mistake is in the notion that the elevation of society, the eliminating of its miseries, is conducive to a religious life and promotive of Christianity. Perhaps the greatest hindrances to the conquest sought by Christianity today . . . are the various agencies intended to reform society.[35]

Princeton theologian Charles R. Erdman, in volume 4 of the same series, hotly repudiated the suggestion that Jesus might be invoked in favor of socialism or the redistribution of wealth. "As to Jesus Christ, it is impossible to identify Him with any social theory or political party. His teachings . . . do not deal with the questions of political economy. . . . The fundamental economic problem relates to the division of wealth; and to that Christ refused to speak."[36]

This repudiation of the Social Gospel was sometimes based on the Social Gospel's supposed destructive effects on evangelism. Sometimes fundamentalists resented the diversion of time and energy away from domestic and foreign evangelism, and into ill-advised efforts at systemic social reforms. Shouldn't one try to rescue eternal souls instead of perishable bodies if the choice had to be made? And it did have to be made, since the world was about to end, at least according to the dispensationalist wing of fundamentalism. Evangelist Dwight L. Moody summed up this philosophy: "I look on this world as a wrecked vessel. God has given me a life-boat, and said to me, 'Moody, save all you can.'"[37] But of course this was hardly the only important segment of the fundamentalist movement. A number of other streams feeding into the coalition had long been enthusiastic in efforts at social reform.[38] The real problem with the Social Gospel was that it was predicated upon the modernist theological assumptions of evolutionary historical optimism (human agents could establish the Kingdom of God in history) and universalism (all people would be saved, or at least the criterion for salvation had less to do with religious orthodoxy than with social compassion).[39] However sympathetic fundamentalists might once have been (or might still be) to the plight of the poor and oppressed, they could never join in religious social reform on such a platform. "How can two walk together, except they be agreed?" (Amos 3:3) It is important to realize that the Social Gospel was not purely and simply a creation of full-blown modernism. The pioneer of the Social Gospel was Walter Rauschenbusch, a Baptist who never sought to deny his evangelical training. While sensing the need to transcend it, he did not think to leave it behind. In a famous quote, Rauschenbusch declared that

> salvation of the individual is, of course an essential part of salvation. Therefore our discussion cannot pass personal salvation by. We might possibly begin where the old gospel leaves off, and ask our readers to take all the familiar experiences and truths of personal evangelism and religious nurture for granted in what follows. But our understanding of personal salvation itself is deeply affected by the new solidaristic comprehension furnished by the social gospel.[40]

Precisely how was it affected? If Rauschenbusch had endeavored merely to suggest that personal salvation, once settled, should be followed by social involvement understood in terms of sanctification (mandatory, but distinct from salvation), it is hard to see how anyone could object. Had not the postmillennialist and holiness advocates said as much? Albert Barnes had made precisely this link between sanctification and reform in 1841:

> One sin is interlocked with others and is sustained by others. . . . The only power in the universe which can meet and overcome such combined evil is the power of the Spirit of God. There are evils of alliance and confederation in every city which can never be met but by a general revival of religion.[41]

William Arthur (writing in 1880) saw the same natural connection:

> Nothing short of the general renewal of society ought to satisfy any soldier of Christ. . . . Much as Satan glories in his power over an individual, how much greater must be his glorying over a nation

embodying, in its laws and usages, disobedience to God, wrong to man, and contamination to morals? To destroy all national holds of evil; to root sin out of institutions; to hold up to view the gospel ideal of a righteous nation [is the duty of sanctified Christians].[42]

The trouble was that Rauschenbusch had waved a red flag by in effect compromising the "finished work" of the atonement. "If we consent to the working principles of the Kingdom of Evil, and do not counteract it with all our strength, but perhaps even fail to see its ruinous evil, then we are part of it and the salvation of Christ has not yet set us free."[43] The issue of an individual's salvation, then, is not settled "once-for-all" by an act of faith in Jesus Christ as personal Lord and Savior, but more generally depends on one's faithful involvement in social causes. Fundamentalists could not help but see here a movement toward a doctrine of "salvation by faith plus works." And it could then be no great distance to the position that any particular decision for religious faith was not as important to salvation as was social involvement. What does come as a bit of a surprise is that today's conservatives have not reacted with similar alarm at the analogous theological shifts being navigated by some rather prominent "Young evangelicals," most notably the influential Sojourners Community. Jim Wallis, founding leader of the group and editor of *Sojourners* magazine, contributed a revealing article entitled "What is Conversion?" to the May 1978 issue. In it he candidly admits:

The thing that is most new about the new evangelicals or young evangelicals, as they have been labeled, is the belief that a concern for justice is central to evangelical faith. However, the more that concern for justice is emphasized, the more the former evangelical identity, which centered on a sole concern for individual salvation, becomes blurred.[44]

That Wallis is moving in pretty much the same direction as that marked out by Rauschenbusch for the Social Gospel, is evident from his own definition of conversion (or redefinition, from any traditional evangelical standpoint): "To convert means far more than to experience the psychological, emotional aspects of change through an inner experience. The biblical accent is clearly on a reversal of direction, a transfer of loyalties, a change in commitment leading to the creation of a new community." Converts may count on experiencing "a change in all their relationships, including their relationship to the world, to their possessions, to the poor and dispossessed, to the violence in their society, to the idols of their culture, and to the false worship of the state." Indeed, it is not going too far in Wallis's judgment to require a specific ideological agenda for salvation. "The meaning of conversion to Jesus Christ in our time must be intimately connected to the mad momentum of the nuclear arms race."[45]

Like Rauschenbusch (and, needless to say, his more radical fellows), Wallis has so broadened the question of salvation that it is no longer clear that a "decision for Christ" could settle the issue for an individual. And the path that led Wallis to this destination seems to be the same one traveled years before by Rauschenbusch and company, namely, the extension of the concepts of "sin" and the "demonic" to include not only the plight (and salvation) of the individual, but also that of society collectively. Whereas Rauschenbusch spoke of "large-scale sins" and "super-personal forces of evil," Wallis now writes of "Principalities and Powers," but both alike tend toward an environmentalist conception of sin, and of course, redemption.

Wallis has already been quoted as to the visible blurring of evangelical identity among his compatriots. In the same issue, Wes Michaelson elaborates: "Those who have emerged from the evangelical world toward a more biblically radical understanding of the gospel are looking to other traditions and movements in the Christian church for the nurturing of their faith." "It is ironic that many of us feel greater ease in fellowship with Christians whose commitment to justice is steadfast, despite other theological disagreements, than with many evangelicals."[46]

Where is all this leading? We are provided a glimpse of what may well be the final destination of the Sojourners and their adherents. In an autobiographical piece, significantly entitled "Mere Orthodoxy," Bill

Lane Doulos recounts how his discovery of the Catholic Worker movement led him to demolish a long-standing theological barrier:

> Those who believe are in; all others are out. Some are going to heaven, some to hell. A lot of us evangelicals have never quite learned to accept this wall that has been built around the orthodox camp. Some of us have had the good fortune to see Jesus bulldozing his way through the cherished creed of his religious culture, and of our own.

Doulos has since been released from his former "enslavement to the abstract quest for propositional purity."[47]

Of course, it is this shift away from personal conversion and toward universalism that makes the pilgrimage of Sojourners distinct from that of other socially aware evangelicals, such as many signers of the 1974 "Declaration of Evangelical Social Concern," including Carl F. H. Henry, Ron Sider, and others. For the dividing line is not simply the fact of social consciousness raising, but rather the precise manner in which this new factor is worked into one's theology. This divide came through clearly, for instance, in the dissenting minority declaration of the 1974 Lausanne Congress on World Evangelism. The Lausanne Covenant affirmed, "Although reconciliation with man is not reconciliation with God, nor is social action evangelism, nor is political liberation salvation, nevertheless . . . evangelism and sociopolitical involvement are both part of our Christian duty."[48] The dissenters objected that politics is no mere "implication" of the gospel but is rather integral to it.[49] Here we see the key difference, which has come to the fore most visibly in the case of Sojourners.

How did these startling departures from Sojourners' originally evangelical stance come about? To answer that question, a complete chronicle of this group would be necessary. For our purposes, it will be enough to note that early on, Jim Wallis made it clear that his group, and his publication, disdained theories about the authority of scripture, in favor of radical obedience to scripture.[50] Apart from some schema of biblical authority, how is one supposed to go about determining just how scripture is to be "radically obeyed"? Would this not seem to be a choice piece of evidence for Harold Lindsell's case? Yet "the strange case" of Sojourners[51] has gone largely unheralded. Stephen E. Berk seems to be one of the few who has noticed that the Sojourners have "jettisoned every vestige of evangelicalism."[52]

So to conclude this consideration of the "Social Gospel" aspect of the fundamentalist-modernist controversy, it may be suggested that, despite Lindsell's surprising lack of attention to it, the transformation of the Sojourners' theological understanding makes plausible the contention that the original drama is being reenacted. The Sojourners' pilgrimage would seem to be traceable to (or at least to be correlated with) their disdain for any doctrine of biblical inerrancy (or any other doctrine of biblical authority). And this pilgrimage away from traditional evangelicalism is not only reminiscent in principle of the old Modernist Social Gospel; perhaps coincidentally, it has followed an almost identical path to that of its predecessor.

HIGHER CRITICISM

The third important issue at stake in the fundamentalist-modernist controversy was that of the higher criticism, that is, that type of biblical criticism which proposed to study the Bible like any other ancient document. Methods of literary and historical analysis had led many scholars to arrive at critical positions regarding the Bible far removed from those of the "Bible-believing" fundamentalists. Charles Augustus Briggs, for instance, noted with some indignation:

> Many theologians have insisted that we must prove that the scriptures were written by or under the superintendence of prophets and apostles. . . . When such fallacies are thrust in the faces of men seeking divine authority in the Bible, is it strange that so many turn away in disgust? It is just here that the Higher Criticism has proved such a terror in our times. Traditionalists are crying out that it is

destroying the Bible, because it is opposing their fallacies and fol-
lies. It may be regarded as the certain result of the Higher Criticism
that Moses did not write the Pentateuch . . . [and that] Isaiah did not
write half of the book that bears his name.[53]

Conservatives, for their part, moved rapidly to stem the tide of
"hyper-criticism." The fundamentalists mounted both offensive and
defensive maneuvers. At first, they sought to drive out the false
prophets in their midst, staging heresy trials, the most famous of these
having C. A. Briggs as its object. But eventually the hole in the dike
widened uncontrollably until the fundamentalists themselves were
cast in the minority role of false prophets. At this point occurred the
great secession of conservatives to found alternative seminaries. Here
the most celebrated instance was that of Princeton Seminary.
Princeton had been the fundamentalist Zion, from whence the inerrant
law of the Lord went forth to the nations. Now J. Gresham Machen,
Harold Ockenga, Carl McIntyre, Cornelius Van Til, Oswald T. Allis,
and others fled like Lot from Sodom, never daring to look back.
Instead, they went on to found Westminster Seminary. And the cry
"Fallen, fallen is Princeton the Great!" has echoed from Chestnut Hill
ever since.

It is important to understand that biblical criticism was not simply
a threat presented fundamentalists from without. Such a challenge
might have caused less alarm. After all, apologists had cheerfully
waged war with infidels real and imagined for generations—why
should the challenge of the Higher Critics be perceived as so much
more frightening? Basically, this time the enemy was within the camp
of the saints. Higher Critics like Henry Preserved Smith and Charles
Augustus Briggs were themselves evangelical Christians, a fact never
denied by their opponents. For instance, B. B. Warfield admitted, "We
are glad to recognize the obvious fact that Dr. Smith does not stand on
the same level with [Abraham] Kuenen. . . . He may triumphantly vindicate his evangelical spirit as opposed to Kuenen's thoroughgoing
naturalism."[54] So the struggle against higher criticism was in the first

instance a family feud. But far from making the problem less serious, this fact only heightened the danger. Fundamentalists contended that while one need not be a modernist to embrace higher criticism, if one did embrace higher criticism, he would sooner or later *become* a modernist! So fundamentalists sought to push the Trojan horse back outside of the gates before Wellhausen, Baur, Strauss, and Renan could come tumbling out of the trap door, sword in hand.

The fundamentalist apologists' fears were not calmed by the professions of evangelical faith made by adherents of biblical criticism. Briggs, described by an observer at his heresy trial as "an ardent lover of the Lord Jesus"[55] gave testimony to the effect that "I affirm before this body that I believe the Holy scriptures to be the Word of God, and the only infallible rule of faith and practice."[56] In his inaugural address at Union Theological Seminary, he had earlier declared that "higher criticism has not contravened any decision of any Christian council, or any creed of any Church, or any statement of scripture itself."[57] Llewellyn J. Evans confided,

> If there is anything in which my whole being is wrapped up, it is the study and teaching of the Word of God. If there is anything that I love with every fiber of every heart-string, it is that blessed old book. If there is anything for which . . . I would gladly lay down my life, it is that this Book may be known and read throughout the length and breadth of the world as the guide of lost souls to heaven.[58]

As far as conservatives were concerned, it was only a matter of time. In the first volume of *The Fundamentals*, J. J. Reeve asks:

> How can so many Christian scholars and preachers accept the views of the critics and still adhere to evangelical Christianity with intense devotion? [For] to accept the results of Criticism is to accept the methods and presuppositions which produced their results. . . . A careful study of the attitude of these mediating critics, as they are called, has revealed a sense of contradiction somewhere of which they are vaguely conscious. They maintain their attitude by an incon-

sistency. . . . This inner contradiction runs through much of their exegesis and they wonder that evangelical Christians do not accept their views. Slowly the Christian consciousness and Christian scholarship are asserting themselves. Men are beginning to see how irreconcilable the two positions are and there will be the inevitable cleavage in the future.[59]

Many years before, C. H. Green of Princeton Seminary made a similar prediction:

No more perilous enterprise was ever attempted by men held in honor in the church than the wholesale commendation of the results of an unbelieving criticism in application both to the Pentateuch and to the rest of the Bible, as though they were the incontestable product of the highest scholarship. They who have been themselves thoroughly grounded in the Christian faith may, by a happy inconsistency, hold fast their old convictions while admitting principles, methods and conclusions which are logically at war with them. But who can be surprised if others shall with stricter logic carry what has been there commended to them to its legitimate conclusion?[60]

To anyone familiar with the more recent jeremiads of Harold Lindsell, Francis A. Schaeffer, and their fellow inerrantists, these statements must sound awfully familiar. Perhaps the forbearing reader will endure two more paraphrases of the same warning, so that the parallel may become completely clear. First, Schaeffer remarked, in a now-famous speech delivered at the Lausanne 1974 conference: "The generation of those who first give up biblical inerrancy may have a warm evangelical background and real personal relationships with Jesus Christ so that they can 'live theologically' on the basis of their limited-inerrancy viewpoint. But what happens when the next generation tries to build on that foundation?"[61] Second, Duane T. Gish laments: "One of the great dangers of compromise is the insidious nature of its influence. Its effect at first is slight, its proponents holding to most of the great cardinal truths. Compromise begets compromise, however, and each succeeding generation, having fed on the ideas of the preceding generation, is willing to compromise more and more."[62]

This parallel between the fears of the original fundamentalists and those of today's inerrantists are interesting for more reasons than their verbal similarity. What it suggests is that Lindsell's claims are not mere alarmism, as is often charged by those whom he (and his Southern Baptist successors today) attacked. Many non-inerrantists would like to think that they and their position are not analogous to those faced by the inerrantists during the fundamentalist-modernist controversy. Instead, they picture the targets of the old fundamentalists as radical Liberals and naturalists in theology, who merely happened to employ biblical criticism (in itself innocent enough) in this framework. Yet it has become clear that the principal objects of the fundamentalists' ire was a group of fellow evangelicals. And, in fact, it can readily be shown that those evangelicals held positions often virtually identical to those proposed by contemporary non-inerrantists. The latter believe themselves to be offering really new solutions that can break the old deadlocks and enable evangelicals to leave the disputes of the past behind. But a brief survey of "modernist" positions regarding inspiration will cast considerable doubt on this perception.

Warfield repudiated "the theory of inspiration which is presented by Dr. [Llewellyn J.] Evans" because he saw it as "that form of 'Limited Inspiration' which confines it to what is called the religious and practical elements of the scriptures: and which therefore, seeks to claim for itself the formula that 'the Bible is the infallible rule of faith and practice.'"[63] In his own words, Evans's position is that

the infallibility of the Bible is pneumatic. . . . It is the infallibility of practical sufficiency, not the infallibility of absolute ideality. It is an "infallible rule," standard measure. . . . Its infallibility is not a microscopic infinitesimal infallibility respecting all particular things in the heavens above or on the earth beneath, or in the waters under the earth. It is an infallible *rule of faith*, i.e., of Christian faith, of Gospel faith, of the faith which is necessary to salvation.[64]

His view sounds for all the world identical to that version of today's "limited inerrancy" position embodied in the doctrinal statement of Fuller Theological Seminary.

Warfield could find little use for a kindred view either. He had particular distaste for any proposal "that only the *mysteries* of the faith are inspired, that is, things undiscoverable by unaided reason."[65] Here, the Princeton apologist repudiates the very theory propounded years later by Daniel P. Fuller as a slight corrective in harmony with Warfield's own doctrine of inspiration. Though he may sound like a clairvoyant, Warfield is not addressing Fuller, but rather the "modernist" evangelicals of his own day, such as Evans, who asks:

> Why was scripture given? The answer of our Confession is: Because "the light of nature was not sufficient." Sufficient for what? "To give [a certain] knowledge." Knowledge of what? Of botany? chemistry? geography? By no means. The light of nature is sufficient for that. . . . What is all secular knowledge compared with "that knowledge of God which is necessary unto salvation?"[66]

Another dead end, in Warfield's estimation, was the suggestion by Henry Preserved Smith that "reasoning on the *phenomena* of scripture is as legitimate as reasoning on their assertions about inspiration."[67] Obviously, Dewey M. Beegle and Virginia R. Mollenkott are far from original when they make the same proposal. Warfield was familiar with, but not persuaded by, attempts to refocus the meaning of "error" from "factual mistake" to "moral lapse" or "willful deception." Jack Rogers and G. C. Berkouwer seek to channel the discussion in this direction today, as will be shown in chapter 4 of the present work. In Warfield's day, it was Henry Preserved Smith. "He seeks to save [the biblical writer's] honesty; he does not accuse him of 'intentional falsification of the record,' 'of asserting what he knew to be false or of suppressing what he knew to be true.'"[68] Finally, James Orr anticipates contemporary non-inerrantists Paul King Jewett and Virginia R. Mollenkott in these words:

> Leaving . . . rationalistic criticism out of account—because that is
> not the kind of criticism with which we as Christian people have to
> deal in our own circles—there is certainly an immense change of
> attitude on the part of many who still sincerely hold faith in the
> supernatural revelation of God. . . . The process of thought in regard
> to scripture is easily traced. . . . Paul is alleged to be still largely
> dominated by his inheritance of Rabbinical and Pharisaic ideas . . .
> and we have to strip off that thought when we come to the study of
> his Epistles.[69]

This is the very rationale invoked by Jewett and Mollenkott in order to
bracket certain Pauline texts regarding women.

The contention of Lindsell that the fundamentalist-modernist contest is being reenacted in the present day, between those evangelicals
who affirm strict inerrancy and those who deny or revise it, seems to
be well founded. This has become all the more evident with the
demonstration that the original controversy also dealt centrally with
disputes *between evangelicals*, often over the very same proposals
being put forth by latter-day non-inerrantists. But does this fact imply
that the dire predictions of apostasy made by Lindsell, Schaeffer, Gish
et al. were equally well founded? Of course they warned that the
(alleged) conflict between evangelical faith and higher criticism would
eventually become evident to the non-inerrantists themselves, or at
least to their students. If the parallel drawn so far is basically accurate,
then the prophecies of spiritual doom uttered by Green, Reeve, and
others should be susceptible of confirmation or disconfirmation by
now. And it is quite obvious that their prediction was borne out, though
the *scale* of the leftward shift they envisioned cannot readily be
judged. It is clear neither just how many evangelicals they feared
would "apostasize," nor how many ever did. Yet the following testimony is important since it probably typified as well as influenced the
pilgrimage of many. Harry Emerson Fosdick concludes his book *The
Modern Use of the Bible* with these remarks:

Let me bear a personal testimony as my closing word. From naive acceptance of the Bible as of equal credibility in all its parts because mechanistically inerrant, I passed years ago to the shocking conclusion that such traditional bibliolatry is false in fact and perilous in result. I saw with growing clearness that the Bible must be allowed to say in terms of the generations when its books were written what its words in their historic sense actually meant, and I saw that often this historic sense was not modern sense at all and never could be. There, like others, I have stood bewildered at the new and unaccustomed aspect of the Book. But that valley of confusion soon was passed. I saw that the new methods of study were giving far more than they were taking away.[70]

Apparently one of the fundamentalist leaders happened upon the same valley, but exited it the way he came. J. J. Reeve recalls: "For some time I thought one could hold these [higher-critical] views . . . and still retain his faith in evangelical Christianity. I found, however, that this could be done only by holding my philosophy in check and within certain limits."[71] Reeve himself teetered close enough to the yawning precipice that he felt the urgency of keeping others from the same danger. These quotes should make it clear that the "danger" (the seriousness of the choice) they described was real. It is not hard in the contemporary evangelical scenario to find examples of the same movement from a non-inerrantist, sooner or later, to a non-evangelical standpoint. One of the more notorious cases of this is Southern Baptist Robert S. Alley who frankly admitted that the use of critical methodology led him to embrace a position not merely "Liberal" in a general sense, but which actually embraced the Christology of Schleiermacher and the demythologizing hermeneutic of Bultmann.[72] The experience of New Testament scholar A. J. Mattill Jr., now a Universalist, was similar:

I would now have to agree with Lindsell that the critical approach and anything resembling orthodoxy cannot long live together. For years I advocated a "reverent-but-rational" method of biblical study, that is, the respectful application of critical criteria to the study of scripture, fully convinced that this was the way to promote an enlightened form of evangelical Christianity. But as I slid down the Lindsellian slide, tossing aside one portion of the Bible after another, it finally dawned upon me as I hit bottom that . . . [my] left hand was peddling piety, my right, a rationalism destructive of that piety.[73]

Again, there is a discernable parallel between what was happening in the days of Warfield and Machen, and what began to occur in the late 1970s. In both periods, there were certainly non-inerrantist evangelicals who eventually did leave their evangelical stance behind, just as inerrantist apologists had predicted they would. But might this be merely the result of a self-fulfilling prophecy? What does such a parallel prove except that some inerrantists and some non-inerrantists eventually came to see the issues the same way? Identifying the same fence, as it were, they agreed to take their places on different sides of it. And, after all, it is quite easy to point to many non-inerrantists in the field of biblical scholarship who have never flinched from their evangelical commitment and show no signs of doing so. Indeed, they *might* be nothing but victims of "biographical inertia" as Schaeffer and other critics suggest. But the point at issue, and it is an important one, cannot be settled by such *ad hominem* attacks. Is there any logical connection between rejecting or revising inerrancy (and thus accepting the critical method) and then coming to reject evangelical faith? This is a question to be dealt with in more detail in subsequent chapters of the present work. But a few preliminary observations may help to set the stage for such a consideration.

EVANGELICAL HISTORICAL CRITICISM?

First of all, non-inerrantist evangelicals feel that any "slide down a slippery slope" toward Liberal theology has little to do with the mere acceptance of critical methodology. Stephen T. Davis has little patience for the claims of inerrantists:

Unless I am badly mistaken, what leads these people to their [Liberal] theological convictions is most definitely not their belief that there are historical and scientific errors in the Bible. [Instead,] what leads them to liberalism, apart from cultural or personal issues, is their acceptance of certain philosophical or scientific assumptions that are inimical to evangelical theology—e.g., assumptions about what is "believable to modern people," "consistent with modern science," "acceptable by twentieth-century canons of scholarship" and the like.[74]

Likewise, George E. Ladd, I. Howard Marshall, R. T. France, and numerous other evangelical New Testament critics have written to the effect that there is nothing improper about employing methods of biblical criticism so long as one does not make the mistake of Bultmann and other Liberals. The latter are said to have imported gratuitous philosophical assumptions—"naturalistic presuppositions" that deny the miraculous element in the biblical narratives, not because of any evidence, but simply on principle.

But is it in fact possible to eliminate such assumptions from the exercise of the historical-critical method? The following discussion will suggest that such a thing is not possible, and that non-inerrantists like Ladd, France, et al. only think it is possible because of a strategic misunderstanding of just what kind of "presuppositions" they are dealing with. This misunderstanding, it will be argued, is the very point of inconsistency hinted at by inerrantists in the position of non-inerrantists. The troublesome "presuppositions" in question in most discussions of the historical-critical method are two: the principle of continuity, and the principle of analogy. The first is what Francis A. Schaeffer meant when he spoke of the secular humanist view of the world as "a closed system of cause-and-effect." Bultmann summarizes the principle of continuity:

The historical method includes the presupposition that history is a unity in the sense of a closed continuum of effects in which individual events are connected by the succession of cause and effect.

... This closedness means that the continuum of historical hap-
penings cannot be rent by the interference of supernatural, transcendent powers and that therefore there is no "miracle" in this sense of
the word. Such a miracle would be an event whose cause did not lie
within history.[75]

The root of the problem is that whereas this principle is taken as
tantamount to philosophical naturalism, it is essentially not a *philosophical* assumption at all, but rather a purely *methodological* one. The
idea is not that the historian necessarily believes that the course of
events actually proceeds in this way and no other. That *would* indeed be
a "philosophical presupposition." Instead the point is that "cause and
effect" is the only thing available for a human historian to trace!
Closely analogous to this principle is the "surprise-free method" of
sociologists. In order to project the probable course of future events,
sociologists must methodologically presuppose "a world in which
present trends continue to unfold without the intrusion of totally new
and unexpected factors."[76] Note that sociologists are not claiming literally to predict the future, or to *know* that nothing now unforeseen will
happen. No more does the historical critic mean to dogmatize on what
did or could occur in the past. Like the sociologist, he must use a probabilistic, surprise-free method, only it is *directed toward the past*. Anything *may* have happened for all he knows, but he can trace only the
traceable! If divine (or magical or whatever) interventions from without
have occurred, they remain invisible to the historian's view.

The historical-critical method remains oblivious to miracles for
another reason. This involves our second principle, that of analogy.
Past events must be assumed to conform in kind to present events.
(Again, it must be underlined that this is strictly a methodological, not
a philosophical assumption.) Historians can only test the probability of
a report if they are acquainted with events like that in the report. If the
reported event is unique in kind (as miracles, by definition, are supposed to be), what criteria may the historian use to try to verify it?
What considerations would allow one to judge a report of, say, a man

turning into a banana as "probable"? Has anyone observed enough similar cases to know what usually does or does not happen when a man turns into a piece of fruit? At most, the historian must simply shrug. Or, to approach the principle of analogy from a slightly different angle: Why is it that any television viewer tuning, halfway through, to a program depicting Godzilla crushing Tokyo, knows instantly that he has found a science fiction movie? Why does it not occur to him that it may be a news documentary? Simply because huge fire-breathing monsters treading armored tanks underfoot are alien, not only to his own experience, but also to the experience of anyone he has ever known. By contrast, if he happened to tune in upon a courtroom scene (something familiar enough to him), it might take a few seconds of scrutiny before he could decide if he were seeing Perry Mason or F. Lee Bailey.

And of course the principle of analogy is indispensable in evaluating nonmiraculous historical claims as well. A famous example concerns the so-called Donation of Constantine, a forged charter purporting to grant the Church eternal possession of the Papal States. Documentary historians had seen enough late Roman land-grant charters to recognize that the "Donation" was not one of them. The only alternative to the twin principles of continuity and analogy is unrelenting credulity. John Warwick Montgomery only confirms this point in his attempt to refute it. Calling the principle of analogy a "naturalistic bias," he argues, "Not knowing the universe as a whole, we have no way of calculating the probabilities for or against particular events."[77] It is quite revealing that on this basis Montgomery argues in the same book for the historical reality not only of Jesus' resurrection, but also of leprechauns, poltergeists, and werewolves. Literally anything must be deemed as probable as anything else.

If the historical critic's methodology enables him to render no positive verdict on miracle stories, may he leave their truth as a toss up? If he could, then the non-inerrantist could at least claim that criticism need not militate *against* the supernatural. But it cannot stop there. For if the historian has no experience of resurrections, walking on water, making axe-heads float, and so on, he does have acquaintance with numerous instances of similar reports (often strikingly close to their biblical parallels) that are demonstrably legendary. Thus biblical miracle stories will usually be judged as probably legendary. (Remember our television viewer. He has never seen any real monsters, but suppose he has taken his children to the cinema to see *Gorgo*, *King Kong*, and *Reptilicus*. Will he hesitate to conclude that *Godzilla* is to be placed among their number as merely one more monster flick?) None of this *disproves* biblical miracle stories. One can believe them if he wishes. But as long as he wishes to play by the rules of the game of historiography (something few people hesitate to do in nonthreatening areas of inquiry), miracles just cannot be affirmed on this basis. So what is one to make of the claims of non-inerrantist biblical scholars that one need only drop a couple of gratuitous antimiraculous assumptions to be able to use historical criticism? These "assumptions" turn out not to be so gratuitous after all, since they form the very basis on which *any* historical report (miraculous or mundane) may be critically sifted. Gerhard Maier has urged evangelical scholars to adopt a "historical-biblical" method instead of the standard "historical-critical method." Similarly George E. Ladd prescribes a "historical-theological method." It is no accident that the word "critical" has dropped out of both versions. For both men, and several others like them, want to pull the reins of biblical criticism when it gets too close to areas still vital to them as evangelical believers. Such a procedure is arbitrary and without rationale in terms either of historical methodology or of traditional biblicism. And here precisely is that "happy inconsistency" alluded to by C. H. Green, the "inner contradiction" that Reeve discerned "running through their exegesis."

INERRANCY: REASON OR RATIONALE?

The old-time fundamentalists and their contemporary counterparts, the strict inerrantists, seem to be clear in their perception of what "higher criticism," or the historical-critical method, entails. They rejected it then and reject it today. But why? Inerrantist apologetics abound for anyone interested in reading them, but one suspects that these scholarly arguments are exercises in rationalizing a position taken on other grounds. And the real grounds are not mysterious. No one even particularly tries to keep them a secret. For example, the first volume of *The Fundamentals* contained several frank admissions. James Orr describes "a satisfactory doctrine of Holy scripture" as "a doctrine which is satisfactory for the needs of the Christian Church . . . , to the place it holds in Christian life and Christian experience, to the needs . . . for edification and evangelization."[78] In the same volume F. Bettex asks rhetorically, "Are the fruits of modern criticism good? . . . Has not this criticism already robbed, and perhaps forever, thousands of people of their love, their undoubting faith, and their joyous hope? . . . Where are the souls it has led to God?"[79] Franklin Johnson, again in volume 1, sums it all up: "As the sheep know the voice of the shepherd, so the mature Christian knows that the Bible speaks with a divine voice. On this ground every Christian can test the value of the Higher Criticism for himself."[80] Needless to say, fundamentalists have been testing biblical criticism on that very basis ever since. Closer to the present day, Carl F. H. Henry recounts the doctrinal and epistemological shortcomings of Liberalism and soon comes to the punch line: "But modern man hungry for spiritual reality will not be flocking there. They will fill up . . . Madison Square Garden . . . to hear Billy Graham preach the New Testament evangel."[81] A fund-raising letter from the International Council on Biblical Inerrancy makes this tear-jerking appeal:

> "Jesus loves me this I know, for the Bible tells me so." As a child sings this song he is reassured of the love of Jesus. But what if the parents, Sunday School teachers, or pastors teaching the child have doubts about the truthfulness of scripture? . . . Will the child continue to be reassured by the Bible of the love of Jesus?[82]

If fundamentalist inerrantists disdained historical criticism primarily out of fear for the consequences of accepting it, they shelved emotion and employed a shrewd logic in developing their apologetical rationale. First, one had to construe the authority of the Bible in such a way that historical criticism would be proscribed from the outset. If it were held to be totally inerrant, then criticism would be pointless. No Bible believer could be tempted to use it to elucidate scripture any more than he would find a Sanskrit-to-English dictionary useful for this purpose. Thus inerrancy was intended as a bulwark to *defend* the Bible's authority, not as a reason for believing in biblical authority in the first place. The latter would imply a completely arbitrary leap of faith. Rather, one should come to faith as to any reasonable conclusion—by the weight of evidence. Warfield contended that he could demonstrate by purely historical reasoning that the gospels seen as ordinary historical accounts were accurate and compelling as to the divine authority of Christ. Building upon this conclusion, Warfield pointed out that if one accepted Jesus' authoritative teaching, he surely must accept the opinion of Jesus and his apostles regarding scripture, namely that it is inspired and inerrant. So inerrancy comes at the end of this argument, not the beginning. This is the reason Warfield could claim that Christian doctrine would not in the least be undermined if the Bible were not inspired in any sense at all. But contrary to some recent non-inerrantist interpreters of Warfield, this did not make inerrancy expendable. Inerrancy could not be given up as far as Warfield was concerned, because if the evidence truly leads us to accept the authoritative opinions of Jesus and the apostles, then we are "stuck" with inerrancy since, like it or not, they believed in this doctrine. Thus to "pick and choose" among the divinely authoritative teachings would be foolishly inconsistent and so would imply the de facto rejection of messianic/apostolic authority. In the final analysis, then, for Warfield the surrender of inerrancy would be epistemologically fatal. And so would the surrender of angelology, the atonement, and the like.

The circuitous route by which Warfield reached this conclusion has provided the occasion for much misunderstanding in the present inerrancy dispute. Some have claimed that Lindsell and company departed from Warfield by making inerrancy absolutely central to religious knowledge, as if inerrancy had become for Lindsell the "essence of Christianity." Some point out that Lindsell contradicted Warfield in precisely this sense when he said, "I am making the claim that had there been no Bible, there would be no Christian faith today."[83] But Warfield himself was close to this view, willing as he was only to surmise "that without a Bible we might have had Christ and all that he stands for to our souls."[84] What Warfield said would theoretically have been expendable was inerrant inspiration, not the biblical record itself, and the latter is what gives us doctrinal security. We are to believe in inerrancy only because of that prior doctrinal security.

Lindsell seemed to agree. No more than Warfield did he make inerrancy some kind of magic that causes the Bible, when rubbed like Aladdin's lamp, to produce true doctrine. Rather, he said, he too "accepts it . . . because it is taught in scripture."[85] In other words, the Bible is authoritative in Lindsell's opinion before he comes to the inerrancy question. This has probably been less than clear to some interpreters of Lindsell because unlike Warfield, he largely omits any discussion of evidence that might lead one to this prior belief in scriptural authority. An expanded but faithful form of Warfield's apologetic is presented by another contemporary battler for inerrancy, John Warwick Montgomery. Elucidating what Warfield had called "the whole mass of evidence . . . which goes to show that the Biblical writers are trustworthy as doctrinal guides."[86] Montgomery writes:

> The historical value of the New Testament records about Christ is, when considered from the objective standpoint of textual scholarship, nothing less than stellar. And in these attested historical documents the Divine claims of Jesus Christ and the Resurrection by which He validated those claims are set forth in the most lucid and persuasive terms. The historical validation of a Divine Christ leads to the establishment of the scriptures as Divine revelation. When one examines, purely on historical grounds, the attitude of Jesus toward the Old Testament, one finds that He regarded it as no less than God's revealed Word. [And] if Jesus were in fact God Incarnate as He claimed and as His Resurrection evidences, then His evaluation

of scripture is no mere human, fallible judgment, but the exact truth.
And the same veracity attaches to His promise to His Apostles . . .
guaranteeing that the New Testament documents, subsequently to be
written by them . . . would have revelatory value also.[87]

It is this "mass of evidence" that Warfield and Montgomery would
set on the scale against any claim to have found an error in the Bible.
In view of the several loopholes in the logic of the argument, they
might be said to have pressed a thumb on the scale. The whole schema
begs several questions of criticism. For instance, Warfield and Montgomery actually invite higher criticism when they offer as evidence for
evaluation the historical trustworthiness of the gospels, the authenticity of strategic sayings of Jesus, and the traditional ascriptions of
apostolic authorship.[88] Obviously to introduce such data into the
debate is to grant the legitimacy of criticism. Besides all this, as has
often been pointed out, it would have been virtually impossible for any
error to run the gauntlet of Warfield's criteria and survive. For the
apologist demanded that any discrepancy be shown to involve a "necessary" contradiction between a Bible passage and "certain" truths of
science and history or between two Bible passages, and that the
problem text was not being eisegeted. More formidable still was the
requirement to do the impossible, to locate the error in the irrecover-
able "autographs."[89] So much for the fundamentalist apologetical
stance whereby Warfield and others sought to protect the Bible from
Higher Critics. But there was also a corresponding internal defense
system. It involved the way in which fundamentalists defined inspiration and its implications for hermeneutics. First, the original fundamentalists believed in de facto dictation, though they made occasional
protests to the contrary in order to cover their tracks. For example,
though they claim to "repudiate" the equation of "verbal inspiration"
with "verbal dictation," Hodge and Warfield also claim that inspiration
extended not only "to the verbal expression of the thoughts of the
sacred writers," but also "to the thoughts themselves."[90] Warfield
seems reluctant to admit that the biblical writers were in a trance state,

but he emphasizes that their own intelligence was merely the instrument whereby they received God's message. The prophets were "in no sense co-authors with God of their messages. Their messages are given them, given them entire, and given them precisely as they are given out by them."[91] He repudiates any application to scripture of the Christological "hypostatic union" concept, and thus feels no qualms about holding what might be called a "docetic" view.[92]

While it is probably true that most fundamentalist lay people have always believed in an exclusively divine scripture, it is interesting that Warfield's own position was considerably more radical (or perhaps merely more forthright) than that of today's inerrantists. The "Reformation Study Center Statement," the earliest creedal affirmation produced by the International Council on Biblical Inerrancy, declared: "The Bible was truly co-authored by God and man." And modern-day fundamentalists never tire of invoking the "hypostatic union" idea, though they seem to affirm it for almost the same reason Warfield denied it; they say that just as the Son of God, though truly human, had no sin, the Word of God, just as human, could have no errors. In both cases, the divine perfection is being stressed, in one case by the absence of the humanity, in the other by its irrelevance. Despite such minor differences, modern inerrantists join with Hodge and Warfield in affirming virtual dictation. The Chicago Statement says that "the very words of the original were given by divine inspiration" (Article VI). And like Hodge and Warfield, they retreat behind the smokescreen question of the "psychology of inspiration," as if to deny a mantic trance state were to deny dictation.[93]

The direct and virtually unmediated writing of the Bible by the Almighty himself is then taken to imply the total inerrancy of all statements dealing with whatever subject, religious, or secular. "What scripture says, God says," so a biblical flaw would convict God of error, or worse yet, call him a liar. Naturally, the application of literary and historical methodologies appropriate for merely human literature are out of place here. The same holds true for any attempt to interpret two biblical texts so that they conflict. Instead, harmonization is always mandatory in the event of "apparent contradictions." No real disunity can be admitted since all texts alike are inspired, inerrant, and authoritative. This being the case, "any text from any part of the Bible was [to be] accepted as a proof-text for the establishment of any truth of Christian teaching, and a statement from the Bible was [to be] considered an end to the controversy."[94]

Such a hermeneutical fortress would seem impregnable, but like Belshazzar's Babylon, its own design proves to be its undoing. In the first place, a close look will make it plain that this fundamentalist blueprint is quietly sacrificing both the Reformation principle of *sola Scriptura* and the normativity of the grammatico-historical method of reading the text. If the reading of "scripture alone" is to determine the legitimacy of any doctrine or tradition, how is it that a prior dogma (of inerrancy) may dictate in advance what one will or will not find in the text? One might as well return to the medieval Catholic practice of simply collecting texts to support dogma as laid down by the Magisterium. Furthermore, how can any heir of the Protestant Reformation find himself saying, as Hague does, "that the ordinary rules of critical interpretation must fail to interpret it aright"?[95] The championing of grammatico-historical exegesis by Luther and Calvin was meant precisely to prevent the ventriloquism whereby any enthusiast or allegorizer could make the Bible mean whatever he wanted. Unlike the *I Ching*, the Bible's sense is to be found by reading it, not by textual divination.[96] But did the fundamentalists really intend to revert to some kind of arcane gematria? Were they not simply concerned to keep higher criticism from dismembering scripture? Certainly they were so concerned, but text-twisting was never far from view. In fact, the stated need to harmonize "apparent contradictions" is a not-quite-tacit admission that the inerrantist has no intention of taking all texts in their "plain meaning." To say that text A "apparently contradicts" text B, is simply another way of saying that the "apparent sense" of text A contradicts that of text B. Now it is precisely the "apparent" or "plain" sense of the text that is said by fundamentalists to be binding! So the inerrantist, like Paul, is "torn between the two" (Philippians 1:22,

NIV). He knows not which to choose. But unlike Paul, his alternatives present him with a "double avoidance conflict"—neither is acceptable, for to hear the plain sense of both texts means to cancel the basis for heeding either, since scripture is seen not to be free of contradiction. On the other hand, to harmonize them is to admit that one employs some type of "canon-within-the-canon" since one must choose which text's plain sense is to prevail as authoritative. The other text will be harmonized into it, as if some "less obvious" sense, unavailable by exegesis of the text itself, would give a more agreeable reading.

In view of these rather serious difficulties, could non-inerrantists be expected to see the traditional inerrantist model as a viable option, no matter what the difficulties of their own views?

This chapter has attempted to portray the setting of the ongoing "crisis of biblical authority" in evangelical circles. Beginning with Harold Lindsell's claim that a new fundamentalist-modernist controversy is brewing, or actually underway, the discussion surveyed recent developments among evangelicals that seemed strikingly to confirm Lindsell's thesis. Next, a critical summary indicated, first, that the non-inerrantist espousal of historical criticism is indeed incompatible with a traditional evangelical stance, even as the inerrantists claimed. But, second, the traditional inerrantist model of biblical authority, apologetics, and hermeneutics was so beset with difficulties that it was unacceptable as an alternative. The remainder of the present work will be devoted to exploring new theological and hermeneutical models presented by non-inerrantists. If they "can't go home again," is there anywhere else to go?

NOTES

1. *Wittenburg Door* (February–March 1980): 10–15.

2. Clark H. Pinnock, *Biblical Revelation: The Foundation of Christian Theology* (Chicago: Moody Press, 1976), p. 228.

3. Harold Lindsell, *The Battle for the Bible* (Grand Rapids: Zondervan Publishing House, 1976), p. 25.

4. Carl F. H. Henry, *God, Revelation, and Authority*, 4 vols. (Waco: Word Books, 1979), 4:182.

5. Charles Caldwell Ryrie, *What You Should Know about Inerrancy* (Chicago: Moody Press, 1981), p. 17.

6. J. Ramsey Michaels, "Inerrancy or Verbal Inspiration? An Evangelical Dilemma," in *Inerrancy and Common Sense*, ed. Roger R. Nicole and J. Ramsey Michaels (Grand Rapids: Baker Book House, 1980), p. 59.

7. Sidney Greidanus, *Sola Scriptura: Problems and Principles in Preaching Historical Texts* (Toronto: Wedge Publishing Foundation, 1970), p. 203.

8. Lindsell, *Battle for the Bible*, p. 144.

9. Ibid., pp. 198–99.

10. Clark H. Pinnock, "The Inerrancy Debate among the Evangelicals," n.p., n d., p. 2. (Mimeographed.)

11. Ben Patterson, "The Battle for the Tent," *Wittenburg Door* (February–March 1980): 2–3.

12. Stephen T. Davis, *The Debate about the Bible* (Philadelphia: Westminster Press, 1977), p. 135.

13. Richard J. Coleman, "Reconsidering 'Limited Inerrancy,'" *Journal of the Evangelical Theological Society* 17 (Fall 1974): 207; also quoted in Lindsell, *Battle for the Bible*, p. 202.

14. Clark H. Pinnock, "Three Views of the Bible in Contemporary Theology," in *Biblical Authority*, ed. Jack Rogers (Waco: Word Books, 1977), p. 70.

15. "The International Council on Biblical Inerrancy Statement of Purpose" (n. p., n. d.), p. 2. (Mimeographed.)

16. *ICBI?* (n.p., n.d.), n.p.

17. Norman F. Furniss, *The Fundamentalist Controversy, 1918–1931* (Hamden, CT: Archon Books, 1963), pp. 50–51.

18. "Input Sheet Responses" (n.p., n.d.), p. 10. (Mimeographed.)

19. Furniss, *Fundamentalist Controversy*, pp. 50–51.

20. Ernest Sandeen, *The Roots of Fundamentalism* (Grand Rapids: Baker Book House, 1978), p. 244.

21. Furniss, *Fundamentalist Controversy*, pp. 50–51.

22. Pinnock, "Inerrancy Debate among Evangelicals," p. 9.

23. J. I. Packer, *'Fundamentalism' and the Word of God* (Grand Rapids: William B. Eerdmans Publishing Co., 1960), pp. 98–99; Francis A. Scha-

effer, *No Final Conflict: The Bible without Error in All That It Affirms* (Downers Grove, IL: InterVarsity Press, 1977), pp. 14–24.

24. James T. Burtchaell, *Catholic Theories of Biblical Inspiration Since 1810* (Cambridge: Cambridge University Press, 1969), p. 114.

25. William Jennings Bryan, *The Modern Arena* (Upland, IN: Taylor University, n.d.), n.p.

26. Kenneth M. Pierce, "Putting Darwin Back in the Dock," *Time*, March 16, 1981, p. 80.

27. Stewart G. Cole, *The History of Fundamentalism* (New York: Richard R. Smith, 1 93 1), p. x.

28. William Jennings Bryan, *The Bible or Evolution?* (Murfreesboro, TN: Sword of the Lord Publishers, n.d.), p. 11.

29. William W. Boardman Jr., Robert F. Koontz, and Henry M. Morris, *Science and Creation* (San Diego: Creation-Science Research Center, 1973), pp. 46, 43.

30. Quoted in Furniss, *Fundamentalist Controversy*, p. 16.

31. Bryan, *Bible or Evolution?* p. 29.

32. Duane T. Gish, *Evidence against Evolution* (Wheaton, IL: Tyndale House Publishers, 1972), p. 20.

33. Schaeffer, *No Final Conflict*, pp. 33–34.

34. David S. Willis, "Creation and/or Evolution," in *Origins and Change: Selected Readings from the Journal of the American Scientific Affiliation*, ed. David S. Willis (Elgin, IL: American Scientific Affiliation, 1978), pp. 6–7.

35. George W. Lasher, "Regeneration, Conversion, Reformation," in *The Fundamentals* 3:139.

36. Charles R. Erdman, "The Church and Socialism," in *The Fundamentals* 4:99.

37. Dwight L. Moody, quoted in *The American Evangelicals, 1800–1900*, ed. William G. McLoughlin (New York: Harper & Row, 1968), p. 185.

38. This is made clear by Timothy L. Smith in *Revivalism and Social Reform: American Protestantism on the Eve of the Civil War* (New York: Harper & Row, 1965); George M. Marsden in *Fundamentalism and American Culture* (New York: Oxford University Press, 1980); William G. McLoughlin in *Revivals, Awakenings, and Reform* (Chicago: University of Chicago Press, 1978); Martin E. Marty in *Righteous Empire: The Protestant*

Experience in America (New York: Dial Press, 1970); and Robert T. Handy in *A Christian America: Protestant Hopes and Historical Realities* (New York: Oxford University Press, 1971).

39. The Social Gospel had moved all the way in this direction in Cincinnati during the Progressive Era. "The city's four Protestant institutional churches also sought to influence a wide and diverse audience. Open to all who might come in, they . . . stressed a vaguely religious gospel of citizenship." For example, Congregationalist Herbert Seely Bigelow, a "disciple of William Jennings Bryan," was involved in the "People's Church" movement. Under Bigelow's leadership, his "church asked its members to hold but one article of faith, the belief that the great work of mankind and of organized religion was to aid in the establishment of the brotherhood of man in a world of social justice. It left theology and philosophy to the individual. According to the People's Church, one's religious duty was to strive for a just social order." Zane L. Miller, *Boss Cox's Cincinnati: Urban Politics in the Progressive Era* (New York: Oxford University Press, 1968), pp. 143, 145.

40. Walter Rauschenbusch, *A Theology for the Social Gospel* (New York: Abingdon Press, 1945), pp. 95, 96.

41. Albert Barnes, quoted in Smith, *Revivalism and Social Reform*, p.152.

42. William Arthur, quoted in Smith, *Revivalism and Social Reform*, p. 154.

43. Rauschenbusch, *Theology for the Social Gospel,* p. 92.

44. Jim Wallis, "What Is Conversion?" *Sojourners*, May 1978, p. 13.

45. Ibid., p. 14.

46. Wes Michaelson, "What Nurtures Us," *Sojourners*, May 1978, pp. 17–18.

47. Bill Lane Doulos, "Mere Orthodoxy," *Sojourners*, December 1976, pp. 25, 24.

48. John R. W. Stott, *The Lausanne Covenant* (Minneapolis: World Wide Publications, 1975), p. 25.

49. "Any man that has been effectively evangelized can never limit that transformation to the realm of the spiritual. It must be a social transformation as well. 'We affirm that in true evangelism salvation is both a spiritual and a social event.'" Clarence Hilliard, "A Dissent," *Sojourners*, November 1974, pp. 15–16. "Repentance is demanded: individuals must experience a change of understanding, attitude and orientation. But the new birth is not merely a subjective experience of forgiveness. It is a placement within the messianic

community: God's new order which exists as a sign of God's reign to be consummated at the end of the age." "A Response," *Sojourners*, November 1974, pp. 6–17.

50. Jim Wallis, *Agenda for Biblical People* (New York: Harper & Row, 1975), p. 4; personal interview with Jim Wallis, Peoples Christian Coalition, by the present writer, Chicago, November 1974; also cf. William Stringfellow, "The Bible and Ideology," *Sojourners*, January 1977, pp. 92–93.

51. Cf. chap. 6, "The Strange Case of Fuller Theological Seminary," in Harold Lindsell, *Battle for the Bible*, pp. 106–21.

52. Stephen E. Berk, "The Radical Christianity of the Sojourners Community," *Agora* (Spring 1980): 13.

53. Charles Augustus Briggs, *The Authority of Holy Scripture: An Inaugural Address* (New York: Charles Scribner's Sons, 1891), pp. 32–33.

54. Benjamin B. Warfield, *Limited Inspiration* (Philadelphia: Presbyterian & Reformed Publishing, 1974), p. 52.

55. *The Trial of Dr. Briggs before the General Assembly: A calm Review of the Case by a Stranger who attended all the sessions of the court* (New York: Anson D. F. Randolph & Co., 1893), p. 15.

56. Ibid., p. 16.

57. Briggs, *Authority of Holy Scripture*, p. 34.

58. Llewelyn J. Evans and Henry Preserved Smith, *Biblical Scholarship and Inspiration* (Cincinnati: Robert Clarke & Co., 1891), p. 4.

59. J. J. Reeve, "My Personal Experience with the Higher Criticism," in *Fundamentals* 1:353, 354, 364.

60. C. H. Green, in *The Old and the New Testament Student* 4 (1886–1887): 368.

61. Quoted in Lindsell, *Battle for the Bible*, p. 142.

62. Gish, *Evidence against Evolution*, p. 21.

63. Warfield, *Limited Inspiration*, p. 3

64. Evans, in *Biblical Scholarship and Inspiration*, p. 61.

65. Benjamin B. Warfield, *The Inspiration and Authority of the Bible* (Phillipsburg, NJ: Presbyterian & Reformed Publishing, 1979), p. 112.

66. Evans, in *Biblical Scholarship and Inspiration*, p. 61.

67. Warfield, *Limited Inspiration*, p. 40.

68. Ibid., p. 37.

69. James Orr, "The Holy Scriptures and Modern Negations," in *Fundamentals* 1:98–99.

70. Harry Emerson Fosdick, *The Modern Use of the Bible* (New York: Macmillan Publishing Co., 1961), p. 273.

71. Reeve, "Higher Criticism," 1:360.

72. Robert S. Alley, *Revolt against the Faithful: A Biblical Case for Inspiration as Encounter* (New York: J. B. Lippincott Co., 1970), pp. 69, 125–29.

73. A. J. Mattill Jr., "The Bible and the Battle of Faith," reprint from Cedar Springs Library, 1977, p. 57.

74. Stephen T. Davis, *The Debate about the Bible*, p. 139.

75. Rudolf Bultmann, "Is Exegesis without Presuppositions Possible?" in *Existence and Faith: The Shorter Writings of Rudolf Bultmann*, ed. and trans. Schubert Ogden (New York: World Publishing, 1964), pp. 291–92.

76. Peter L. Berger, *A Rumor of Angels: Modern Society and the Rediscovery of the Supernatural* (Garden City, NY: Doubleday, 1970), p. 16.

77. John Warwick Montgomery, *Principalities and Powers: A New Look at the World of the Occult* (Minneapolis: Bethany Fellowship, 2nd ed., 1975), p. 214.

78. James Orr, "Holy Scriptures," p. 100.

79. F. Bettex, "The Bible and Modern Criticism," in *Fundamentals* 1:89.

80. Franklin Johnson, "Fallacies of the Higher Criticism," in *Fundamentals* 1:63.

81. Carl F. H. Henry, *Frontiers in Modern Christian Theology* (Chicago: Moody Press, 1968), p. 153.

82. James Montgomery Boice, fundraising letter, (n.p.: International Council on Biblical Inerrancy, n.d.), p. 1.

83. Lindsell, *Battle for the Bible*, p. 18.

84. Warfield, *Inspiration and Authority*, p. 126.

85. Ibid., p. 162.

86. Ibid., p. 173.

87. John Warwick Montgomery, *The Suicide of Christian Theology* (Minneapolis: Bethany Fellowship, 1975), pp. 38, 39, 40.

88. "The inspiration, the canonicity, and the authority of the Bible depends, therefore, upon the results of the Higher Criticism. We are obliged, first, to prove that a writing was composed by an 'inspired prophet or apostle whose name it bears, or, as in the case of the gospels of Mark and Luke, written under the superintendence and published by the authority of an apostle.' But we cannot prove this for all the writings of the canon." Charles

Augustus Briggs, *Whither? A Theological Question for the Times* (New York: Charles Scribner's Sons, 1890), p. 84.

89. Archibald A. Hodge and Benjamin B. Warfield, *Inspiration* (Grand Rapids: Baker Book House, 1979), p. 36.

90. Ibid., p. 19.

91. Warfield, *Inspiration and Authority*, pp. 92, 91.

92. Ibid., p. 162.

93. "The Chicago Statement on Biblical Inerrancy," Article VIII; and Packer, *'Fundamentalism' and the Word of God*, p. 78.

94. Hague, "Higher Criticism," 1:32–33.

95. Ibid., p. 12.

96. Hans Frei, in his *The Eclipse of Biblical Narrative* (New Haven, CT: Yale University Press, 1977), addresses several related abuses of the text, in which the meaning of the text as *read* is bypassed in favor of some element underlying the text. Orthodox apologists, rationalist skeptics, form-critics, and questers after the historical Jesus all sought their various kinds of data *behind* the story actually told by the text. Also see Greidanus, *Sola Scriptura: Problems and Principles in Preaching Historical Texts*.

Chapter 2

PRODIGAL
FUNDAMENTALISTS

The Neo-evangelical Ferment

TIME TO REGROUP

*A*s the smoke began to clear following the fundamentalist-modernist Armageddon, inerrantists resumed business as usual, or as nearly "usual" as possible in light of the recent reorganizations and realignments. There were the usual pursuits of missions, Bible teaching, "soul winning," and internecine theological bickering. In the "postwar" environment, fundamentalists had to accustom themselves to a sectarian and minority status. They were no longer the dominant religious voice as they had been during the old days of the "Righteous Empire" (Martin E. Marty). Perhaps the voice of the turtle-dove was no longer to be heard in the land, but at least, thank God, neither was the hissing of the serpent. Higher Critics would no more whisper "Yea, hath God said . . . ?" among the ranks of the faithful. Or so it was hoped. But after that, a new generation grew up who knew neither Warfield nor what he had done for fundamentalism. A group of angry young men were to set a new controversy ablaze. These thinkers and writers for the most part represented the heirs of the fundamentalist struggle. They had come up through the evangelical educational establishment, and in the relatively settled aftermath of the fundamentalist-modernist controversy they had time to devote their attention to learning, culture, and the larger ecclesiastical scene. They fairly burst on the scene with demands for a reassessment by fundamentalists of their priorities. With books like *The Uneasy Conscience of Modern Fundamentalism* by Carl F. H. Henry and *The Case for Orthodox Theology* by Edward John Carnell, these Young Turks announced an agenda of issues ranging from social reform to respectable hymnody, from ecumenical openness to theological renewal. Henry, Carnell, and others including Harold J. Ockenga, Bernard Ramm, and Gordon H. Clark were not simply voices crying unheeded in the wilderness, for soon they headed a whole movement, whose most prominent new monuments included *Christianity Today*, Fuller Theological Seminary, the National Association of Evangelicals, and the Billy Graham Evangelistic Association. Clearly, there was significant action on a variety of fronts.

And any movement that does this is bound to make some waves of controversy. The "new evangelicals" or "neo-evangelicals" (variant forms of nomenclature contributed by Ockenga) generated and received flack on several of their positions. Probably the most volatile issue was that of ecumenical openness. Ockenga, Carnell, Henry, and the rest publicly repented of their fundamentalist past with its ill-mannered separatism. They supported "co-operative evangelism" and so made countless fundamentalists faint with outrage at seeing Billy Graham invite Liberal clergy to assist in crusade meetings. What other reaction could be expected from people who had paid a high price for "doctrinal purity"? Following the neo-evangelicals' path would force them to admit they were mistaken. Cognitive dissonance of that magnitude was simply out of the question.

Neo-evangelicals also sought to reopen dialogue with theologians of a more liberal persuasion. Some, like William F. Hordern, clasped this hand of fellowship, as can be seen from his surprisingly positive treatment of the movement in his *A Layman's Guide to Protestant The-*

ology. Other mainstream theologians were a bit skeptical. And they had some reason to be, since the neo-evangelicals (perhaps to defend their posture to right-wing critics) had made little secret of the fact that "dialogue" was primarily a device for obtaining a more effective platform for apologetics. Daniel B. Stevick, a neoorthodox critic of neo-evangelicalism, was a former fundamentalist himself and had a keen perception of what was going on. "We cannot," he wrote in *Beyond Fundamentalism*, "sit down together showing the 'mutual signs of humility' that Carnell desires if one party to the conversation wants it understood from the outset that it represents a 'classic' normative truth which is that of the Bible and the church throughout the ages. . . . The spokesmen for the newer conservatism remain unwilling to review their own complete theological stance. At the vital center of thinking, they cling to the absolute of the 'inscripturated' revelation and a finally formulated orthodoxy."[1]

Certainly Harold Ockenga could take no exception to the last assertion. In an important *Christianity Today* editorial, "Resurgent Evangelical Leadership," he had written: "Evangelical theology is synonymous with fundamentalism or orthodoxy. In doctrine the evangelicals and the fundamentalists are one."[2]

Others doubted this was so. Far-right fundamentalists like Charles Woodbridge, Carl McIntyre, and Robert P. Lightner never ceased vilifying the "neo-evangelicals" (whom they amalgamated with today's "young evangelicals")[3] as doctrinal compromisers and "wolves-in-sheep's-clothing." Ockenga is even to this day singled out as the pied piper of apostasy, apparently because it was he who christened the movement "new evangelicalism." How did Ockenga himself respond to such criticisms? In his adulatory preface to Harold Lindsell's *The Battle for the Bible*, Ockenga explained:

> Because no individual carried the banner for the new evangelicalism and no one developed a theology or a definitive position, many younger evangelicals joined the movement and claimed the name, but did not confess the doctrinal position of orthodoxy. This brought

neo-evangelicalism into criticism and often, both unwisely and unfairly, transferred these criticisms to the original leaders of the movement.[4]

There is certainly an element of truth in Ockenga's statement. As has already been mentioned, Ockenga's radical right-wing detractors fail to draw clear lines between "neo-evangelicalism" and the "young evangelicalism" of Richard Quebedeaux, Jim Wallis, and others. (Of course what can one expect, when the same critics lump Billy Graham together with Rudolf Bultmann?) But in the present chapter it will become clear that Ockenga's recollections are revisionist history. In fact, it was Ockenga's own neo-evangelical movement (though admittedly perhaps not Ockenga himself) that raised anew the questions of biblical reliability and critical study, thus prying open the floodgates through which gushed the non-inerrantist tide of today. *The Battle for the Bible* written by Lindsell and prefaced by Ockenga might even be seen as an effort to undo some small part of the "damage" they had done years before.

REOPENING THE DISCUSSION

That neo-evangelical thinkers themselves had begun to have some doubts about their fathers' model of biblical authority was apparent even to outsiders. Liberal L. Harold de Wolf (who, it may be remembered, authored another volume in the same series with E. J. Carnell's *The Case for Orthodox Theology*) mused: "There is a noticeable, though indecisive change in the doctrine of biblical inspiration and authority. Some of the new evangelicals . . . avoid teaching 'verbal' inspiration of the Bible, stressing rather plenary or full inspiration."[5] William F. Hordern (the third collaborator with Carnell and de Wolf) also saw signs of a modification of the earlier fundamentalist position.[6] And Carnell himself made two much-quoted statements that lent weight to this perception. First, in *The Case for Orthodox Theology*, he wrote: "Contemporary orthodoxy does very little to sustain the classical dialogue on inspiration. The fountain of new ideas has apparently run dry, for what was once a live issue in the church has now ossified into a theological tradition."[7] In the second remark, made in public on the occasion of sharing a forum with Karl Barth, Carnell admitted that how to "harmonize [the] appeal to scripture as the objective Word of God with [the] admission that scripture is sullied by errors, theological as well as historical or factual" was "a problem for me, too."[8]

Carnell never dealt extensively, or very explicitly, with the problems of inspiration and their possible solutions. Nevertheless there is a small number of statements in his *The Case for Orthodox Theology* that are far more significant than their length or number might imply. Other neo-evangelicals did deal at greater length with these issues, however. Important works include Dewey M. Beegle's *The Inspiration of Scripture*, Bernard Ramm's *Special Revelation and the Word of God*, and Everett F. Harrison's essay "Criteria of Biblical Inerrancy," which appeared in the January 20, 1958, issue of *Christianity Today*. An observation made in the last named work served as the entry point to a discussion of the issues. Harrison made the perhaps surprising admission: "Inerrancy is not a formally stated claim made by the scriptures on their own behalf. It is rather an inference that devout students of the Word have made from the teaching of the Bible about its own inspiration."[9] Ronald H. Nash in *The New Evangelicalism* reiterated Harrison's statement, adding that in his judgment most of the neo-evangelicals were willing to make the same qualification. So the Bible, contra Warfield, did *not* teach its own inerrancy, but merely taught its own inspiration, from which its inerrancy might be inferred. What Harrison and Nash left unspoken was of course more important than what they did say: Might inerrancy *not* be inferred? This must surely be the implication, yet neither Harrison nor Nash took the implied option themselves. Presumably anyone who did would not have been blamed. But Harrison and Nash were content rather to nuance and qualify the battle-weary term. Several means for doing this were at hand.

The basic presupposition for this task was that in formulating one's understanding of biblical authority, the "phenomena of scripture" must be given equal weight with its explicit teaching on the subject. In other words, one must pay attention to "what scripture does" as well as "what it says." In the midst of the fundamentalist-modernist controversy, of course, Henry Preserved Smith made the same point, to which Warfield responded by simply demanding that such a comparison conclude by harmonizing the phenomena with the scriptural claims![10] But the matter would not rest. Dewey Beegle repudiated as specious "any attempt to let scripture speak for itself" that did not also "reckon with the facts . . . of the Biblical record."[11] Beegle took off the kid gloves as he proceeded to enumerate just which "phenomena" (factual data) he had in mind. These included chronological errors in the record of Israel's kings, quotations from spurious pseudepigraphical texts, scientific inaccuracies, historical blunders in Stephen's speech, and so on. Beegle admitted that the industrious apologist might well be able to produce a harmonization for any given problem. But just how long could he keep doing it with a straight face? Soon he would find himself bound hand and foot in a long chain of such weak links. Better to admit once and for all that the inspiration of the Bible did not include its inerrancy.

Harrison, starting from the same premise ("the form that our view of inerrancy ought to take is to be derived inductively from the data of the text"),[12] chose instead to modify inerrancy rather than discard it. His ensuing discussion yields two basic ways to do this. At the outset, it is very important to note that both are indeed "inductive." They are drawn from within the text itself, not applied from without, say, in the form of prior theological criteria. First, Harrison reminds his readers, "It is anachronistic to apply the standards of our own time to the scriptures."[13] Thus inexact quotations, descriptions of nature in naive popular terminology, and the imprecise and symbolic use of numbers, though disallowed by modern historiography, do not implicate the Bible in "error." Similarly, Bernard Ramm warns, "scripture does refer to history but from the perspective of literature and not scientific historiography."[14] In other words, what would someone in the Bible writers' own day have considered an error? Incidentally, would the same criteria apply to the Hellenistic historian Luke as to the ancient Semitic chronicler of the book of Joshua? A closely related consideration should be mentioned, namely that of literary genres. Bernard Ramm recalls, with evident approval, James Orr's willingness to see in scripture the use of various literary forms considered legitimate in ancient times, including pseudonymity and even legend![15] Such a suggestion has never been accorded much of a welcome in evangelical circles. Dyson Hague, writing in *The Fundamentals*, indignantly refuses "to completely readjust his ideas of honor and honesty, of falsehood and misrepresentation" just to accommodate the instances of pseudepigraphy allegedly to be found in the Bible.[16] The Chicago Statement on Biblical Inerrancy similarly rejects what Clark H. Pinnock had, in an early work, called "deceitful literary forms."[17]

But to return to E. F. Harrison, his second criterion for nuancing inerrancy was that "scripture must be judged in terms of faithfulness to the purpose in view."[18] For instance, if Luke's Hellenistic audience will be confused by the mention of the thatched roof through which the paralytic was lowered, why should Luke hesitate to replace the dried grass with familiar clay tiles in his re-telling? Is he to be charged with "error" for having done so? In fact the roof did not have tiles, but so what? The same would apply to Jesus' calling the mustard seed the smallest of all seeds. Much can be said of this "inerrancy of intention" view, and more will be said on it in a later chapter where it is discussed in connection with more recent writers. For present purposes, it is enough to note that this suggestion had already surfaced in the evangelical discussion this far back. One of the more ironic admissions made by E. J. Carnell in *The Case for Orthodox Theology* concerned apparent discrepancies between the Old Testament books of Chronicles and earlier biblical histories. After considering various attempts at sidestepping the difficulties, Carnell asks what would happen should evangelicals drop the pretenses and admit the discrepancies. Surprisingly, "the doctrine of Biblical inerrancy would *not* be demolished.

Orthodoxy would simply shift its conception of the thing signified" by the term *inerrancy*. In what may seem to be a flirtation with "suicide by a thousand qualifications," Carnell goes on to explain this fail-safe strategy. Rendering what we might call an "inerrant record of errors," the Chronicler (and presumably any other inspired writer in the same bind) may be said to have given "an infallible account of what was said in the public registers and genealogical lists." As if embarrassed by his own suggestion, Carnell immediately reminds readers that such maneuvers are "already at work in orthodoxy."[19] Perhaps Carnell meant to refer to the traditional evangelical explanation of the cynical book of Ecclesiastes. Commentators had always blushed at this book's presence in the canon of scripture, rather as one winces at having to invite an obnoxious relative to a family get-together. They usually found themselves retreating to explanations of which that offered in the *New Scofield Reference Bible* is typical: "The philosophy it sets forth . . . makes no claim to revelation but . . . inspiration records [it] for our instruction."[20] How many readers will see such a statement for what it is: an unassimilated piece of out-and-out Liberalism, whereby a biblical document represents merely the "world-view" of a man in his search for God, rather than an oracle from heaven to humanity? Such an irony cannot have escaped Carnell, and one is driven to wonder if his suggestion regarding Chronicles is not made tongue-in-cheek as a *reductio ad absurdum*. Carnell left the whole matter standing unresolved. Later Clark H. Pinnock would try to salvage this possibility by combining it with Harrison's criterion of intentionality. Using Carnell's own example, Pinnock would suggest that the errors in the Chronicler's sources were irrelevant to his larger purpose in compiling the historical record as a whole.[21]

At any rate, Carnell had broached a significant problem posed at about the same time by Beegle, albeit in slightly different fashion. Beegle started from the other end of the problem, so to speak. In *The Inspiration of Scripture*, he took considerable pains to demolish Warfield's strategic retreat to the long-lost inerrant autographs. Beegle assailed this notion from every conceivable direction. In what seems to have been his favorite line of attack, Beegle contended that in their attribution of inspired authority to scripture, Jesus and Paul were referring without qualm to the textually corrupt copies in their possession. In other words, it never occurred to them that Warfield's autographs were superior to contemporary Torah scrolls. Of course, Beegle's own argument is vitiated by the very same kind of conclusion jumping of which he rightly accuses Warfield. For Beegle's point to be established, Jesus and Paul would have to have consciously *rejected* Warfield's distinction, and not merely remained oblivious to it. As it is, Beegle's erasure of any qualitative gap between autographs and copies (that is, neither being inerrant) is as much sheer inference from Jesus and Paul's statements about scripture as is Warfield's original inference of inerrancy. The texts simply do not seek to address either concern.

CANONICAL ADOPTIONISM

Another, apparently more cogent, critique was Beegle's calling attention to the fact that in many cases there simply *were no* autographs in Warfield's sense. This was obviously the situation with a compilation of any kind. Here we must choose between positing the (non-inerrant) inspiration of the material in all precanonical stages of development (Beegle's own option), or the inerrant inspiration of only the very last stage of compiling and editing. The latter alternative was implied in Carnell's efforts on behalf of the Chronicler. The model of inspiration implicit here has become clear only with the development of the discipline of redaction-criticism, to which it would seem almost ideally suited.[22] For Carnell the inspired writer is identified as the editor of the final form of the book. Thus the only directly "inspired" activity in the production of a biblical book would be the process of editing itself, most visible in redactional alterations such as that made by Matthew in the material provided him by his sources Q, M, and Mark. The material taken over unaltered by the inspired redactor would receive his imprimatur by virtue of its inclusion, but it would not be "inspired" in its own right. Nor would it necessarily be strictly inerrant, any more than the Chronicler's genealogies.

It should be admitted that some powerful difficulties attach to this suggestion; for example, would the nonentity who appended the longer ending of Mark (16:9–20) be the only "inspired writer" of that gospel? But the really strategic question has already been glimpsed: What is to be said when one biblical writer uses the work of another as a source for his own work, as is the case when Matthew and Luke use Mark, 2 Peter uses Jude, the Chronicler uses Samuel and Kings, and so on? The precise problem is that on Carnell's suggestion, the redactor provides an "infallible record" of source material that need be neither inspired nor inerrant, and this would seem to negate the inspiration of the earlier writers used by the later ones.

But is this necessarily implied? Why not simply say that one inspired writer "borrowed" from another, also inspired? This will not work, because occasionally the later redactor can be seen to have edited the very editorial work of his predecessor, as, for example, where Mark has split one pericope in two and inserted another one in the middle (for example, the entry into Jerusalem to purge the temple and the cursing of the fig tree), and Matthew has restored their original integrity, placing them side by side (cf. Matthew 21:10–12, 18–19 with Mark 11:11–15). A similar problem arises when Matthew "corrects" the words of Jesus, reversing the sense of his absolute prohibition of divorce (cf. Matthew 19:9 with Mark 10:11). Also, sometimes the later writer corrects the first writer's original assertions (not the first writer's preservation of someone else's), as when Matthew omits Mark's comment that Jesus "declared all foods clean" (Mark 7:19b).

If the final issue of all this is that the inspiration of one biblical book is collapsed into that of any other which incorporates most of it, must the "source material" books like Mark, Jude, Samuel, and Kings be relegated to a "deutero-canonical" appendix to the Bible? Such a result might so stretch plausibility that the whole line of reasoning would have reduced itself *ad absurdum*. But this is not the only possible conclusion to the matter. What if instead it was these secondary "source material" books that called the tune for all the others? Then all alike would be secondary to the final "redaction," wherein inspiration would ultimately repose. The final redaction would be the "compilation" of these books as a canon of scripture. But would this picture not imply that "inspiration" really applies more to the canonizing Church than to the canonized writings? Is the authority of the canon merely a function of the Church's authority, as if the act of canonization were inspired simply as one of the many inspired acts of an infallible Church Magisterium? The resulting picture would be more Catholic than evangelical. Evangelicals generally resist making the Bible's inspiration secondary to that of its source. They have rejected the claim of C. H. Dodd and other Liberals that the biblical writings were inspired insofar as they represented the work of "inspired men," or "religious geniuses."[23] Against this view, the biblical writers were held to be inspired and infallible only *as they wrote*. The Catholic view whereby the scriptures derived their infallibility from that of the infallible Church which canonized them was just as objectionable to evangelicals. The present model, it is true, would shift "inspiration" from the earlier stage of writing to the later stage of *collecting* and *canonizing*. But the Catholic view may be neatly avoided if the inspiration of the Church is restricted as present only in the special, once-and-for-all act of canonization. This, it will be recognized, is exactly parallel to that maneuver by which the Liberal "inspired man" model was avoided. The Church, like the biblical writers on the traditional understanding, is here taken to be simply the human vessel used by God on a unique occasion to produce inspired scripture. Let it be clear that inspiration *is* being attached to the Bible subsequent to the composition of the texts, but coterminous with it. Inspiration occurs at the point of canonization, not of composition. Thus, just as some evangelicals have compared the verbal inspiration model with the doctrine of incarnation, the present model would aptly be called "canonical adoptionism."

Has not the discussion run very far afield? What can "canonical adoptionism" conceivably have to do with the questionings of the neo-evangelicals about scripture? Did any of them propose a view of scripture even remotely resembling this one? In fact, they did, albeit indirectly. In possibly the most intriguing comment in his essay "Criteria of Biblical Inerrancy," Harrison mused, "If the Bible were of such a nature that it was composed by man and only subsequently was adopted by God and breathed into by the Holy Spirit, then it might conceivably be allowed that God was so concerned with the spiritual message that he tolerated a measure of error in the factual material."[24] And it has already been shown that Carnell's teasing remarks on the Chronicler raised questions that seemed to point for their answer in the direction, ultimately, of canonical adoptionism. Apparently, this model of biblical inspiration has never been explored in detail, much less explicitly embraced by evangelicals. Yet here and there, glimpses of it have appeared. Charles H. Kraft has described scripture as "a selection of . . . recorded materials [that] has been preserved by the people of God and, following God's leading, elevated to the status of scripture."[25]

Herman N. Ridderbos has also written words concerning inspiration that from the perspective of canonical adoptionism become even more interesting than they seem at first glance:

> The Word of God exists in eternity, is perfect. Inspiration consists in this, that God makes the words of men the instrument of his word, that he uses human words for his divine purposes. As such the human words stand in the service of God and participate in the authority and infallibility of the Word of God, answer perfectly God's purpose, in short, function as the Word of God and therefore can be so called.[26]

The language of "participation" recalls Paul Tillich's discussion of Christology, where "Jesus as the Christ" is to be thought of as "divine," not in his own right, but by virtue of his participation in the divine. And he so "participates" because, like the "words of men" in Ridderbos's remarks, he answers the call of God in perfect obedience. As Tillich suggested that "adoption" was not an alternative to "incarnation," but rather the corresponding human "underside" of it, may not Ridderbos's statement imply that "canonical adoption" similarly describes the "underside" of "inspiration/inscripturation"?

Before changing the direction of the discussion to focus on other problems dealt with by neo-evangelicals, two final notes on "canonical adoptionism" may be in order. First, it is quite interesting that a similar notion was proposed in the heat of nineteenth-century Catholic discussions of biblical inerrancy. In his account of this debate, *Catholic Theories of Biblical Inspiration Since 1810*, James Burtchaell describes the premise as employed at that time: "A book might be reckoned as scripture solely on the strength of a later guarantee by God or the Church that it was free of all error."[27] "Canonical adoptionism" as sketched out in the present work differs from the suggestion of the nineteenth-century Catholics in at least two respects: inerrancy is not the criterion for subsequent adoption, and the entire Bible, not simply disputed sections of it, is the subject of adoption. Incidentally, Burtchaell says that this idea "came to grief." It never caught on, but it was productive in the developing discussion as a foil for other, ultimately more successful, theories. Even so, Harrison in "Criteria of Biblical Inerrancy" no sooner mentions the adoption idea than he dispenses with it: "But this [that is, later adoption] is not the scriptural doctrine of its own origin. Rather it is insisted that the Spirit was active and controlling in the very production of the Word in its entirety."[28] However if one saw merit in canonical adoptionism otherwise, such an objection need not deter him. As Daniel Stevick, James Barr, and others have shown, the claim that "scripture" (as if it were a unit) makes *any* claims for "it"-self involves one in insuperable difficulties. Basically, such a claim is fatally circular, presupposing by far most of what it seeks to prove, that "it" can speak authoritatively as a harmonious unity.[29]

THE CANON WITHIN THE CANON

The preceding discussion took its rise in part from the difficulties and possibilities implicit in E. J. Carnell's efforts to deal with the question of errors taken over by biblical writers from their sources. Carnell's tentative speculations might be extrapolated in the direction of Harrison's hypothetical suggestion of an adoptionistic model. But Carnell himself ended his musing with an observation that pointed in an altogether different direction. He granted that "orthodoxy may never officially decide whether the Holy Spirit corrected the documents from which the Chronicler drew his information. But this irresolution does not affect the theology of the church, for Paul received his theology directly from Jesus Christ (Galatians 1:11–12). He did *not* draw on *existing* documents."[30] Thus Carnell chose in effect to settle the question by means of a "canon-within-the-canon." He makes this fact explicit in a famous passage in *The Case for Orthodox Theology*: "If the church teaches anything that offends the system of Romans and Galatians, it is cultic."[31] Was this choice purely arbitrary, one of mere personal preference? Or did Carnell have some real reason for it? He had at least two. First, having granted that preserved source material might not be completely trustworthy, Carnell took the corollary to be that material received directly by revelation would provide a safety zone. Had Carnell supposed, as some fundamentalists have, that the first chapters of Genesis were received by Moses (or whomever) via visions or automatic writing, presumably this, too, would have been more reliable than the dubious genealogies of the Chronicler. But he is concerned with theology first and foremost.

And this observation leads to Carnell's second criterion for his canon-within-the-canon, namely, that didactic statements in scripture always "interpret" (actually, *take precedence over*) any other literary form. And in Galatians and Romans, Carnell finds the clearest didactic exposition of all. Bernard Ramm agrees with Carnell here. Though he takes special pains to safeguard the integrity of various literary genres in scripture, he insists that "our guide" in doctrinal matters must finally be "those passages of scripture which are clearly didactic, theological, and hence, transcultural."[32] Ramm does not indicate any particular preference for Paul, much less any specific epistles of his; nevertheless the principle is basically the same. Though both Carnell and Ramm employed the concept of a canon-within-the-canon, the main function of it seemed to be to mediate among the various genres in scripture. The idea was that readers of the Bible might find themselves confused (and that many, especially non-evangelicals, did) if they tried to derive doctrine from texts not intended to provide it. Only strictly didactic texts were so intended. But neither of these neo-evangelical theologians came to grips with the possibility of real differences between didactic texts, or between different theological positions represented by their writers. It was his struggle with this problem that made Ernst Käsemann give the canon-within-the-canon idea new currency. And among major neo-evangelical writers only Dewey Beegle seems to have used the "inner canon" idea in the latter fashion. He recognized that the New Testament writers differed theologically on this or that secondary point. With uncharacteristic diplomacy, Beegle asked rhetorically, "Is it not . . . possible that details of doctrine tend to get fuzzy as one nears the fringes of truth?" If they do, where does the would-be believer of the Bible find "the standard for determining trustworthy and authoritative doctrine?" That is, how does he spot it among the various possibilities *within the text*? "According to the New Testament writers, Christ and the gospel are determinative. . . . The Biblical writers shared unequivocally some doctrines that cluster around Jesus, the incarnate Christ, and the way of salvation."[33] So Beegle differs with both Ramm and Carnell on this question. Unlike the first, he does not hold as normative over the rest of scripture *all* didactic texts. But unlike the second, he does not limit his choice to the texts of one author, whether Paul or anyone else. Instead, he finds a sort of "central common denominator" that at the same time both unites all the New Testament writers and screens out their individual differences from one another. This hermeneutical schema obviously deserves more attention than it receives in this brief mention. It will be taken up in more detail in a later chapter.

CONCEPTUAL INSPIRATION

It is by now plain that the theoreticians for the "new evangelicalism" were concerned to deal with biblical inaccuracies and contradictions in more realistic ways than the earlier fundamentalists had. One might imagine that an obvious way to have done this would be to dispense with, or at least significantly modify, the old "verbal" model of inspiration. And at the start of the present chapter, L. Harold de Wolf was quoted as noticing precisely such a change. He sensed a trend away from "verbal" toward simply "plenary" inspiration. But an examination of the major neo-evangelical literature, as well as contemporary criticism of the movement, indicates that De Wolf was at most only half-right. Instead of "plenary inspiration," the controversial alternative proposed to "verbal inspiration" was "conceptual inspiration." Actually, it seems that most neo-evangelicals never accepted this theory. But at least it was important as a foil against which they could more carefully define the positions they *did* hold. First of all, just what is a "conceptual" model of inspiration supposed to mean? Burtchaell devotes an informative chapter of his historical study to this model, which he calls "content inspiration." It seems to have been formulated and popularized by Jesuit theologians in the nineteenth century. One of them, Leonhard Leys (or "Lessius"), explains the point of such a model: "For any thing to be Holy scripture, its individual words need not be inspired by the Holy Spirit. . . . That is, by the sort of inspiration that would have the Holy Spirit forming the individual material words in the writer's mind."[34] Another of the proponents of this theory, Giovanne Perrone, further elaborates, stating that "this model would require for inspiration an impulse and . . . the *assistance* of the Holy Spirit touching the content and statements . . . but a sort of *positive* assistance whereby God plants all the ideas, and stands by the authors to guide and influence them as they pick and choose their words and compose sentences—without, however, dictating the individual words."[35]

Did any of the neo-evangelicals propound this view? Many of their contemporary right-wing critics thought they did, and did not sit idly by. Spokesmen for the movement denied this charge, claiming that their critics were merely heresy-hunters so eager to pounce on any deviation from orthodoxy that they did not wait to analyze carefully what was being said. Ronald Nash claimed this with some justification, but there was definitely something in the wind. For instance, John Walvoord of Dallas Theological Seminary pointed to Bernard Ramm's *Special Revelation and the Word of God* as a statement of the content or conceptual inspiration theory. He was probably right. The key passages in Ramm's book are these:

> When we speak of inspiration setting the language of scripture we must not think atomistically (i.e., as if the words were doled out to man as individual pearls) but we must think in terms of units of meaning . . . [rather than] an inspiring of individual words divorced from their meaning. . . .
>
> The essence of the doctrine of inspiration, is that there is a limit to which words can be rearranged, altered, or substituted. To put it another way, if the scriptures are an authentic and sufficient form of special revelation, this inspiration must in some comprehensive sense be verbal. The meaning of special revelation can be expressed in a certain limited number of possibilities, and inspiration secures the language of scripture in such a way that the language of scripture remains within these possibilities.[36]

Ramm does seem to be proposing the conceptual inspiration model, though his language at one point suggests that he means merely to explain what he sees as the proper connotation of the rubric "verbal inspiration." Nonetheless, it would be hard to deny that he is defining it in terms of *conceptual* inspiration. Ramm seems to have been alone in holding this view, even among neo-evangelicals. Others in the movement shared the substance of Ramm's concern but expressed it in a somewhat different manner. The direction they took will receive more attention momentarily. Why was conceptual inspiration so scorned? When they believed they had detected it among the neo-evangelicals, fundamentalist critics showed no mercy in their invectives, vilifying the neo-evangelicals as compromisers with modernism. In reply, most neo-evangelicals in effect threw Ramm to the wolves, hastily repudiating the hated "concept" theory. The "content" doctrine had even disappeared from among the Catholic circles where it had once been so widely received. There, it had finally lost ground because it came to be seen as synergistic, implying a "half-and-half" team effort on the part of God and the human writers. The schema was viewed as analogous to Semi-Pelagianism in soteriology and Arianism in Christology, and as being equally unacceptable. As in both of these cases, scripture was more properly to be conceived by Catholics as fully divine *and* fully human at the same time.

But the later Protestant distaste for conceptual inspiration had little to do with such considerations. Instead, they protested that this view tended to drive an impossible wedge between ideas and their expression. From the neo-evangelical standpoint, Nash calls "such a view of inspiration . . . not only theologically but also philosophically unsound." He gives his blessing to the words of James Orr: "Thought of necessity takes shape and is expressed in words. If there is inspiration at all, it must penetrate words as well as thought."[37] James Barr has as little patience with what he calls "inspiration of ideas." "As in any other literary work, the verbal form is its mode of communicating meaning. If the verbal form of the Bible were different, then its meaning would be different."[38] Naturally, there is no one who believes ideas may be transmitted apart from words. But this is so obvious that it hardly needs refuting, and certainly not with such vehemence. But is this what Ramm was suggesting? Was he not rather maintaining that ideas may exist in the mind prior to being articulated in words? True, an "idea" so vague that it cannot find articulation in specific words is probably no real idea. But no one really doubts that one idea can be variously expressed in several possible word combinations without serious distortion in meaning. Of course, even synonyms of a word differ at least slightly in meaning from the original. But would such a small degree of difference be enough to disqualify Ramm's conceptual inspiration model, as if the Holy Spirit's "original idea" becomes too diffused in that grey zone of the human writer's freedom to articulate it?

This does seem to be the grounds on which evangelicals have rejected this model. That they have done so is rather ironic for two reasons. First, the same line of reasoning necessitates a virtually univocal and exact correspondence between God's thoughts, and those of man. In fact, the objection even implies that the writer initially gets a verbal message from God and proceeds to paraphrase it in a manner more to his own liking, rather like Kenneth Taylor reading the American Standard Version of 1901 and rephrasing it as the Living Bible. But evangelicals are not supposed to believe this: Francis A. Schaeffer, for example, maintains that "propositional revelation" implies only that there be enough continuity between divine and human thoughts for them to be adequate and not exhaustive communication of truth.[39] (One is tempted to observe mischievously that Schaeffer seems to be saying the same thing as Ramm—*only in different words.*) The universal rejection of conceptual revelation by evangelicals is even more ironic for a second reason. The issue of how exact a correspondence is needed between a thought and variant words would seem to be the same as that underlying the process of translation. For just as a word and its synonym in the same language never mean *precisely* the same thing, neither does a word in one language correspond *exactly* in meaning to its corresponding word in a different language. Yet evangelicals, however devoted to studying "the original Greek," do not deny that translations into other languages are truly God's Word! Muslims, by contrast, do make exactly this claim concerning the Koran (which incidentally is why Mohammed Marmaduke Pickthall called his English translation *The Meaning of the Glorious Koran*): "The Koran cannot be translated. That is the belief of old-fashioned Sheykhs and the view of the present writer. The Book is here rendered almost literally. . . . But the result is not the Glorious Koran. . . . It is only an attempt to present the meaning of the Koran . . . in English."[40]

Now, if evangelicals also wanted to make such a claim, they would find the requisite theological categories ready to hand. Just as the scriptures are said to be inerrant only in the original autographs, they might as easily be said to be *inspired* only in the original *languages*. A la Pickthall, the New International "Version" of the Bible (for example) would then have to denote that its reader is not holding the real scriptures.[41] So perhaps evangelicals were a bit hasty in rejecting conceptual inspiration. But, as mentioned above, some neo-evangelicals who did not fully agree with Ramm nevertheless were trying to make a similar point. Ronald Nash contended that while neo-evangelicals did not embrace conceptual inspiration, they did wish to reemphasize the conceptual dimensions of (a more-or-less standard view of) verbal inspiration. Granted that inspiration extended to the words, what were the words *saying*? Wasn't this the important thing? Neo-evangelicals by no means wished to rid themselves of belief in verbal inspiration. They merely sought to correct a distortion in focus produced by the older fundamentalists' defensive posture regarding the real divine origin of the words. Neo-evangelicals wished to say, in effect: "That battle is over. Now let's turn to other issues—what did God want to tell us with those inspired words?"

Interestingly, this corrective can be seen as the mirror image of the critique leveled by Nash, Orr, and Barr (above) against conceptual inspiration. If there are no ideas without words, neither are words meaningful unless they denote ideas. And then, surely the ideas are the important thing. Recent writers on inspiration have said it well. Charles Kraft affirms:

> I believe strongly that the scriptures are inspired and that this inspiration may properly be labeled "verbal" . . . and "plenary." . . . These terms label what is inspired (i.e., all the words). But the words are inspired almost incidentally. For the primary focus of inspiration (as of all ethnolinguistic communication) is on the meaning. [42]

And G. C. Berkouwer reminds verbal inspirationists that the "God breathed character is a witness which at no time can or may be severed from what is testified to by the words."[43] For Berkouwer, this shift in perspective has some rather searching implications that the neo-evangelicals may have missed. If the inspiration of the words serves primarily to secure the message, then it may no longer be (and may never have been) appropriate to speak of the formal inspiration of anything but the message. This significant shift will claim more attention in a later chapter.

All in all the present overview of neo-evangelical thinking on scripture has shown that the neo-evangelical period was a transitional period between fundamentalism and today's evangelicalism in a much more significant sense than is usually thought. The change from the fundamentalist posture was neither merely one of manners and tactics, as Daniel B. Stevick claimed,[44] nor simply one of ecclesial and social openness as Ockenga claimed at the time and apparently still claimed in 1976. Instead, the neo-evangelical movement, insofar as it took seriously its own call to theological creativity and intellectual challenge, set in motion important changes, particularly vis-à-vis the doctrine of inspiration. By and large the neo-evangelicals (with the exceptions of Beegle and Ramm) hesitated to pursue these insights. The next generation (the "Young evangelicals") did begin to follow through on the path marked out for them, as will become clear in the next chapters. But when they did, Ockenga, Lindsell, Carl Henry, and Gordon H. Clark[45] recoiled in shock, announcing a "new fundamentalist-modernist controversy." Having left the old fundamentalist homestead, these men had journeyed to a far country, carrying with them their share of the evangelical inheritance. Leaving older brothers like Carl McIntyre and Bob Jones indignantly fuming back home, the prodigals enthusiastically sought to engage the world on its own terms. But one day, they came to their senses and realized that all they had to show for their labors was a pen full of non-inerrantist pigs. No time was lost returning home in bitter tears of repentance.

NOTES

1. Daniel B. Stevick, *Beyond Fundamentalism* (Richmond, VA: John Knox Press, 1964), pp. 74–75.

2. Harold John Ockenga, "Resurgent Evangelical Leadership," in *A Christianity Today Reader*, ed. Frank E. Gaebelein (New York: Meredith Press, 1966), p. 136.

3. Richard Quebedeaux, *The Young Evangelicals* (New York: Harper & Row, 1974).

4. Lindsell, *Battle for the Bible*, p. 12.

5. L. Harold de Wolf, *Present Trends in Christian Thought* (New York: Association Press, 1960), p. 40.

6. William F. Hordern, *A Layman's Guide to Protestant Theology* (New York: Macmillan Co., 1975), p. 110.

7. E. J. Carnell, *The Case for Orthodox Theology* (Philadelphia: Westminster Press, 1959), p. 110.

8. Carnell quoted in Robert P. Lightner, *Neoevangelicalism Today* (Schaumburg, IL: Regular Baptist Press, 1978), p. 81.

9. Everett F. Harrison, "Criteria of Biblical Inerrancy," in *A Christianity Today Reader*, p. 63.

10. Warfield, *Limited Inspiration*, p. 41.

11. Dewey M. Beegle, *The Inspiration of Scripture* (Philadelphia: Westminster Press, 1963), p. 14.

12. Harrison, "Criteria of Biblical Inerrancy," p. 63.

13. Ibid., p. 64.

14. Bernard Ramm, *Special Revelation and the Word of God* (Grand Rapids: William B. Eerdmans Publishing Co., 1968), p. 68.

15. Ibid., pp. 63–64.

16. Hague, "Higher Criticism," 1:31.

17. "Chicago Statement on Biblical Inerrancy," Article VIII, despite Article XVIII; Pinnock, *Biblical Revelation*, p. 94.

18. Harrison, "Criteria of Biblical Inerrancy," p. 66.

19. Carnell, *Orthodox Theology*, p. 31.

20. Frank Gaebelein, ed., *The New Scofield Reference Bible* (New York: Oxford University Press, 1967), p. 696.

21. Clark H. Pinnock, "Limited Inerrancy: A Critical Appraisal and Constructive Alternative," in *God's Inerrant Word*, ed. John Warwick Montgomery (Minneapolis: Bethany Fellowship, 1974), p. 148.

22. Carnell's hesitant location of inspiration in the editor of source materials had been anticipated by Llewelyn J. Evans: "Shall we say that the inspiration of the Gospel of Luke, e. g., is to be sought for not in the material, not in the documents which he confessedly used, but in the editorial compilation and elaboration of the material? Surely this is a most unsatisfactory solution. Of all the makeshifts to which the theory of absolute inerrancy

compels its adherents, this is to my mind the weakest. . . . The idea that inspiration resolves itself into the correction of a date, substituting one man's name for another, changing a number, inserting a caption—important as such particulars may be in their way—such an idea of inspiration is suitable only for Theology in Lilliputia." Evans and Smith, *Biblical Scholarship and Inspiration*, pp. 38–39.

Actually, the more recent labors of redaction critics have shown that such "minor" editorial changes are not so Lilliputian in importance as Evans thought. Hans Conzelmann's *The Theology of St. Luke*, trans. Geoffrey Buswell (New York: Harper & Row, 1961) and Heinz Joachim Held's "Matthew as Interpreter of the Miracle Stories" (pp. 165–300 of Günther Bornkamm, Gerhard Barth, and Heinz Joachim Held, *Tradition and Interpretation in Matthew*, trans. Percy Scott. New Testament Library [Philadelphia: Westminster Press, 1976]) are particularly revealing examples of the usefulness of such data in reconstructing the theology of the individual redactor. John Drury, *Tradition and Design in Luke's Gospel* [Atlanta: John Knox Press, 1977]) and Michael D. Goulder, *Midrash and Lection in Matthew* [London: SPCK, 1974)] have laid the groundwork for the recognition of broad literary creativity on the part of the redactor. The latter is now hypothesized to have employed Midrashic expansion actually to create significant amounts of the narrative. This activity, on Carnell's theory, would be inspired by the Spirit.

23. C. H. Dodd, *The Authority of the Bible* (New York: Harper & Bros., 1958), pp. 30–31.

24. Harrison, "Criteria of Biblical Inerrancy," p. 63.

25. Charles H. Kraft, *Christianity in Culture: A Study in Dynamic Biblical Theologizing in Cross-Cultural Perspective* (Maryknoll, NY: Orbis Books, 1979), p. 213.

26. Herman N. Ridderbos, *Studies in Scripture and Its Authority* (Grand Rapids: William B. Eerdmans Publishing Co., 1978), p. 25.

27. Burtchaell, *Biblical Inspiration*, p. 52.

28. Harrison, "Criteria of Biblical Inerrancy," p. 63.

29. Stevick, *Beyond Fundamentalism*, p. 91; James Barr, *Fundamentalism* (Philadelphia: Westminster Press, 1978), p. 78.

30. Carnell, *Orthodox Theology*, p. 111.

31. Ibid., p. 59.

32. Bernard Ramm, *The Christian View of Science and Scripture* (Grand Rapids: William B. Eerdmans Publishing Co., 1974), p. 54.

33. Beegle, *Inspiration of Scripture*, p. 173.

34. Quoted in Burtchaell, *Biblical Inspiration*, p. 88.

35. Ibid., p. 93.

36. Ramm, *Special Revelation*, pp. 177, 178.

37. Ronald H. Nash, *The New Evangelicalism* (Grand Rapids: Zondervan Publishing House, 1963), p. 41.

38. James Barr, *The Bible in the Modern World* (New York: Harper & Row, 1973), p. 178.

39. Francis A. Schaeffer, *He Is There and He Is Not Silent* (Wheaton, IL: Tyndale House Publishers, 1973), pp. 93–95.

40. Mohammed Marmaduke Pickthall, trans., *The Meaning of the Glorious Koran* (New York: New American Library, n.d.), p. vii.

41. Pretty much the same point was made by Briggs in *Whither? A Theological Question*, pp. 64–65. It may readily be noted that this argument parallels Beegle's argument that Warfield's distinction between the "inerrant autographs" and relatively corrupt present-day copies is self-defeating. The whole reason for drawing the distinction was the claim that an inspired work must be inerrant. Thus to say that only the long-lost autographs were inerrant must also mean that they alone, exclusive of today's "errant" copies, are inspired! To protect the inspiration of the originals, Warfield was shown by Beegle to have sacrificed the inspiration of the only Bible available today!

42. Kraft, *Christianity in Culture*, p. 206.

43. G. C. Berkouwer, *Holy Scripture*, trans. Jack Rogers (Grand Rapids: William B. Eerdmans Publishing Co., 1975), p. 162.

44. Stevick, *Beyond Fundamentalism*, p. 75.

45. Gordon H. Clark, *The Concept of Biblical Authority* (Phillipsburg, NJ: Presbyterian & Reformed Publishing, 1980).

Chapter 3

"INERRANCY, LTD."

The Inerrancy of (Some) Assertions

SHORTENING THE LINE OF DEFENSE

> For "plenary inspiration" . . . we are asked to substitute a sort of "inspiration with limited liability," the limit being susceptible of indefinite fluctuation in correspondence with the demands of scientific criticism. This Parthian policy is carried out with some dexterity; but like other such maneuvers in the face of a strong foe, it seems likely to end in disaster.[1]

*T*his was the assessment by agnostic Thomas Henry Huxley of what is today called "limited inerrancy." Obviously Huxley, the defender of Charles Darwin in debates against churchmen, scorned the doctrine as a policy of appeasement, in fact meant to appease *him*! But his victory seemed sure, so why should he bother to take such compromise measures seriously? Many who have fought on the opposite side of the "battle for the Bible" have had an equal lack of enthusiasm for "limited inerrancy." Let no one think it prudent, they warn, to shorten the lines of defense. All that will result is an even speedier siege of one's own castle.[2] Everett F. Harrison, who advised carefully qualifying the claim for inerrancy, warned against any avowal of limited

inerrancy. "The history of biblical inspiration shows that the abandonment of the inerrancy of scripture in non-doctrinal items has a tendency to make criticism of the doctrinal data much easier."[3]

The present chapter will consider some of the principal attempts
among contemporary evangelicals to salvage the fundamentalist doctrine of "inerrancy" by limiting it in some way. In the course of the discussion it will become clearer just what motivates such limiting, what
sorts of limits are imposed, and what is done with that biblical material falling outside those limits. Perhaps increased insight on some of
these matters will make possible an evaluation of limited inerrancy as
a hermeneutical tool and as an apologetical strategy.

DANIEL P. FULLER'S PROPOSAL

As the quotation from Huxley indicates, theologians have sought to
limit the scope of biblical inerrancy on other occasions of theological
controversy in the past. But the entrance of this position into the most
recent controversy was brought about by Daniel P. Fuller in a series of
addresses from 1967 through 1970 to the Evangelical Theological
Society at Toronto, to the American Scientific Affiliation at Fuller
Seminary, and to the student body at Wheaton College. Later published in the form of two articles ("Benjamin B. Warfield's View of
Faith and History, A Critique in the Light of the New Testament" and
"The Nature of Biblical Inerrancy"), Fuller's remarks occasioned a
storm of controversy. He fanned the flames of a debate begun a few
years earlier by Dewey M. Beegle's book, *The Inspiration of Scripture*, referred to in the previous chapter. Beegle had flatly rejected
inerrancy as a legitimate predicate of inspired scripture. This was outrageous enough to conservatives, but in some ways Fuller's proposal
seemed even more insidious since it intended to *retain, but revise,*
inerrancy. Real fundamentalists could, as it were, spot Beegle's Con-
federate bills and refuse them readily enough. But Fuller's counter-
feiting was another story.

Whereas Beegle had made no bones about attacking the fundamentalist patriarch Warfield, Fuller was humbly seeking to remain faithful to the old master. Fuller used a study of Warfield as a point of departure for a critique of fideism. While some evangelicals were content to rest on the "testimony of the Spirit" as the sole warrant for their faith, Fuller saw this as subjectivist, arbitrary, and unconvincing. And so did Warfield. Fuller felt much more at home with Warfield's appeal to the *indicia*, the weight of evidence, "which vindicates for us the trustworthiness of Christ and His apostles as teachers of doctrine."[4] In other words, there were good *reasons* why one should convert to Christian faith in the Bible. Warfield (and Fuller) admitted that the resulting conviction, no matter how "certain" emotionally, was only probabilistic by nature. But the probability was quite high, and a little theoretical uncertainty seemed a small price to pay to be able to offer faith respectably in the marketplace of ideas. There was only one problem with Warfield's view as Fuller saw it. It will be remembered that Warfield suspended his doctrine of total inerrancy on the very same argument. And Warfield had thus allowed his a priori belief in inerrancy to prejudice his consideration of the problem data of scripture. With his famous list of criteria for "proved errors," Warfield had in effect lifted the Bible out of the field of historical verification. Fuller realized that this constituted a particularly embarrassing case of special pleading for someone like Warfield who sought to be an evidentialist in apologetics. This was the point at which Fuller sought to apply his corrective. Upholders of Warfield's apologetics (of whom there were many, for example, John Warwick Montgomery) would be well-advised, said Fuller, to remove the preferential zone of immunity from the troublesome phenomena of scripture. If, with Warfield, one maintained that the evidence was far heavier on Christ's side of the scale, why not allow for the possibility that an insignificant fact or two might be placed on the other side of the balances?

But could Warfield's position accommodate such retooling? Or had he painted himself inextricably into the corner described by Fuller? After all, Warfield felt compelled to uphold inerrancy precisely because most of the evidence *did* stack up on the side of Christ and the apostles as reliable teachers. It was they who taught inerrancy! Warfield always claimed to have been willing to renounce his scruples vis-à-vis inerrancy if it could be shown that the "doctrinal verses," for example, 2 Timothy 3:16, did not teach inerrancy as well as inspiration.[5] It was at this point that Fuller was convinced Warfield had (unwittingly) left himself and his disciples a loophole through which to escape. For did not the "biblical reliability" propounded in these "doctrinal verses" refer in context only to "doctrinal" matters? If so, why stretch their meaning, especially in a direction so embarrassing for apologetics as Warfield had done? It was enough that scripture was inerrant insofar as it made us wise *unto salvation*, that it was profitable for doctrine, reproof, correction, and instruction. Why need it make us wise unto meteorology, geography, biology, botany, or incidental facts of history?

Or, in Fuller's own words, "since the Bible declares that its purpose is to impart revelation, we run no risk of distorting its message as we credit its revelational teachings and admit the possibility that its non-revelational statements and implications are a reflection of the culture of the writer and his original readers."[6] Fuller's mention of "non-revelational statements" denotes his belief that some biblical assertions may be necessary for the structural composition of the work as a whole, yet have no importance as teaching revelational or salvific doctrine in their own right. Who cares if such statements are technically correct? Who would even think to ask, had not strict inerrantists made an issue of it? Did Jesus heal the blind man on his way *into* or *out of* Jericho? Did the blind man care? Should anyone else? "Implications" in Fuller's statement refers to incidental features of an assertion revelatory in its thrust. Here the classic example is Matthew's mustard seed. According to Fuller, anyone with common sense can see that Jesus is not concerned to teach botany, but to teach about the Kingdom of Heaven. So why scruple if the mustard seed turns out *not* to be the smallest? Now one could always simply rewrite the text as the translators of the New International Version did (now it conveniently reads "The smallest of all *your* seeds"). Compared to such a tactic, "limited liability inerrancy" hardly seems so desperate an expedient at all. By contrast, it must be noted that Fuller is quite willing to allow that there are at least some historical assertions in scripture that fall under the rubric of inerrancy, since they are absolutely fundamental to the revelational point thus established. They are not mere incidentals, since the most important "revelational matters" are "God's mighty acts in history."

For the sake of historical interest, it is worth observing that strikingly similar views had been put forth by Jesuit theologians in the nineteenth century. For instance, Burtchaell describes the view that Marcantonio de Domini held, namely, "that not all matters related in the Bible are matters of faith. Anything which might have come to the sacred writer by way of simple observation could not be presented by him to us to be believed." Similarly, theologian August Rohling limited inspiration to the "scope" of faith and morals, which he construed as the real intent of revelation. Historical passages were guaranteed inspired and inerrant only when they were necessary to establish a spiritual assertion in the text.[7] Warfield dismissed such attempts with little sympathy in his survey of historical modifications of inspiration. It is ironic that Fuller would come to suggest such a reworking of inerrancy as a "tightening-up" of the loopholes and inconsistencies of Warfield's own view. Two brief points of comparison with the older Catholic views bear mention. First, like Rohling, Fuller wanted to limit the "scope" of inerrancy (not inspiration, however). This implied that the concept was applicable only to revelational statements. It is not that non-revelational assertions are "errant" instead of inerrant. They are simply not in view. Second, Fuller's schema is similar to that of Marcantonio de Domini in that Fuller defines "non-revelational matters" as those "capable of being checked out by human investigation."[8] But whereas the Jesuit theologian referred to the ability of the biblical writers to discover certain information for themselves, Fuller's concern has more to do with the contemporary apologetical task; the "investigation" he has in mind is carried out by historians today, rather than by biblical writers of yesterday. This is a point of some importance for understanding Fuller's intentions, and it will receive more attention presently.

CLARK H. PINNOCK' S "ALTERNATIVE"

Daniel P. Fuller's theories were criticized not only by strict inerrantists, but also by those sympathetic to his concerns. Many simply thought his efforts, though well intentioned, made the situation worse. Perceived inadequacies in his solution might lead others to conclude that no attempt at all should be made to deal more realistically with the "phenomena" in the context of some kind of "inerrancy." If Fuller's efforts were less than satisfactory, might there seem to be no alternative to Warfield except Beegle? So others volunteered to stand in the breach. The most important of these was Clark H. Pinnock, who had begun to move both attitudinally and conceptually from an earlier position of militancy.

Pinnock, like Fuller, was both a disciple of Warfield and an evidential apologist. And, like Fuller, he had long been concerned to present a viable and intelligible doctrine of scriptural inerrancy. Though Pinnock would not have sought novelty for its own sake (after all, the whole point was preserving the truth), his approach to inerrancy may be said to have been somewhat distinctive. Throughout his writings on the subject, he has held fast to the criterion of "intentionality." In his earlier apologetics for inerrancy, Pinnock used the criterion in pretty much the same way Warfield had. The second of Hodge and Warfield's criteria (see above) for proving an error in scripture was: "Let it be proved that the interpretation which occasions the apparent discrepancy is the one which the passage was evidently intended to bear. . . . The true meaning must be definitely and certainly ascertained, and [only] then shown to be irreconcilable with other known truth."[9] Pinnock gave almost central importance to this criterion. For Warfield and Hodge, it seemed to imply merely that no one should charge error in a passage if the problem element might be simply the result of careless interpretation. The "error" might be of one's own making. But Pinnock's writings began to turn the "intention" rule subtly toward new uses. He began to ask just what point the biblical writer had intended to make. Inerrancy applied only to that intended assertion, and not to other features of the text incidental to the main point. The distinction being drawn was analogous to that implied in modern scholarship on the parables of Jesus. For centuries the parables had been interpreted as allegories, each detail bearing separate symbolical significance. But Adolf Jülicher had suggested that such an approach was badly anachronistic. Instead, the parable should be seen as making one point. The various details of the story were nothing more than they seemed to be: details. It was the parabolic story as a whole that made its impact. And, Pinnock said, so with any biblical assertion. What was the point? What was the writer driving at? Biblical authority and inerrancy alike were located only here. The subsidiary details were not in and of themselves proper sources for theological authority. For example, no one should begin baptizing vicariously for the dead merely on the basis of Paul's sidelong reference to the practice in the course of making a different point. And no more should such incidental references be targets for the accusation of error. Only the writer's intended point might or might not be in error (and of course Pinnock held it was not). Note the difference from Warfield here, who had merely sought to disallow accusations of error based on bad exegesis.

At first Pinnock's use of intentionality did not allow for very much flexibility. One reason for this was his attitude toward the "thought/ taught" distinction employed by traditional inerrantists. Warfield had written, "No one is likely to assert infallibility for the apostles in aught else than in their official teaching."[10] In *The Fundamentals*, James M. Gray similarly denied that the biblical writers were "always and everywhere inspired, for then always and everywhere they would have been infallible and inerrant, which was not the case. They sometimes made mistakes in theory and erred in conduct. But . . . such fallibility or errancy was never under any circumstances communicated to their sacred writings."[11] Thus they wrote infallibly *ex cathedra* so to speak, so that a boundary was drawn coterminous with that of the canon, between what erroneous views a biblical writer may have entertained privately, and those inerrant truths asserted by him in the text. Thus apparently Pinnock did not need to check "incidentals" in the text for divinely censored apostolic eccentricities.

At first, Pinnock also shared the strict inerrantists' antipathy for what he himself characterized "deceitful literary forms." While "symbolism, parable, allegory, or proverb" were legitimate biblical genres, myth, legend, and pseudepigraph were not so lucky.[12] These all seemed less than straightforward, relating non-events as unassuming narrative, claiming apostolic authorship for someone else, and so on. And unlike E. J. Carnell, Pinnock rejected as wrong-headed the allowance that source materials occasionally went uncorrected by the scriptural writer. As far as he is concerned, an inspired redactor's task would include such corrections. No errors may be allowed for in this manner.

All these categories might seem ideally conformable to the criterion of intentionality since no such material would bear on the author's intended point. But it was only somewhat later that Pinnock began to take advantage of this fact. Continued study both of the text and of modern scholarship led him to conclude that quite a bit of "erroneous" material could be accommodated by the intentionality rule. Eventually he could write that "one could fairly say that the Bible *contains* errors but *teaches* none, or that inerrancy refers to *subjects* rather than all the *terms* of scripture or to the *teaching* rather than to all the components utilized in its formulation." "But let it be plainly stated that according to this understanding of inerrancy, the Bible is *not* free of all 'errors' in its whole extent, but free of errors where its intended teachings are concerned. Inerrancy has been qualified hermeneutically."[13]

This later view parallels that of the nineteenth-century Catholic theologian Marie-Joseph Lagrange, who wrote

Again, what is important for us is not what [the biblical writer] believed, but what he wanted us to believe. Nevertheless it can happen . . . that we may discover an error on his part; but an error that, thanks be to God—and why not attribute this happy preservation to inspiration?-—he did not teach us formally.[14]

But is it not all too apparent that Pinnock's later position bears just as striking a resemblance to Fuller's "limited inerrancy" view, described earlier? Pinnock balks at the suggestion that his own thinking has moved into the limited inerrancy camp, though "to be candid and fair, we must admit to limiting inerrancy ourselves."[15] What *is* the difference, then? Basically, this: Pinnock objects to Fuller's invocation of 2 Timothy 3:16ff in the attempt to limit the scope of inerrancy to one particular element of scripture as a whole ("revelational matters"). Such a criterion (the "mega-purpose" of scripture) imposed from without, cuts jaggedly across individual biblical assertions, including some and excluding others. Pinnock believes Fuller has, in Walter Kaufmann's phrase, "gerrymandered" the text. True to Warfield, Fuller would seem to be silencing the phenomena of scripture—in this case the "non-revelational" assertions. Instead, Pinnock thinks that if "all scripture is inspired," then each passage should be allowed to speak for itself. And when it has so spoken, it must be deemed inerrant in whatever assertion (salvific or mundane) it has made.

Another critic of Fuller on this point is Stephen T. Davis, who complains that there seems to be

> an ambiguity in Fuller's argument between the intention of the whole Bible [Pinnock's "mega-purpose" of scripture"] and the intention of a particular Biblical writer in a particular passage. It may be that Fuller is correct that the intention of the Bible is to make us "wise unto salvation," but it would be odd to claim that this is the purpose of every single passage in the Bible. . . . Can it ever be a Biblical writer's intent to write a non-revelational . . . proposition?[16]

Davis is indicating the need for the very corrective proposed by Pinnock—the recognition that some assertions do not directly contribute toward the mega-purpose, and that some sense is to be made of them. The sense Pinnock makes of them is, of course, that they too are infallible.

It may be doubted that Pinnock and Davis have rightly construed or criticized Fuller here. In the first place, it is hard to see the difference between Fuller's use of "mega-purpose" texts like 2 Timothy 3:16 and the role played by the same texts in Pinnock's larger doctrine of inspiration. In both, such texts are the warrant for predicating inspiration and authority to biblical assertions at all. One could as well object that Pinnock takes 2 Timothy 3:16 as a license to ride roughshod over texts like Luke 1:1–4, which make no claim to be inspired.[17] In any case, it can be shown that Fuller *is* careful to heed the "mini-purpose" of each biblical statement. Insofar as inerrancy is concerned, "the Biblical writers are to be judged only in terms of the revelational teachings they intended to communicate." Still, inerrancy *does* concern most of the Bible taken text by text (as distinct from scripture *as a whole*), since "Most of its propositions are directly revelatory." As for the rest, their meaning is not suppressed. Fuller openly recognizes that "the Bible's non-revelational statements . . . do not have the same function as its revelational propositions."[18] This does not imply any lack of inspiration, only of inerrancy; the mundane texts fall outside the scope of the second, but not of the first. In fact, Fuller is only able to draw such a distinction because he has listened honestly to the intention of each text and does not strong-arm the texts into appearing to bear some spiritual meaning alien to their natural sense.

So Fuller is not so far from Pinnock as the latter seems to think. Not only so, but Pinnock may not be so far from Fuller as he thinks, either. Pinnock objects to Fuller's arbitrary preference for "revelational" over other material. Yet, surprisingly, the very same distinction may be implied in Pinnock's own position. The question arises in connection with Pinnock's willingness to redraw the old "thought/taught" boundary *through* the text, instead of *around* it as formerly. Now the text may contain erroneous *assumptions* on the part of the writer as long as it makes no erroneous *assertions*. Long ago, Warfield dealt with this possibility, indicating an interesting irony, namely, that to isolate only the writers' explicit "teachings" from their assumptions is, ironically, to retreat from the "Biblical theology" procedure of reconstructing their system of thought, and to return instead to mere proof-texting:

From [the] standpoint [of Biblical theology] it is incredible that one should attribute less importance and authoritativeness to the fundamental conceptions that underlie, color and give form to all of Paul's teaching than to the chance didactic statements he may have been led to make by this or that circumstance at the call of which his letters happened to be written. This certainly would be tithing mint and anise and cumin and omitting the weightier matters of the law.[19]

But surely this cannot be Pinnock's point. He certainly has no intention of inserting such a wedge, as if Paul's theological system might be quite errant so long as the assertions he chances to make are, providentially, correct. It is obvious to read Pinnock and other evangelical New Testament scholars (George E. Ladd, Herman Ridderbos, I. Howard Marshall, Ralph P. Martin, and so on) that for them apostolic assertions and theological assumptions (that is, their systems) all partake of a uniform "apostolic" authority. Warfield's words make it apparent that Pinnock implicitly intends that only the biblical writers' *nontheological* assumptions (for example, flat earth cosmology) be considered dispensable. When this distinction is made explicit, it becomes evident that Pinnock has really been making the same sort of "revelational vs. non-revelational" distinction as Fuller all along.

IS NOTHING SACRED?

One important question remains concerning the comparison of the surprisingly similar viewpoints of Fuller and Pinnock. If both tend to find mundane factual and historical matters expendable, are there *any* historical assertions in scripture that must finally be maintained as inerrant and inviolable? And if so, on what basis is this invulnerability predicated? Beginning with Fuller, it is time to recall the importance of apologetics in his model of limited inerrancy. It makes a great deal of difference that whereas Pinnock's "limited inerrancy" model is a *hermeneutical* device, Fuller's is an *apologetical* device. As noted above, Fuller began his deliberations with the incompatibility of Warfield's views of evidential apologetics on the one hand and of inerrancy on the other. Fuller's first priority was a consistent evidentialist apologetics, for which he was willing to pay the price of having only a "highly probable" conviction instead of the implicit certitude provided by fideism. Furthermore, when he spoke of the extent of inerrancy, the real question was: Just how much of biblical history would have to be disproved before Christian faith would be in serious trouble? (By contrast, Pinnock's question would be something more like: What elements in the text can be safely relied upon for purposes of theology?) That Fuller's real concern is to identify an apologetical "safety-zone" in scripture is clear from the following: "Knowing that verbal inspiration kept the writers free from all error in revelational matters, we are not afraid that what we can learn about history or science ourselves may jeopardize the validity of what the Bible teaches."[20] "I sincerely hope that as I continue my historical-grammatical exegesis of scripture, I shall find no error in its teachings."[21]

The basic strategy to ensure the safety of the doctrinal "teachings" is to make them nonfalsifiable; hence Fuller's definition of "nonrevelational matters" as those which are "capable of being checked out by human investigation." The amazing irony is that Fuller is an evidentialist apologist, and in his *Easter Faith and History*, he contends that the resurrection of Jesus *is* "capable of being checked out by human investigation." In fact, "I argue historically that the risen Jesus must have appeared to Paul and have commissioned him to become an apostle."[22] Fuller pursues this apologetic (to little effect) in his *Easter Faith and History*. Davis is willing to leave this admission as a mere "ambiguity" in Fuller's position, susceptible perhaps to further clarification. But the logic is really quite clear enough: the resurrection narratives *cannot* be inerrant, otherwise they would be useless for evidential apologetics, which seeks precisely to "check out" and verify the resurrection *to a high degree of* (mere!) *probability*. This much is no doubt intentional, however underemphasized in Fuller's essays. What may not be so intentional is the further implication that if (on Fuller's terms) the verifiable is *not* the revelational, and if the historical is the verifiable, then the revelational can not be historical! So Fuller must eventually find himself locating God's revelatory "act" in "raising Jesus" *outside* of the realm of verifiable history (in *Geschichte*), no matter what interesting or odd (*historische*) "facts" he might be able to prove regarding Easter morning. And he might *not* be able to prove any. The text's assertions about a tomb and some apparitions, being in principle verifiable, are therefore also falsifiable, falling outside the scope of inerrancy and into the category of mere instrumental "implications" of the "revelation assertion" of "resurrection."[23] Thus the "revelational truth communicated" about the resurrection would stand as inerrant even should Fuller's apologetical efforts fail to prove the *historical* assertions of the texts! Revelation (in this case, the resurrection) has in principle become dehistoricized (removed from the verifiable realm of "science and history") and could stand apart from any events. Finally, his version of "limited inerrancy" guarantees *no* historical events in the commonly understood sense, not even the resurrection. Fuller has unwittingly recapitulated Bultmann's gulf between history and revelation, and only the latter can be protected by inerrancy in Fuller's sense.

Does Pinnock's version fare any better? At the outset, it may be safely assumed that the problems will at least be different. If nothing else, the focus on hermeneutics rather than apologetics here will change the picture. The prima facie implication of Pinnock's position is that certainly some historical assertions will finally stand as inerrant. This would be expected since the text is supposed to be free to make real assertions (and thus inerrant statements) on any subject. But Pinnock has increased the scope of his "intentionality" criterion (as described above) to accommodate factual and historical "assumptions" as long as they are incidental or instrumental to the intended assertion of the text. And an important element of ambiguity has thereby been introduced. There comes to be an ever-increasing latitude in the concept of "intention." As more and more errors (inaccuracies or contradictions) come to be honestly recognized, the "intention," or "main point" (Davis's suggestion), tends to recede further and further from the external referent. Before he had widened the scope of "intentionality," Pinnock was able to say, "When the scripture records a historical fact, we presume a real event occurred which corresponded to it. . . . In short, infallibility operates under the rubric of a normal 'correspondence idea of truth.'"[24] Not any more. For as more and more errors are acknowledged, virtue is automatically made of necessity, and more and more items slip quietly from the category of "inerrant assertion/main point" into that of "errant instrumental term."

This process is easily illustrated from the works of two other limited inerrantists, Henry P. Hamaan and Harry R. Boer. In *The Bible Between Fundamentalism and Philosophy*, Hamaan declares that it "indeed would be an attack on the inerrancy of the scripture [if] clear biblical statements regarding what happened [were to] be made into statements of what did not happen." So the integrity of narratives must be preserved. Yet Hamaan is not greatly concerned in cases "where the central concern [that is, 'main point'] is clear as clear could be, but where there is irreconcilable disagreement way out on the periphery." For example, whether Jesus entered Jerusalem riding one donkey (Mark) or two (Matthew) is really immaterial; the fact is that he entered. "There is a formal discrepancy in the actual wording, but complete agreement in what is really said [the 'intended assertion']."[25] But how would Hamaan feel about, say, Matthew's account of Jesus walking on the water, where he is joined by Peter, as opposed to the other accounts where Jesus walks alone? Certainly "it is as clear as clear could be" that we are to understand that Jesus walked on water, but poor Peter's adventure is now not only relegated "way out to the periphery," but is *also* "made into a story of what did not happen." Indeed, "Lord, save, we perish!"

Similarly, Boer assures his readers that "it is important to note that the traditional understanding of infallibility is by no means confined to the harmony or harmonizability of data in the several books of scripture." For example,

That Jesus *left* Jericho and was appealed to by *two* blind men (Matthew 20:29–30) is not the same as his leaving Jericho and being appealed to by *one* blind man (Mark 10:46–49) or as his *entering* Jericho and being appealed to by *one* blind man (Luke 18:35–39). That Jesus is the compassionate Savior who responds to all who call on him is the common and abiding teaching.

Note that Boer does not flinch at leapfrogging every historical referent to get to the "abiding teaching." One wonders about the nature of the abiding teaching to be drawn from the disparity between the risen Jesus having "become a . . . spirit" without "flesh and blood" (1 Corinthians 15:45, 50), and his *not* being "a spirit" since he *does* "have flesh and bones" (Luke 24:39). Boer asks, "With these distinctions before us, what must we understand by the infallibility of the Bible?"[26] What indeed ?

As James Barr points out, whenever interest shifts to the "intention" of the writer, the focus shifts from an external, factual referent to an internal, mental referent: "The question is not [any longer] whether Jesus walked on water, but why the Gospel [writer] depicted him as walking on water."[27] Theoretically, could not *any* narrative account, even the resurrection of Jesus, be included among those errors "contained but not taught" in scripture? It is on the basis of just this kind of distinction that Bultmann dispenses with any factual resurrection. It is a legend, but what of it? Its "inerrant assertion" or "intention" or "main point" is that in the kerygma we are offered a new possibility for existence.

In retrospect, the fundamental stone of stumbling for both Pinnock and Fuller seems to be the role played by scripture as the sole warrant for believing in the historical events of revelation. For hermeneut Pinnock, belief is allowed in miraculous redemptive events only if an authoritative scripture can inerrantly guarantee them. For apologist Fuller, belief in such events is forbidden unless the scriptures *as evidence* can bear the scrutiny of historical proof. But Pinnock cannot finally keep hold of any inerrant assertions of historical facts. And because of Fuller's hermeneutical definition of inerrancy (applying only to non-historical, non-*historische*, matters), inerrancy would not only fail to guarantee any events, but it logically separates God's revealing acts from the realm of events anyway! So if scripture is still to be the epistemological channel of access to God's saving acts, they must be dehistoricized. But can evangelical theology survive such major surgery? It would mean a decided step in the direction of Bultmann. Indeed it would mean reaching that destination in a single giant step.

But evangelicals might also be able to follow a path marked out by Karl Barth, who also separated faith from history but in a significantly different manner from Bultmann. Basically, Barth seems to have recognized more clearly than the non-inerrantist evangelicals the implications of historical methodology. As the brief discussion of the principles of continuity and analogy (chapter 1 above) sought to explain, historical-critical study can lend no support to credence in miracles. (Thus the futility of Fuller wanting to approach scripture critically enough to be able to find errors, but hoping still to be able to prove the resurrection.) But at the same time, the methodological inability to find miracles did not prove them never to have occurred. It simply made clear that epistemological contact with such historiographically invisible events must be made via an act of pure faith.

It was apparently on the basis of such a distinction that Barth could affirm the space-time reality of Jesus' resurrection even as he repudiated attempts to verify it historically. Faith, after all, is faith, and why should a Christian balk at it? And history, too, is history; it does no good to balk at it. No matter how long one holds his breath, historical method will not change to appease him. Evangelicals have never found Barth's stance very congenial. Some were evidentialist apologists who would have looked askance at fideism whoever suggested it. But John Warwick Montgomery expressed a more serious concern:

> I get the impression that [Barth] would prefer not to speak of the historical method at all in connection with the resurrection. He is willing to use it in connection with the death of Christ—with those

events that are of a natural and normal type. But it appears to me that with regard to the resurrection, for example, there is a hesitancy that doesn't arise simply from Barth's refusal to take a rationalistic position on miracles. He seems unhappy with any use of historical method in relation to the resurrection.

Montgomery feels that, instead, one must either claim that the resurrection objectively happened "and is subject to empirical investigation, or contend that it [didn't], by the very fact that there is [supposedly] no way of determining the fact. . . . To claim objectivity [for the resurrection], but to remove any possibility of determining it, is by definition to destroy [its] objectivity."[28]

Montgomery quite properly questions the meaningfulness of an asserted "resurrection" that is so ambiguous in nature that one cannot even say how one would go about trying to verify or falsify it! He is no doubt thinking of Liberal "ideas" of the resurrection, for example, Hans Küng's: "There was nothing to photograph or to record."[29] But Montgomery is mistaken in charging Barth with such equivocation. When the latter calls the resurrection "unverifiable," he means it in a very different sense. For Barth, there *was* something, so to speak, to photograph or record, but unfortunately we have arrived on the scene several centuries too late. Cameras and recorders we may have, but time machines we do not. The resurrection is not unverifiable (better, unfalsifiable) in *principle*, but it is unverifiable in *fact* because of the inescapable methodological limits of historical investigation.

Is this merely a return to rude biblicism ("I believe whatever the Bible reports, and historical study be damned!"), and so a renunciation of "limited" inerrancy? In other words, with such "immunity" from historical-critical disproof of miracles, would Pinnock and Fuller have any basis left for admitting errors on mundane matters, for example, Pekah's reign or the mustard seed? Yes, they would, since such matters are not supposed to be extraordinary or miraculous, and thus can readily be confirmed or disconfirmed by the historian. In other words, it would be meaningless to suggest any legitimate alternative epistemological path to *these* biblical claims. A miracle may have occurred, and historians may have to dub the report of it a "legend" for want of any closer analogy in experience. But with King Pekah, it never even gets to this stage. Logically, his reign *cannot* have been two different lengths. A miracle may have occurred and be inevitably mistaken for a legend, but one reign lasting eight years and twenty years at the same time is just nonsensical.

A "LIMITED" ADJUSTMENT

With the adjustments suggested here, a viable and natural criterion for limiting inerrancy would be available. All parties to the inerrancy debate admit that *some* sections of the Bible (for example, the poetry) cannot fall under the "inerrancy" rubric either negatively or positively since they are not "assertions" and thus do not ask to be "believed." A viable limitation principle would recognize that there are also different kinds of assertions, or that various assertions by nature invite various kinds of responses. While all assertions by definition intend to be believed, they may implicitly invite and expect belief on different criteria. Historical and scientific statements are put forth with the understanding that evidence will bear them out, and their reader/hearer is responding as intended if he goes to check before he agrees. (If he refrains from checking this time because checking in the past has convinced him of the trustworthiness, competence, or whatever, of the speaker/writer, this is the same thing.) An assertion like "I love you" invites a response of the emotions, which is not exactly cognitive belief, but which does accept and agree with the assertion. Revelations (for example, "Behold, I show you a mystery, we shall not all sleep," and so on) are in a different class still. Here a cognitive agreement, or belief, is invited and expected. But on what basis? Not investigation, "for flesh and blood has not revealed it to you." On what basis is the assertion being presented? "Not by persuasive words of wisdom, but a demonstration of the Spirit's power." If we respond by investigating, we violate the nature of the assertion and reject it. We respond appropriately, we believe or agree, on the basis of what would perhaps formally be called "intuition." Materially, we would call it "the testimony of the Spirit."

The point is that assertions based on revelation invite belief in the sense of "faith," not in the sense of "studied agreement." They are the assertions of which one says, "They are inerrant," though this is a rather odd way of saying it. After all, "inerrant" only means "correct." It would be better to say revelational assertions are those by nature able to invite our verdict of "inerrant" or simply "true" *automatically*. Other kinds of statements cannot expect and do not even implicitly invite automatic belief of this kind. By contrast, mundane claims invite "trust" in the sense either of "Look, I haven't steered you wrong yet, have I?" (that is, sufficient verification in the past) or "Hey, *trust* me!" (that is, take an acknowledged risk—no confidence implied at all). Not all biblical assertions are of a revelational nature. Psalms, as no one denies, may invite sympathy, but in the nature of the case could not command "belief." Assertions in the form of Proverbs appeal to the obvious congruency of the proverb to the facts of experience to which it refers. Its observation is to be accepted as *wisdom* (inductively derived), not *revelation* (deductively derived). Assertions as to how long a king reigned invite verification before agreement (even if only implicitly, as when someone says, "If you can show me different, I'll gladly change my mind"). Assertions of any event, even the occurrences of miracles, are no different, and none are to be taken simply "on faith." For instance, see 1 Corinthians 15:6b where Paul implicitly invites verification ("Most of them are still living," that is, "Go ask them, if you don't believe me."). (That there turns out to be a special difficulty in verifying reports of miracles does not change this.) Assertions and injunctions regarding decorum, morals, or doctrine invite assent on various kinds of grounds, depending on the basis on which the assertion or injunction is being made. If Paul forbids women to teach on the basis of debatable Old Testament exegesis (1 Timothy 2:12–14), the proper response is quite different than if he forbids Pentecostal chaos by the authority of his own inspiration ("If anyone thinks he is a prophet, let him recognize that what I say is the command of the Lord," 1 Corinthians 14:37). If Paul calls homosexuality a reprobate perversion (Romans 1:26–27) because of his prescientific assumption that such sexual preference is "against [their] nature,"[30] our assent is not expected to be different in kind from our confidence in the original assumption. He is *reasoning* with us, and invites our *evaluation* of his arguments. But if he affirms that Christ has risen and is the end of the Law for anyone who believes, he makes it on the implied grounds that "I received it by revelation from Jesus Christ" (Galatians 1:12), and the response invited is one of faith. We believe it implicitly.

Only this kind of assertion invites that sort of unqualified assent implied in "inerrancy" language. Others imply, "Come, let us reason together," and should we come away unconvinced as to the claim, even this will not be an inappropriate response. Basically, then, if one recognizes that, by nature, only some kinds of assertions expect automatic (faith) assent, it becomes superfluous to invoke a "doctrine of inerrancy" over the ones that *do* invite faith, and arbitrary and artificial to invoke it over those that do *not*.

Thus, there is available a viable "limitation" criterion. It satisfies Pinnock's desire to let each text make its own (kind of) claim. It satisfies Fuller's desire to limit unqualified assent to revelational statements. And it safeguards the historical reality of the crucial salvific acts of God. It can do this while Pinnock's and Fuller's criteria could not, because it derives this historical element not from *historical* assertions but from *revelational/kerygmatic* assertions entailing events, such as Galatians 1:12 and 1 Corinthians 15:1, 3ff. Incidentally, the anchoring of the salvific acts by deriving them from kerygmatic texts also enables us to tell just which ones are the "necessary" ones to believe (just which ones we are being asked by revelation to believe, and so to which we have legitimate extra-historiographical epistemological access). It should be apparent that the limited-inerrancy approach outlined here also meets the objection usually aimed at limited inerrantists, "False in one, false in all," or truer to the intention of the objector, "If false at one point, then possibly false at any point." The implied problem is a real one for most limited inerrantists, because they agree with the strict inerrantists in flattening all biblical assertions out to the same level; all are imagined to claim belief in the same way. The strict inerrantist cannot see any criterion for denying some texts' claims and not others. Fuller offered a criterion, but an unworkable one: Texts dealing with mundane matters could be denied at the reader's discretion, but some revelational statements were arbitrarily placed in a safety zone, with others outside it. For Pinnock, all affirmations were to be accepted, but it was made difficult or impossible finally to locate the "assertion" in the text. For Stephen T. Davis, *any* statement may be denied at the reader's discretion, as long as he feels he has a good reason for doing so! "I believe it is a Christian's responsibility to accept *whatever* the Bible says on *any subject whatsoever* unless there is compelling reason not to accept it. That is, everything in the Bible is authoritative and normative for the Christian until he comes across a passage which for good reasons he cannot accept."[31]

For Davis, then, scripture is "presumed inerrant until proven guilty." In terms of the present model of limited inerrancy, Davis is regarding all texts as if their claims to assent were of one kind, as if all alike were empirical assertions inviting assent only subject to verification. (His standpoint, then, is the mirror-image of that of the strict inerrantist, who treats all biblical assertions as if they were revelational in our sense and thus able to expect implicit acceptance.) Actually, Davis's schema is the most clearly suicidal of all the limited inerrancy positions. If he followed it out consistently, his attitude would be, "All biblical claims are guilty until proven inerrant." Having introduced the possibility of falsification across the board, he should *not* believe *any* text unless he has a good reason for doing so. It can tell him nothing he doesn't already know. All Davis can really justify doing is to "agree" with the Bible when it matches what he already knows, and, otherwise, to decide naively to believe in the absence of prior knowledge either way. Anyone attracted to this model of biblical "authority" should keep in mind an extra-biblical aphorism: "Fool me once, shame on you; fool me twice, shame on me." Whereas Davis's model invites the strict inerrantist's objection like Saul invited his armor-bearer's sword-thrust, the model proposed in this chapter meets that objection by providing a criterion for accepting and rejecting the claims of each text by *responding as invited* to each, whether with investigative scrutiny, with empathy, with evaluation, or with implicit faith. This last response (the kind usually intended by "inerrancy" language) is reserved only for revelation assertions, since *no other* biblical assertions even invite it. A "doctrine of inerrancy" (limited or otherwise) is seen to be simply redundant. The only question is, Does one "believe" the Bible where it asks to be "believed"?

This chapter has discussed various attempts to "limit" inerrancy, primarily those of Daniel P. Fuller and Clark H. Pinnock. Other limited inerrantists including Harry R. Boer and Henry P. Hamaan tended to echo Pinnock, while Stephen T. Davis's limitation of inerrancy proved to be virtually a self-drawn caricature of the limited-inerrancy position. As such it served as a foil in the discussion of other models, since it clearly illustrated dangers which the others attempted to avoid. On the surface, the differences between Fuller and Pinnock would seem to fulfill the predictions of the strict inerrantists, that once the Bible is admitted to be mistaken at any point, then it must be deemed at least potentially "errant" everywhere. As Charles Caldwell Ryrie puts it, "If the Bible is not completely without error, then it must have at least one error in it. Now if we could all agree on where that one error is, the problem might conceivably be tolerated."[32] But Fuller and Pinnock hardly seem to agree on where the error, or the category of admissible errors, may be found. Yet, on closer examination, it became apparent that Fuller and Pinnock were after all not so far apart. Both tended to make pretty much *any historical* datum negotiable in the effort to safeguard doctrinal or salvific texts. By the same token, both also proved unable to draw any hard-and-fast line safeguarding the "mighty acts of God in history." The discussion concluded with some suggestions as to how such a line might be drawn, by distinguishing the various grounds of assent implied in the various kinds of biblical assertions.

NOTES

1. Thomas Henry Huxley, quoted in John C. Greene, *Darwin and the Modern World View* (New York: New American Library, 1963), p. 21.

2. Cf. Warfield, *Inspiration and Authority*, p. 112; and Pinnock, "Limited Inerrancy," pp. 156–57.

3. Harrison, "Criteria of Biblical Inerrancy," p. 63.

4. Benjamin B. Warfield, quoted in Daniel P. Fuller, "Benjamin B. Warfield's View of Faith and History," *Bulletin of the Evangelical Theological Society* 11 (Spring 1968): 77.

5. Naturally, this passage has reference only to the Old Testament, as the New was not yet written. Here presupposed is the formulary invocation of the text by evangelicals as a warrant for the inspiration of the whole Protestant canon.

6. Daniel P. Fuller, "The Nature of Biblical Inerrancy," *Journal of the American Scientific Affiliation* (June 1972): 50.

7. Burtchaell, *Catholic Theories*, pp. 58, 62.

8. Fuller, "Nature of Biblical Inerrancy," p. 48.

9. Hodge and Warfield, *Inspiration*, p. 36.

10. Warfield, *Inspiration and Authority*, p. 196.

11. James M. Gray, "The Inspiration of the Bible—Definition, Extent and Proof," in *Fundamentals* 2:11.

12. Clark H. Pinnock, *A Defense of Biblical Infallibility* (Nutley, NJ: Presbyterian & Reformed Publishing, 1975), p. 28.

13. Pinnock, "Inerrancy Debate among Evangelicals," pp. 7, 8.

14. Burtchaell, *Catholic Theories*, p. 145; also cf. p. 154.

15. Pinnock, "Limited Inerrancy," p. 148.

16. Davis, *Debate about the Bible*, p. 47.

17. Subsequent writings suggest that Pinnock has come to see things in precisely this way. If so, then Pinnock may be said to have entered a third major period of thought. But the present discussion deals only with the model of inerrancy manifest in the mid to late-seventies, when he was interacting with Fuller.

18. Fuller, "Nature of Biblical Inerrancy," p. 50.

19. Warfield, *Inspiration and Authenticity*, p. 199.

20. Fuller, "Nature of Biblical Inerrancy," p. 50.

21. Daniel P. Fuller, "On Revelation and Biblical Authority," *Journal of the Evangelical Theological Society* 17 (Spring 1973), quoted in Davis, *Debate about the Bible*, p. 42.

22. Fuller, "Nature of Biblical Inerrancy," p. 88.

23. As his writings "Biblical Theology & the Analogy of Faith" and *Easter Faith and History* show, Fuller has affinities with the *Heilsgeschichte* School of Oscar Cullmann, Werner Georg Kümmel, Gerhard von Rad, et al. According to one of the leading proponents of this movement, G. Ernest Wright, this "is a theology of recital or proclamation of the acts *of* God, together with the inferences drawn therefrom. These *acts are themselves interpretations of* historical events . . . described within the conceptual frame of . . . a certain historical continuum." G. Ernest Wright, *God who Acts* (London: SCM Press, 1966), p. 11. (Emphasis mine.) Of course this is the very sense intended by Bultmann when he speaks of the "act" of God in Christ's death and resurrection. The resurrection is the *geschichtliche*, interpretative, part of the "act," whereas the death is the *Dass* or bare *historische* event. Fuller's fellow evangelicals (and others like James Barr) have always had difficulty pinning down just what kind of an "act" in "history" we are talking about here. Fuller might have done well to ask himself the same question.

24. Pinnock, *Defense of Biblical Infallibility*, p. 13.

25. Henry P. Hamaan, *The Bible Between Fundamentalism and Philosophy* (Minneapolis: Augsburg Publishing House, 1980), p. 60.

26. Harry R. Boer, *Above the Battle? The Bible and Its Critics* (Grand Rapids: William B. Eerdmans Publishing Co., 1977), pp. 82, 83.

27. Barr, *Bible in the Modern World*, pp. 173–74.

28. John Warwick Montgomery, *History and Christianity* (Downers Grove, IL: InterVarsity Press, 1974), pp. 89, 87–88.

29. Hans Küng, *On Being a Christian*, trans. Edward Quinn (New York: Pocket Books, 1978), p. 349.

30. John Boswell, *Christianity, Social Tolerance, and Homosexuality* (Chicago: University of Chicago Press, 1980), pp. 107–13.

31. Davis, *Debate about the Bible*, p. 75.

32. Charles Caldwell Ryrie, *What You Should Know about Inerrancy* (Chicago: Moody Press, 1981), p. 21.

Chapter 4

ENIGMA AND KERYGMA

An Infallible Central Message

A HIDDEN DISTINCTION

*A*lmost alone among commentators on the recent evangelical controversy, Robert K. Johnston has noticed a division among those who reject the strict inerrancy position of Lindsell, Henry, and Schaeffer. He describes the basic difference between what he calls "complete infallibilists" and "partial infallibilists." The first are those who take all scriptural *assertions,* but not all scriptural *assumptions*, as infallible (or at least take all revelational/doctrinal statements as infallible). These of course are the "limited inerrantists" discussed in the previous chapter. The second group is constituted by those who "believe that the [biblical] authors' intended message is in error at points, but their witness to the gospel is trustworthy and authoritative."[1] As a matter of fact, it is difficult to understand how this distinction has not occupied a more important position in the present debate. Even Johnston's own ensuing discussion seems largely to ignore it. It is easy to see why strict inerrantists would bypass this difference; errancy is errancy is heresy, after all. But those who reject strict inerrancy really have some further choices to make.

Pinnock rejects the defining of inerrancy or infallibility according to a "mega-purpose" of scripture as a whole. Such a strategy, he feels, gives up too much ground unnecessarily. Thus, his own approach seeks to salvage some kind of infallibility of each text's assertion. While his attempt has serious difficulties, the "limited inerrancy" model as a *type* of framework we found to be viable in dealing with the kind of textual data found to be problematical by limited inerrantists ("complete infallibilists"), namely *factual inaccuracies and narrative contradictions*. The "partial infallibilists" also seek to deal with this data. In fact, reading most presentations of their views, one might receive the impression that the "partialist" model was developed in response only to such difficulties. If this were the case, Pinnock's implied criticism of "partial infallibility," that its "mega-purpose" acts as a Procrustean Bed within the Bible, would be justified. But the partial infallibility model is actually concerned with a far more serious problem. The limited inerrantists seemed to suppose that if those irritating mistakes could be gotten rid of, biblical authority would have found a safe haven at last. Not so fast, say the partial infallibilists; factual contradictions are unfortunately not the only kind. There are also *theological contradictions* within the Bible, perhaps lots of them, and it does no good to ignore them. In a sense, no evangelical has ever ignored them. This problem is at the root of fundamentalist attempts to harmonize, which have resulted in an embarrassing de facto repudiation of the grammatico-historical (or "plain sense") approach at selected points. J. I. Packer writes "As for the principle of harmony, this . . . is dictated by the doctrine of inspiration, which tells us that the scriptures are the product of a single divine mind. . . . Scripture should not be set against scripture. . . . The basis for this principle is the expectation that the teaching of the God of truth will prove to be consistent with itself."[2] John Warwick Montgomery supplies the consequent strategy: "A passage of Holy scripture is to be taken as true in its natural, literal sense unless . . . an article of faith established elsewhere in scripture requires a broader understanding of the text."[3] Alas, one might have hoped that strict inerrantists would at least require of a harmonization what Hodge and

Warfield required of an alleged error—that it faithfully represent the probable intention of the author.

Limited inerrantists reject the effort to harmonize narrative discrepancies (for example, Peter's *six* denials) as being beneath scholarly dignity. It would be painful to see them suddenly refurbishing their gymnastic skills in order to maintain that their "infallible" scripture had no *doctrinal* discrepancies. And while the limited inerrancy (complete infallibilist) model does not seem to allow for the possibility of doctrinal conflicts, the entire partial infallibilist effort is predicated directly upon the problem. The basic strategy is to reach a sort of "lowest common denominator" or "central message" that may be claimed as infallible. These evangelicals, innovators though they are in their own recent context, are following directly in the footsteps of the "Biblical Theology" or *Heilsgeschichte* School of the 1940s and 1950s.[4] This chapter will briefly explore the "central message" model of the partial infallibilists, testing its viability in an evangelical context by comparing it with both the *Heilsgeschichte* School and traditional evangelical criticisms of that movement.

THE BIBLICAL THEOLOGY MOVEMENT

Heilsgeschichte means "sacred history" or "history of salvation." And it was this element that provided the theme in terms of which biblical scholars construed "the message of the New Testament." This last phrase occurred constantly in the literature of the Biblical Theology Movement, for example, in titles like Joachim Jeremias's *The Central Message of the New Testament* and A. M. Hunter's *The Message of the New Testament*. In the latter, Hunter declared, "The central message of the New Testament is . . . the record of the completion of God's saving purpose for his People through the sending of his Son the Messiah."[5] The redemption in Christ was the last of a series of "mighty acts of God," another phrase appearing with incessant regularity in this literature, for example, G. Ernest Wright, *God Who Acts*, and G. Ernest

Wright with Reginald H. Fuller, *The Book of the Acts of God*. From the latter comes the statement, "The central concern is to bear testimony to the story of what [God] has done to save men and to bring his kingdom into being on this earth."[6] Wright also set forth a key distinction that marked the thought of the whole movement, as well as, it was thought, that of the Bible itself: "Biblical theology . . . is *not propositional and systematic dogmatics. . . .* It is a theology of recital or proclamation of the acts of God, together with the inferences drawn therefrom."[7] (Emphasis mine.)

George E. Ladd was probably the first well-known evangelical scholar to embrace this approach openly, but several other major figures have followed him. A few representative statements will demonstrate the particular value seen by partial infallibilist evangelicals in this model:

Our thesis is that the unity of New Testament theology is found in the fact that the several strata share a common view of God, who visits man in history to effect the salvation of both man, the world, and history; and that diversity exists in the several interpretations of this one redemptive event.[8] (Ladd)

Every word about the God-breathed character of scripture is meaningless if Holy scripture is not understood as the witness concerning Christ. . . . It is only regarding this centrality that it is legitimate to speak of the unity of Holy scripture. It is a unity of witness and cannot be derived a priori and deductively from the revealed character of the entire scripture.[9] (G. C. Berkouwer)

Infallibility is limited only by the intention of the author and the kerygmatic nature of the biblical message. As a Christian historian, I see the Bible as *the* remarkable account of the historical acting out of God's love and man's response. The tensions, difficulties, and possible contradictions we encounter are not the blemishes of a system of doctrine and practice, but the natural result of writers who were compelled to preach the Gospel in the language and forms of their contemporaries.[10] (Richard J. Coleman)

From these pragmatic statements it can be seen not only that these scholars have recapitulated the basic *Heilsgeschichte* model, but also that they have a special concern with theological diversity and the consequent difficulties of systematizing biblical teachings. Of course this is no new concern, having been important in the Biblical Theology Movement as well.

As is well known, evangelicals were mightily disturbed by what they perceived as a shift in the Biblical Theology camp from "propositional revelation" to "personal encounter." This shift, too, can readily be discerned in the partial infallibilists' model: "The Biblical writers are witnessing to their experiences of a person. They are not primarily outlining a system of abstract ideas"[11] (Jack Rogers). "Scripture is not composed of a number of isolated words, theses, and truths expressed, but a centered witness. . . . [The] purpose of the God breathed scripture is not at all to . . . increase human knowledge and wisdom, but to witness of the salvation of God unto faith"[12] (Berkouwer). "So he has provided us with a casebook rather than with a theology text book"[13] (Charles Kraft). "Men and women encounter in the Bible's pages a Person whose words and deeds meet our central human needs. . . . We should not impose on scripture a demand that it produce rational . . . rules, objective, impersonal truths"[14] (Rogers). Finally, George Ladd admits that he no longer adheres to "the older orthodox view . . . that 'revelation, in the biblical sense of the term, is the communication of information.' [Rather] revelation moves in the dimension of personal encounter . . . God reveals himself."[15] It is perhaps worth noting that this change in emphasis does not imply that the Bible yields no "truths" or "information," as traditional evangelical critics of the Biblical Theology School used to allege. Rather, what information there is, is in the form of proclamation, directing the reader to experience a personal encounter with God. Evangelicals often pointed out with indignation that propositional revelation was not "nonsense."[16] Certainly, the Bible mediates "personal encounter," as evangelicals must be the last to deny. But isn't it reasonable that "propositions" *about* this God would be helpful? Otherwise, one is embarking on a rather

dangerous "blind date." The original proponents of "Biblical Theology" and the new heirs of this model agree that propositional revelation is an intelligible enough idea. The problem lies elsewhere,
namely, in that critical study of the Bible makes it impossible to see
much of the text as literal propositional revelation, since various theological assertions in the text contradict each other. Traditionalists had
always welcomed "diversity" in the text, since this sort of difference
could be ascribed to the "multifaceted" nature of revelation. But this
rubric, as inerrantists readily admitted, could not accommodate the
presence of different interpretations of the same point that *disagreed*
with each other. So some alternative formula had to be found, whereby
the "proposition" or "information" category would be restricted to a
defensible common core. And this in turn required a modified understanding of revelation and inspiration.

Room was made for just such an adjustment by clearing a bit of
space between the saving "acts of God" and the human witness to
those acts preserved in the Bible. Wright gave clear expression of what
was envisioned here: "Israel's doctrine of God . . . was not derived
from systematic or speculative thought, but rather in the first instance
from the attempt to explain the events which led to the establishment
of the nation. . . . The knowledge of God was an inference from what
actually had happened in history."[17] Traditional evangelicals,
including at one time George Ladd, saw this view as severely inadequate and set themselves squarely against it. Ladd wrote, "Revelation
[indeed] occurred in specific concrete events . . . but essential to the
events are the divinely inspired words of the prophets . . . setting forth
. . . the revelatory meaning of these events. Men were not left to spec-
ulate, to infer what events might mean: God spoke His Word."[18] But
many evangelicals, including some of Ladd's colleagues at Fuller Theological Seminary, began to sound increasingly like G. Ernest Wright.
Jack Rogers speaks not so much of the normative prescriptions of the
Bible in doctrine and practice, but rather of "how the Biblical writers
understood and applied the gospel."[19] Charles Kraft states, "The purpose of scripture is . . . not to tell us about God's essence (though . . .

we deduce much on this subject), but to show us how he relates to us."[20] Compare Kraft's statement with one by Wright: "The being and attributes of God are nowhere systematically presented but are inferences from events."[21]

EVANGELICAL OPPOSITION

Mention has already been made several times of traditional evangelicals' criticisms of the Biblical Theology Movement. What were the basic objections? If non-inerrantist evangelicals are now espousing the important tenets of the *Heilsgeschichte* School, have they been able to overcome those objections? First, the objections: from the outset, evangelicals were suspicious of both Barthians and the Biblical Theology thinkers, because while both allegedly wanted to go "back to the Bible," neither rejected the critical study of the Bible, "higher criticism." Granted, they had repudiated many of the more radical conclusions of early critics, but they were far from espousing inerrancy or verbal inspiration. So just as in the fundamentalist-modernist controversy, it was the very closeness to evangelical conservatism that made the remaining differences seem all the more dangerous. For example, see the contemptuous and disdainful rejoinder of J. I. Packer to the Biblical Theology Movement in *'Fundamentalism' and the Word of God*: "If they were consistent in reading the Bible 'from within' and receiving what its authors were concerned to teach, they would be led to the doctrine of scripture which we have expounded."[22] And of course there was Cornelius Van Til's dismissal of Barthian neoorthodoxy as *The New Modernism*, a title after which, what more need be said? It was beginning to look as if what one thought about Wellhausen or Kant were more important than what one thought about Jesus Christ.

But the failure to reject higher criticism in the name of inerrancy would have disqualified any competing theology. What specifically were the problems besetting the *Heilsgeschichte* School? Could the demon be forced to name itself? The fundamental problem was the gap perceived to exist between God's "mighty acts" and their interpretation. Biblical Theology spokesmen seemed to attribute the biblical interpretations of the saving acts to purely human inference, possibly even mistaken ones. This poisoned stream went on to split into two channels.

First, talk about the "mighty acts" sometimes seemed so hazy (evasive?) that it was doubtful whether any "acts" were thought to have occurred anywhere but in someone's imagination. Wright's foundational book *God Who Acts* was typical of this tendency. It criticized demythologizing, but seemed less than straightforward on whether any supernatural phenomena occurred. And suspicions were inevitably aroused when he himself said of the saving "acts" that they "are themselves interpretations of historical events."[23] Thus it was understandable that Kenneth S. Kantzer should charge that "the contemporary cliché 'mighty acts' of God, . . . skirts the issue of a supernatural miracle. . . . The significance of the Biblical miracle is to be found primarily in that God is acting directly."[24] James Barr (hardly a fundamentalist) had some doubts along the same lines. He thought it "not unfair to say that the 'event' of the biblical narrative is [construed by the Biblical Theology writers as] a mythical representation of an actual saving event which is however of quite a different character."[25] Behind such comments lurks healthy commonsense skepticism: Had we been there, and seen chariots mired in the *Reed* Sea, instead of covered by the *Red* Sea, would we have been so sure it was a "mighty act of God," or maybe just an awfully lucky break?

It will be remembered that in the preceding chapter, Daniel P. Fuller was criticized on the basis that his particular limited inerrancy model tended toward the very dichotomy in question here. That is, he wound up having to place the revelatory aspect of the resurrection in a suprahistorical, nonverifiable realm, even as the historical facts of Easter morning were in principle verifiable, but thus nonrevelatory. Of course he never said (or intended) as much, yet his confusing treatment of the resurrection as revelational in some sense, yet verifiable in another, led logically to this end. Partial infallibilists espousing a *Heils-*

geschichte approach do not fall into the same trap. They never suggest that miracles (at least those deemed integral to the central message) were anything but supernatural, though on occasion there is the admission that their *significance* would be unavailable to the historian *as* historian. While this admission might be enough to rile the ire of extreme evidentialists like John Warwick Montgomery, it should provide no grounds for suspicions like those understandably directed at Wright.

The second result of the new evaluation of God's "acts" as purely human in interpretation was the denial of propositional revelation. The original *Heilsgeschichte* writers were perceived by many evangelicals as rejecting *in toto* the divine origin of the interpretive word of the biblical writers. Warfield had already anticipated the difficulty. "Scripture," he contended, is "not merely . . . [as Warfield's opponents claimed] the record of the redemptive acts by which God is saving the world, but [is] itself one of these redemptive acts."[26] Later, during the controversy with the Biblical Theology Movement, J. I. Packer reiterated, "Doctrines, on this view, are not revelation, though they are formulated on the basis of revelation. . . . [God's] teaching us truths about himself is hereby ruled out. . . . We are to regard scripture as a human response and witness to revelation, but not in any sense revelation itself."[27] Though there is quite a large measure of truth in Packer's assessment, it is still seriously misleading at one important point. His opponents did not actually deny that revelation was also in play in the interpretation of the "acts." Wright himself sounds like an evangelical when he claims that "such events need interpretation before their true meaning can be understood. . . . By means of human agents God provides each event with an accompanying Word of interpretation."[28]

By themselves, these words may also be as misleading as Packer's. Certainly there was still a major difference between the two camps somewhere. Taking into account the belief of Wright and others in the God-given nature of the interpretation, Carl Henry's criticism is more modest and more helpful than Packer's:

> The spiritual meaning of these sacred events is divinely given, not humanly postulated. Here . . . *Heilsgeschichte* and conservative

scholars agree. But how is this divine meaning of sacred history given to faith? Conservative scholars insist that . . . the New Testament documents as they testify to divine deed-revelation give, or *are* themselves, divine truth-revelation. . . . The *Heilsgeschichte* scholars compromise the conservative view because of their prior critical rejection of the historical Christian understanding of revelation in terms of the infallible divine communication of propositional truths. Their emphasis falls instead upon individual spiritual encounter . . . as the focal point of the revelation of divine meaning.[29]

Or, as Richard J. Coleman sums up the problem, "It is an issue not of whether God acts and man interprets, but whether . . . man's interpretation is received *directly* from God."[30] (Emphasis mine.) Though God gives the interpretation, he does not communicate "absolute truths" about himself "because man cannot be delivered from his historical environment and his sinful nature for a moment in order to perceive utterly new and unknown divine truths."[31] Coleman has located precisely the point of difference. So Wright does indeed believe that God revealed himself not only in the events, but also in their interpretation, but "all that the Biblical writers present they inevitably cast in terms of the world-view of their day. . . . The revelation of God occurred within the conceptual life of the people then."[32]

Here is the real difficulty with "propositional revelation." Let it be noted that both evangelicals and *Heilsgeschichte* theologians agree that revelation comes to the human interpreters in "time-bound" or "culture-bound" forms. But the latter are willing to include under this rubric major theological concepts. The former, on the other hand, limit the time-bound character to the words themselves, so that basically all that is necessary is translation.[33] By contrast, the "didactic thought models" (Pinnock) of today's theology must be those of the biblical writers, since these are integral to the revelation itself, and not just the culture-bound forms in which revelation is given. So depending on which side of the temporal/eternal divide the biblical thought-forms are placed, one is deciding for or against "propositional revelation." Or, probably more accurately, one would be deciding just how *literally* true the propositions are to be taken, or how exact they are in their correspondence to the divine realities.

At this point it is evident that the question has resurfaced as to whether human language can represent divine truth in more than an equivocal or analogous way. This had become an issue earlier in the debate over "conceptual" versus "verbal" inspiration (see chapter 2). Only now the issue is drawn far more seriously. Neo-evangelicals balked even at Bernard Ramm's mere suggestion that while the concepts *were* of heavenly origin, the words were supplied by the human author (within a providentially demarcated range). Might our partial infallibilist evangelicals take this significant step beyond even Ramm? Could the "didactic thought-models" themselves be human in origin (though, again, apparently within an allowable range)? It seems so; but is such a step inevitably a departure from evangelical orthodoxy? Jack Rogers and Donald K. McKim do not think so. They are able to make creative use of the traditional category of "accommodation" to accomplish the shift. Some evangelicals had already used the notion of accommodation to discount the seriousness of undeniably prescientific cosmology in the Bible. God, it was said, accommodated himself to human cultural limitations by revealing, say, the fact of creation in terms understandable to "the people back then" as one often hears it said. Even this fairly modest use of the idea has occasioned controversy. The rare evangelical who denies the literal understanding of demon-possession as depicted in the Synoptic gospels, feels that if *he* knows that demons were just neuroses and psychoses, surely *Jesus* must have been privy to the fact, too. He merely "accommodated" himself to the people's (lack of) understanding. This kind of explanation seldom passes unchallenged. This would make Jesus a deceiver. Apparently it is a good deal easier to agree that the earth is not flat despite Genesis chapter 1, than to agree that demons were really psychological aberrations. Since for most evangelicals, demons are purely hypothetical, rather like the "Pre-Tribulation Rapture" or the Trinity, it is harder to disconfirm them. At any rate, accommodation has a long if uneven acceptance among evangelicals.

Rogers and McKim's use of the idea seems to mark something of a new departure, at least in the American evangelical context. For they take God to have accommodated the revelation of his truth not only to his audience, but in the first instance to the mediators of the revelation themselves. In other words, it is not so much that "Moses wrote you this for the hardness of your hearts," as that "God wrote Moses this for the hardness of his heart," or at least for the limits of his vision. This is most clearly visible when, for example, Paul Jewett deals with Paul and his "rabbinic" teaching on the status of women (more about this in chapter 6 below). And for Rogers this means that theologians today are not by any means bound by any system of thought present in the Bible.

"Persons in other parts of the world neither think nor express their thoughts the way we do." "The cultural setting of the Bible is different from our culture both because of time and place. It is ancient and it is Near Eastern." Thus for the Bible, religion "is not an ideology, a system of thought, or a code of ethics, but a way of life in which one walks." And the result for the contemporary theologian? He or she must "take the central message of scripture . . . and translate it into the forms of our . . . contemporary culture."[34] Or as A. M. Hunter had put it during the heyday of the Biblical Theology Movement, today's theologian must "do for our generation what they [the biblical writers] so magnificently did for theirs."[35]

It has by now become evident that while the partial infallibilist evangelicals have embraced the old *Heilsgeschichte* or Biblical Theology model in most of its essentials, they have not done this uncritically. They managed to avoid completely the traditional evangelical objection that this model tended to make God's saving acts nonmiraculous. And the other major criticism (that propositional revelation is rejected), while definitely not avoided, was considerably blunted in force. This was done by showing how this very "relativization" could be brought about by the consistent extension of principles already held by evangelicals. Indeed, in so doing, they have in effect given a belated defense on behalf of Wright and others censured in the past by Packer, Kantzer, and Henry.

THE CENTRAL MESSAGE AND
ITS IMPLICATIONS

The essence of the discussion so far is that theological disunity within the Bible has been accommodated by the postulation of a normative core or "central message" of salvation to which all else is peripheral in both authority and importance. Now more detailed attention must be given to the implications of this change for the doctrine of inspiration and for hermeneutics. First of all, if inspiration has been relativized by the admission that biblical thought-forms are not directly revealed, then it is not initially clear why a "central message" would be any more authoritative than peripheral matters. Are not both types of material relativized? Inspiration clearly does not count for quite as much as it did in more traditional evangelical models. One might think to object to this assertion, saying for instance, "Inspiration is as important as previously, only construed differently; now it is understood to ground salvific encounter with God." Yes, but whereas this is equally true in traditional models, their construal of inspiration also guaranteed the didactic normativeness of each biblical assertion, something the newer view cannot do. Of course, the whole point of resorting to the "central message" approach (and no one would if he didn't have to) is to escape from such extravagant claims for scripture. They are incapable of delivery on account of the stubborn doctrinal disunity in the text. So the change is certainly advisable, but this does not alter the fact that it is a sort of theological deficit spending. The inevitable result is the inflation of the currency, in this case, of the doctrine of inspiration. It is made larger in meaning, but buys less.

Anyway, on the understanding of traditional inerrantists, any lowest common denominator of scriptural teaching remaining after the excision of contradictory texts would be useless. Since for inerrantists any statement is authoritative simply because of its presence in the inspired text, then any single acknowledged contradiction would obliterate (debunk) the very basis for authority. This would be so even if *all* other texts were in clear agreement. But for advocates of the central message approach, the locus of authority has moved from the inspired text per se (or in Berkouwer's terms, "formally") to the inspired quality of the writers' *witness to* the central kerygma. In fact, it has moved a step further, to the kerygma of Christ to which the writers variously attest. (The variety of their witness is, of course, provided for by the more indirect understanding of inspiration.) Equally important as the location of authority in the kerygma, is the reason that *these* writers, the authors of the New Testament, are the ones whose witness is inspired. The New Testament authors are understood as representatives of the foundational stage of the Christian faith, or of the original generation of hearers of the kerygma. Hans Küng reflected this understanding in his book *The Church*: "The preaching of the apostles, as it has come down to us in the writings of the New Testament, is the original, fundamental testimony of Jesus Christ, valid for all time. . . . Later generations in the Church are dependent on the words, witness and ministry of the first 'apostolic' generation."[36] Thus the New Testament writers, whether members of the original circle of the twelve or not, are seen as representing and preserving the original Christian kerygma. In turn, their writings bear witness to this witness of theirs. Seen in this light, the contradictions that do exist between the New Testament writers actually help *define* the real authority of the text instead of *destroying* it, as would be the case in the traditional model wherein authority is based on the formal inspiration of the text itself. The contradictions perform this service in that they serve to differentiate the basic kerygma from the individual interpretations and applications of it. (These last, then, cannot claim normative authority except in a looser sense as models for our own attempts at application.) As John Charlot summarizes C. H. Dodd's position, we would have a "dogma/opinion" distinction within the text itself.[37]

Though the above sketch is seldom made explicit, it would seem to be the rationale for statements like the following:

> Biblical theology . . . seeks . . . to determine and set forth . . . the essential and normative content of the faith of the Old Testament and

the New . . . as distinct from transient, peripheral, aberrant, and individual features within their own structure.[38] (John Bright)

The gospel is . . . the essence of scripture. It is scripture attaining its acme. . . . It is the "canon within the canon."[39] (Ramm)

For most Christians today the *kerygma* . . . of . . . the "gospel of Christ" is still the authoritative standard for doctrinal formulations. . . . But when the Biblical writers move away from the basic doctrinal statements . . . there is generally less uniformity of teaching.[40] (Beegle)

We should keep clear the distinction between two levels of approach to the Bible. The first level is the central, saving message of the gospel. . . . Around that saving center lies a vast body of supporting material that is often complex, difficult to interpret, and subject to a variety of understanding.[41] (Rogers)

Ordinarily . . . one is said to "break" the analogy of faith when one teaches something deemed contrary to scripture. . . . We are using the phrase to describe what may be regarded as a disparity or incongruity within scripture itself.[42] (Jewett)

Not all scripture attests equally to the . . . Gospel of reconciliation and redemption, which is the formal norm of scripture. . . . It is only when [the writers'] testimony is related to and refined by the self-revelation of Jesus Christ that it has the force of infallible authority.[43] (Donald G. Bloesch)

The range of these statements indicates both the gradual and wide influence of this model.

Interestingly, the central message/periphery distinction, like the limited inerrancy model, can be helpfully viewed in light of the old "thought/taught" boundary, originally drawn by inerrantists around the canon. Any erroneous opinions held by biblical writers were supposed to have been providentially kept out of the text. Limited inerrancy, at least Pinnock's version, tended to redraw the line down the middle of the canon, ascribing errors in the text to assumptions of the writer that were expressed only incidentally in making the (inerrant) *assertion*, what he "taught." In the present model, however, that of the central message, it might be said that, while the line is again drawn through the canon, it is so to speak drawn in the other direction. Now it is what the writers "thought" (that God had acted salvifically in history) that is infallible, whereas what they "taught" (their various interpretations and applications of the saving acts) is fallible.

Yet in still another sense, the "thought/taught" line has been drawn *behind* the canon. It has already been explained how the reference of biblical statements has changed; from being in and of themselves inspired propositional pointers to a system of eternal truths, as it were external to the text, they have become pointers *inward*, representing the witness of the writers to the central message within the text. In the same way, to enable the exegete to reconstruct the "witness" of each writer, individual texts are now used as pieces of evidence for mapping out the system of thought of each writer. (Ironically, some of the same scholars who protest that the Bible cannot be systematized, proceed to outline "Pauline" or "Johannine theology.") This is the approach followed by George Ladd (*A Theology of the New Testament*) and Herman Ridderbos (*Paul: An Outline of his Theology*), and it might seem to presuppose something like the old "inspired man," as opposed to "inspired text," model of Liberal theology. But that is another question. Now what exegetical studies like these render is the details and contours of the writers' respective "witnesses" from which the "central message" is then abstracted. The normative core never appears in the text in pure form, since the whole text is but raw material for reconstructing it. This means that in an important sense, *everything* in the text, both what the writer *thought* (his various assumptions) and what he *taught* (his interpretations and applications of the underlying kerygma), is *outside* the line. Only the hypothetical "prime kerygma" is normative.

Though the application of the "thought/taught" distinction may be somewhat novel, the real point here has never escaped the notice of those like James Barr who have criticized this model in its original context, that of the Biblical Theology Movement. He noted that this is a schema whereby authority resides in the skeleton of *events* interpreted, rather than in the interpretations themselves (that is, what we actually have before us in the text). Can one still speak of "the authority of *the Bible*," or must we now speak only of "the authority of the theology/structure *of* the Bible"?[44] It might even be asked if the "central message" model does not reestablish Semler's distinction between the text of the Bible and the Word of God. Actually, the problem is probably not as serious as it seems at first. Berkouwer, not surprisingly, has anticipated this difficulty. "Calling scripture a human witness . . . does not at all mean a separation of scripture and revelation, but rather an honoring of integral scripture. The witness is indeed directed to that which is witnessed to."[45] Berkouwer seems to be aiming at the insight of Paul Tillich that every word of the Bible is at one and the same time revelation and the reception of revelation. After all, we cannot properly speak of revelation at all without taking into account both the objective "giving" side, and the subjective "receiving" side of revelation. If it is not received, can anything be said to have been revealed? Thus precisely *as* the receptive witness to revelation, the text of scripture *is* revelation. Or, better, the textual witness/ reception *together with* the kerygma witnessed/received are revelation. And on a more basic level, *no* theology takes texts as authoritative in isolation. Instead, texts are recognized as always *referring to* something else, whether to an underlying kerygma, or to an external system of timeless truths. Probably the only alternative is bibliomancy, the medieval use of biblical texts to tell fortunes. (Whether Hal Lindsey falls into this category, the reader may decide.)

One more important version of this problem concerns the boundaries of the canon of scripture. Can the understanding of inspiration implied in the central message justify traditional canonical limits? The seriousness of the problem is only heightened by the obviously strained character of George Ladd's defense for the canon in a Biblical Theology framework:

> The canonical books . . . share in a unity of redemption history that
> is intrinsic within them rather than superimposed upon them from
> without. No collection of 66 books drawn from the Jewish apoc-
> ryphal writings and from the Christian apocryphal literature can be
> assembled that will share in any sort of unity such as that which we
> find in the books of scripture.[46]

The flagrant special pleading is such that it refutes its own case by
stating it. Naturally, no other books, say I and II Maccabees, fit into
the sacred history of the Protestant canon, simply by virtue of the fact
that such books are not canonical. If they were, why then, the acts of
God through Judas and his brethren would be part of that history of
redemption into which, however, Judith would still not fit. Besides, it
is far from obvious that all of the material in the present canon can fit
under the Biblical Theology rubric for canonicity. Witness the difficulty of fitting the Old Testament wisdom literature into either of the
theological schemas of Eichrodt or Von Rad.[47]

Berkouwer is somewhat more successful in his efforts to make
sense of the canon:

> The nature of the canon does not demand that in order for the canon
> to be authoritative, its boundaries must be readily provable and per-
> spicuous. . . . Such a formulation can only be understood when the
> message of salvation is held to be the central core of the canon. . . .
> This is additional evidence for the fact that we cannot and may not
> view the canon formalistically.[48]

Berkouwer seems to mean that his view actually has an advantage
over the traditional model, which found itself embarrassed by the fact
that the *antilegomena*, or "disputed books," were finally accepted on
the basis of redundancy. At least they did not *contradict* the basic
"apostolic" doctrine of the undisputed books. This criterion seems
strange if all the books, as formally "inspired" documents in their own
right, "authenticated themselves." If they had, why couldn't books be
accepted containing material substantially supplementary to the basic

list? By contrast, Berkouwer's "central message" model makes exactly this kind of center/periphery distinction *on principle*, and so does not blush at the actual history of the canon.

However, there *is* a serious diversion from traditional "canonicity" in Berkouwer's view. The less normative "peripheral" material must become "deutero-canonical," perhaps even on the level occupied by the Apocrypha among some Protestants—the material is "edifying" and "profitable" in some sense, but need not govern belief. Berkouwer tries to cover his tracks here. His model need not lead us to "make distinctions between 'center' and 'periphery' in the canon in the manner which presupposes that the periphery is unimportant."[49] Mere denial of the implications will not make them go away. And why should they? As Barr points out, virtue is quite profitably made of necessity here. In the old canon model, there would be real danger if the canonicity of this or that book were to be doubted. If Jude were dropped, what would become of the vitally important doctrine of Satan's haggling with Michael over Moses' corpse? But if the central message alone is really normative, neither Jude nor the ghoulish bargaining would much be missed.

Probably the most unpleasant aspect of the whole picture is that the canonical status of the Old Testament really becomes problematical. If peripheral elements of the New Testament are essentially deutero-canonical, what value can be attached to the Old Testament? Is it not an indispensable portion of the salvation history culminating in Jesus Christ? It is actually surprising that critical scholars still maintain this, since their own exegesis shows plainly that the strained and implausible hermeneutical ventriloquism whereby New Testament writers pretended to link the Old Testament to Jesus was itself part of the culture-bound peripheral element surrounding the New Testament kerygma. Indeed, the New Testament history of salvation is unintelligible apart from the Old Testament, but the same is true, as the same scholars are quick to affirm, of the Qumran scrolls, the Pseudepigrapha, and perhaps a good deal of other material that no one wants to see stapled onto the canon. But the seemingly insurmountable difficulty in justifying the Old Testament as Christian scripture on the assumptions of the central message model is best demonstrated by John Bright's argument in *The Authority of the Old Testament*. Like Ladd's, his enterprise is convincing in its self-refutation. Rejecting various "Marcionite" ways of treating the Old Testament, Bright attempts to let this material speak with its own voice, as it were, without a Christian accent. The proposal is to employ both Old and New Testament to reconstruct a central message and structure of beliefs growing throughout both, whereby the peripheral and aberrant elements may be pruned. The trouble is that anything "sub-Christian" is thus excised from the Old Testament, and we are back to the "redundancy" criterion for canonicity.

To conclude this consideration of the central message model promoted by partial infallibilist evangelicals, a glance will be taken at the greatest difficulty looming for this attempt to salvage biblical authority. Having provided a rationale whereby New Testament disunity may be relegated to a not-quite-normative periphery, a virtually deutero-canonical status, are partial infallibilists prepared to live with the consequences? If all that material is really as secondary as is being asserted in order to preserve something like traditional normative status for the residual central message, it simply cannot be made the basis for theological constructions of the kind evangelicals have always built on such texts. The partial infallibilists *seem* to recognize these new limitations.

Jack Rogers says he sees "scripture, not as a general encyclopedia of information, [nor] a computer printout of concise technical information."[50] Thus, clearly it could no longer be what Barr calls a "problem-solver" among whose pages one could readily turn in order to answer this or that question of doctrine or practice. But is Rogers prepared for this? He and Donald McKim offer their work *The Authority and Interpretation of the Bible* as an instrument to facilitate healing among the ranks of the Presbyterian Church, strife-torn over issues like the ordination of women and homosexuals. Yet do they not see that what they offer is a charter precisely for the flexible, situational approach that alienated conservatives to begin with? *This* is precisely the sort of hermeneutical posture that excludes the use of the Bible made by denominational conservatives like Richard Lovelace. An even more striking example is that of Donald G. Bloesch, who admits frankly, "It is inadmissible to treat the Bible as though it were a source book of revealed truths that can be drawn out of scripture by deductive or inductive logic."[51] If this is truly so, then how can Bloesch go on in the same work to map out in detail the relative positions of heaven, hell, Sheol, and Hades; to mediate the intricacies of pre-, post- and a-millennialism, and all on little apparent basis other than proof-texting? A few years previously, Bloesch had lamented the identical inconsistency in Karl Barth. "In practice Barth seems to take for granted the essential reliability and trustworthiness of scripture, but in principle he allows for errors even in the matters of theological judgment."[52]

There seems to be a large range of issues raised implicitly by the adoption of the central message model. If adducing normative propositions is no longer available to decide questions of eschatology, soteriology, even Christology, then on what basis are such questions to be decided? A rethinking of theological method is called for, such as was not necessitated in the limited inerrancy model, where "didactic thought models" were neither relativized nor relegated to effectively deutero-canonical status. And without the ability to appeal to normative thought models, can partial infallibilists consistently object to the demythologizing or reconceptualizing going on in theology outside of the evangelical community? Will they themselves remain within that community?

NOTES

1. Robert K. Johnston, *Evangelicals at an Impasse* (Atlanta: John Knox Press, 1979), p. 19.

2. J. I. Packer, "Hermeneutics and Biblical Authority," *Themelios* 1 (Autumn 1975): 7.

3. John Warwick Montgomery, "The Fuzzification of Biblical Inerrancy," *Faith Founded on Fact* (New York: Thomas Nelson, 1978) p. 225.

4. While these two movements are historically distinguishable, they do share significant points of similarity. But, more important, evangelicals seem to have merged the two in their criticisms. And it is that evangelical picture of the combined systems which seems also to have served as the model for emulation by those non-inerrantists discussed in this chapter.

5. A. M. Hunter, *The Message of the New Testament* (Philadelphia: Westminster Press, 1944), p. 122.

6. G. Ernest Wright and Reginald H. Fuller, *The Book of the Acts of God* (Garden City: Doubleday, 1960), p. 43.

7. G. Ernest Wright, *God Who Acts* (London: SCM Press, 1966).

8. George Eldon Ladd, *The Pattern of New Testament Truth* (Grand Rapids: William B. Eerdmans Publishing Co., 1968), p. 41.

9. Berkouwer, *Holy Scripture*, p. 166.

10. Richard J. Coleman, "Another View: The Battle for the Bible," *Journal of the American Scientific Affiliation* (June 1979): 78.

11. Jack Rogers, *Confessions of a Conservative Evangelical* (Philadelphia: Westminster Press, 1974), Incidentally, note the striking parallel of Rogers's view just quoted, not only to the views of neoorthodox and Biblical Theology Movement thinkers, but also to modernist Llewelyn J. Evans, who suggested that God's intention was "not in the first instance to give a book, not to transmit a revelation *about* Himself, not to write, or to cause to be written, a series of definitions, logical categories, abstract propositions relating to his person, his nature, his attributes; but to reveal Himself." Evans and Smith, *Biblical Scholarship and Inspiration*, p. 52.

12. Berkouwer, *Holy Scripture*, pp. 178, 180.

13. Kraft, *Christianity in Culture*, p. 199.

14. Rogers, *Conservative Evangelical*, pp. 82, 104.

15. Quoted in Donald W. Dayton, "Where Now Young Evangelicals?" *Other Side* (March–April 1975): 34–35.

16. Francis A. Schaeffer, "Is Propositional Revelation Nonsense?" *He Is There and He Is Not Silent* (Wheaton, IL: Tyndale House Publishers, 1973), pp. 91–97.

17. Wright, *God Who Acts*, p. 44.

18. George E. Ladd, *The New Testament and Criticism* (Grand Rapids: William B. Eerdmans Publishing Co., 1967), p. 32; also cf. George E. Ladd,

"The Saving Acts of God," in *Basic Christian Doctrines*, ed. Carl F. H. Henry (Grand Rapids: Baker Book House, 1973), pp. 12–13.

19. Rogers, *Conservative Evangelical*, p. 35.

20. Kraft, *Christianity in Culture*, p. 32.

21. Wright, *God Who Acts*, p. 57.

22. Packer, '*Fundamentalism*' p. 152.

23. Wright, *God Who Acts*, p. 11.

24. Kenneth S. Kantzer, "The Communication of Revelation," in *The Bible, the Living Word of Revelation*, ed. Merrill C. Tenney (Grand Rapids: Zondervan Publishing House, 1976), p. 71.

25. Barr, *Bible in the Modern World*, p. 83.

26. Warfield, *Inspiration and Authority*, p. 161.

27. J. I. Packer, "Contemporary Views of Revelation," in *Revelation and the Bible*, ed. Carl F. H. Henry (Grand Rapids: Baker Book House, 1976), pp. 96–97.

28. Wright, *God Who Acts*, pp. 83, 84.

29. Henry, *Frontiers in Modern Theology*, pp. 45–46.

30. Richard J. Coleman, *Issues of Theological Warfare, Evangelicals and Liberals* (Grand Rapids: William B. Eerdmans Publishing Co., 1972), p. 87.

31. Ibid., p. 82.

32. Wright, *God Who Acts*, p. 128.

33. Cf. Carl F. H. Henry, *God, Revelation and Authority*, 4 vols. (Waco: Word Books, 1976–1979), 1 (1976): 49.

34. Rogers, *Conservative Evangelical*, pp. 32, 34, 35.

35. Cf. John A. T. Robinson, *The Human Face of God* (Philadelphia: Westminster Press, 1973), "To *mean* what the New Testament writers or the Fathers *intended* to say of Jesus' humanity or divinity we may well have to say different things" (pp. 16–17).

36. Hans Küng, *The Church* (Garden City: Doubleday, 1976), p. 456.

37. John Charlot, *New Testament Disunity* (New York: E. P. Dutton, 1970), p. 103.

38. John Bright, *The Authority of the Old Testament* (Grand Rapids: Baker Book House, 1975), p. 125.

39. Ramm, *Special Revelation*, p. 119.

40. Beegle, *Inspiration of Scripture*, p. 174.

41. Rogers, *Conservative Evangelical*, p. 62.

42. Paul K. Jewett, *Man as Male and Female* (Grand Rapids: William B. Eerdmans Publishing Co., 1975), p. 136.

43. Donald G. Bloesch, *Essentials of Evangelical Theology*, 2 vols. (New York: Harper & Row, 1978–1979), 1 (1978): 55, 68.

44. Barr, *Bible in the Modern World*, pp. 85–86.

45. Berkouwer, *Holy Scripture*, p. 165.

46. George E. Ladd, *A Theology of the New Testament* (Grand Rapids: William B. Eerdmans Publishing Co., 1974), p. 32.

47. Also see James Barr's discussion in Barr, *Bible in the Modern World*, pp. 85–86.

48. Berkouwer, *Holy Scripture,* p. 89.

49. Ibid., p. 90.

50. Rogers, *Conservative Evangelical*, pp. 102, 104.

51. Bloesch, *Essentials of Evangelical Theology*, 1:69.

52. Donald G. Bloesch, *The Evangelical Renaissance* (Grand Rapids: William B. Eerdmans Publishing Co., 1973), p. 97.

Chapter 5

THROUGH A KALEIDOSCOPE DARKLY

Authority as Authorization in a Pluriform Canon

BACK TO THE PERIPHERY

*I*n the preceding chapter, it was argued that whereas the limited inerrancy model of some non-inerrantists skirted the vital issue of disunity and contradiction in the "safe" area of revelational texts, the central message model of the partial infallibilists sought to make up this lack by confining such doctrinal disunity to the periphery of the canon. Such a strategy seemed to preserve a viable core of biblical authority, an area reduced somewhat in size, but with something like the original "hard" authority of a propositionally revealed, inspired text. Presupposed in this approach was that there was indeed such a broad area of agreement between biblical, at least New Testament, writers. For instance, John Bright, one of the original framers of the *Heilsgeschichte* model, characterized the "biblical understanding of and witness to God's action in history" as "diverse in its expression, and it can by no means be reduced to a harmonious system of doctrine. But it is not, for all that, a cacophony of discordant voices."[1] Daniel B. Stevick agrees: "A central message can make itself so clear that by it the form in which it comes can be questioned."[2] Interestingly, Stevick, like Bright, uses a musical analogy to explain his point. The Bible is compared to a symphony score, wherein a lost *ritardando* is detected and restored by a conductor because the thrust and contours of the piece were so distinctive that the *ritardando* was conspicuous by its absence. Such analogies suggest that there is far more harmony than disharmony in the Bible.

But another group of scholars on the contemporary evangelical scene detect something of a sour note in this analysis. In fact, in their estimate, it would probably not be too exaggerated to compare the Bible to an orchestra pit where everyone is tuning up before the performance gets under way. For they challenge the notion of a single kerygma representing most biblical (or New Testament) thought. Instead, the disunity of the canon is by far more pronounced. Partial infallibilists spoke of a central message, but these scholars (to be referred to here as "pluriform canonists") can speak only of a bare minimum of common New Testament, or biblical, teaching. The lowest common denominator has become quite low indeed. Old Testament scholar John M. Goldingay assures us that "we may believe that underneath the diversity there is a fundamental agreement on the nature of God and his ways with men." Is there any clue to the outlines of this "fundamental agreement"? Goldingay only alludes to "basic attitudes," without specifying them.[3] By contrast, New Testament scholar James D. G. Dunn identifies a "unifying center" canonizing "Jesus-the-man-now-exalted." "Christianity begins from and finally depends on the conviction that in Jesus we still have a paradigm for man's relation to God and man's relation to man." If this seems modest, Dunn claims that biblical "diversity prevents us from insisting on a larger or different canon within the canon."[4]

Missionary anthropologist Charles Kraft approaches the same question from a slightly different angle. He points out that an estimate of the Old Testament as really canonically authoritative beside the New Testament requires that the doctrines and ethics in both must somehow be equally binding in some way. In order to make sense of the huge diversity thus produced, Kraft compares Old and New Testament notions of justification, with significant results:

> We learn from the New Testament . . . how God went about making it possible for him to be legitimately just and simultaneously to justify Old Testament peoples and New Testament peoples alike on the basis of faith alone (Romans 3:26). However, such justification was never based on knowledge of how God worked it out. . . . [Abraham], like us, was saved *through* Christ—for there is no other way to God (John 14:6). There is no other "name" through which salvation can be granted (Acts 4:12). But note that "name" in such contexts signifies the *authority* of the person of the bearer (Christ), not any magic that might attach to the knowledge and utterance of a word. My point is that, though the inspired information concerning *how* God brought about our eternal salvation is extremely valuable, *God's message is no different since the occurrence and Spirit-guided interpretation of these redemptive events than it was in Abraham's or Adam's time.* It was then, and still is today, the message of the eternal God who exists and who "rewards those who search for him" in faith (Hebrews 11:6).[5]

The idea is that, given the normativity of the entire biblical corpus, no doctrine not taught universally throughout all biblical writings can be requisite for saving faith. On the other hand, what is taught only in some biblical books may be quite true in its elaboration of faith, ethics, and redemption. Kraft's unifying center is far smaller than Dunn's since unlike him, Kraft takes on the challenge of both Testaments. In fact, since the Old Testament does not teach the salvific work of Jesus Christ (even claims of "double fulfillment" messianic prophecies depend upon the New Testament), Kraft has even said he would much rather speak of "Biblianity" than of "Christianity."[6] This might be seen as a creative reworking of the typical fundamentalist exaltation of the Bible over Christ (cf. John Warwick Montgomery: "Scripture's Christ"). Kraft, in a radical departure, actually seeks to let the Old Testament speak with its own voice(s), instead of subjecting it to the traditional hermeneutical ventriloquism.

If the unifying center has so far receded that it threatens merely to become a mathematical point, then clearly a new evaluation of the "periphery" is necessitated. If the disunity in the text is seen to be so comprehensive, can "biblical authority" somehow be shifted in focus from the center onto precisely the diverse elements, so as to make *them* somehow normative? If this challenge can be met, then two of the difficulties besetting the central message model may be ameliorated. First, the "peripheral" material will no longer be implicitly relegated to deutero-canonical status. Second, the Old Testament will, as anticipated just above, receive a genuine role in the hermeneutical task, no longer in effect "put out to pasture." To understand how Goldingay, Dunn, and Kraft go about redefining "biblical authority" to these ends, it will first be necessary to delineate just how they construe biblical disunity theologically. Then the way will have been cleared to examine the implied notions of inspiration and religious language.

All three writers agree as to the first cause of biblical diversity, namely, situational application. Dunn explains that "the Spirit of God inspired the writers of the New Testament to speak the word of God to people of the first century A.D., reinterpreting faith and life-style diversely to diverse circumstances." This situational reinterpretation accounts for the diversity. "In different situations and environments that strand [of the unifying center] was woven into more complex patterns, and . . . by no means did they always complement each other."[7] Goldingay is equally clear on this:

> Diversity within the teaching of the Bible is surely clear enough. . . .
> Can all these attitudes [expressed by biblical writers] be infallible?
> In approaching this question, we need to begin from [the] description of the books of the Bible. . . . They comprise a series of divine-human responses to specific situations. . . . The Bible is not a corpus of theological generalisations. . . . [What instances of doctrinal diversity] show is how the message is ever matched to the situation.[8]

Similarly, Kraft explains the diversity in the canon with reference to the revelation by God of the "single message within a diversity of the cultural frames of reference in terms of which that message and the responses to it are illustrated."[9]

On the surface, none of this may seem at all extraordinary. Yet all three writers are willing to let some pretty strategic theological data become relativized in this way. For instance, Goldingay offers such theological situationism to explain the difference between James and Paul: "James says that Abraham was justified by works, Paul denies it."[10] This would seem to be a significant departure from the standard evangelical dismissal of this as an "apparent contradiction," since Goldingay frankly admits the clash. The situational aspect is used to *explain* the contradiction, not to explain it *away*. And in the bargain "justification" is implicitly relativized. Whether "works" (though certainly indispensable to both New Testament writers) are *requisite to* justification (James) or *consequent upon* justification (Paul) is left up in the air, not settled by the final claim of either text.

The second cause of diversity in the biblical canon is something akin to the traditional doctrine of "progressive revelation." Kraft combines this idea with that of a varied situational application of God's "supracultural truth." According to Kraft, certain aspects of culture in a given biblical epoch facilitate the revelation/acceptance of information or directives further elucidating God's perfect truth/will. Such new information might have been irrelevant or incomprehensible earlier simply because of different cultural perspectives prevailing at the time. "This accumulation of information is what has been traditionally labeled 'progressive revelation' but is here termed 'cumulative revelational information.'" This means that "The Bible shows us a range of ideal, subideal but acceptable, and unacceptable behavior and belief."[11] "Regressive revelation" might describe a very similar notion espoused by Goldingay. He reasons that the real diversity of perspectives to be found within the canon "does not, however, imply that every message is equally near to the heart of divine truth. . . . [Rather] sometimes we will be able to establish some hierarchy amongst the varied expressions

of the will of God." Some of the elements of biblical teaching that
Goldingay recognizes as not so near and dear to God's heart are
Matthew's qualification of Jesus' ruling on divorce, and the development of "early Catholicism" in the New Testament. But their "presence
... within the canon indicates that God accepts [them], ... perhaps as
an inevitable though regrettable development, as he accepts the expressions of Old Testament faith that seem further from the heart of its message (Chronicles, Ecclesiastes, Daniel)."[12] No one in the context of
evangelicalism seems to have too much trouble accepting Jesus' depre-
cation of the Mosaic divorce provisions as merely an accommodation
to hard-heartedness. What is new about Goldingay's suggestion, however, is that the same kind of accommodation was not confined to the
earlier stages in the history of revelation. In certain cases, then, the
interpreter may detect the occurrence of "regressive revelation."

Both Kraft and Goldingay, then, feel compelled to admit the presence of "subideal" elements in the diversity of the canon, although neither would seem to want to explain all diversity on this basis. Dunn,
however, refuses to recognize this kind of evaluative distinction. "For
if the canon is the New Testament as such, then why should the earlier, less developed expressions [or, with Goldingay, the later elements
that seem to "backtrack"] not be equally normative, normative in their
very uncertainty or unwillingness to head [e.g.] in the [Christological]
direction John followed so boldly?"[13]

Incidentally, Clark Pinnock, generally in sympathy with Dunn up
to this point, wants to inject here something like Goldingay's hierar-
chical evaluation:

> If a person is able to affirm the Christology of Luke but not able to feel
> comfortable in the Christology of John, surely we can be thankful for
> this much faith and applaud it. The canon of scripture protects the
> diversity that lies within its bounds and we dare not limit it.[14]

The difficulty of such evaluation is hinted at in Pinnock's own
words, with the implication that one ought also to be thankful that

poor Luke had "this much faith"! Beyond this, Pinnock would like to attempt a synthesis "which captures amid the diversity the main thrust of the larger whole."[15] But if Dunn's exegetical diagnosis is on the right track, will the data allow us to speak of such a "main thrust"? On his own estimation, Dunn is able only to derive a narrow "unifying center."

Thus far, the views of Dunn, Goldingay, and Kraft are marked by significant differences from standard evangelical conceptions of the canon, though their continuity on several points is apparent, too. They seem to have creatively modified traditional evangelical categories like "progressive revelation." What picture of inspiration emerges from the discussions of the "pluriform canon" model? Goldingay's definition of infallibility would seem to give evangelicals little reason for alarm: "The infallibility of scripture implies that whatever the author meant to convey was exactly what God wanted said. The author did not mistake the truth and thus, when rightly interpreted, his work will not mislead us."[16] Goldingay himself admits that the "rightly interpreted" proviso is already a source of potential mischief, but the doctrine of inspiration implied in the theories of Goldingay, Kraft, and Dunn is another area of considerable latitude. But it is not left vague, even if it is not explained in detail. The important features of their doctrine of inspiration are readily distinguishable.

Goldingay is able, first of all, to distinguish two different modes of inspiration in scripture, "according as the divine or the human initiative is primary. The first . . . we might call the prophetic mode. . . . The other mode one might call scribal." The first would refer to works like the prophetic books, the Gospel of John (cf. John 16:14–15), and the Revelation; the second would include the histories of Luke and the Chronicler, Proverbs, and Genesis. Interestingly, this seems to be virtually the only instance in the entire evangelical discussion of anyone adducing something like Aquinas's distinction between "revelation" affecting the "speculative judgment" (the direct divine communication of information or truth) and "inspiration" affecting the "practical judgment" (the divine influence to prompt the writer's skills and will to use already-extant material for certain ends). This distinction has figured largely in Catholic discussions concerning the limitation of inerrancy and related matters.[17] According to this distinction, the material in given texts would be "what God says" in significantly different ways depending on whether the speculative or the practical judgment were involved in the text (whether the text were inspired in the prophetic or the scribal mode).

Actually, despite the possible utility of this distinction for questions of factual inerrancy, he does not attempt to apply it to the question of theological diversity. However, Goldingay might easily have postulated that the application of divine truth to various situations and environments was a function of the inspiration of the scribe, bringing forth from his storehouse new treasures as well as old. Dunn's words, already quoted, suggest a similar mode of inspiration, since the Spirit is spoken of as inspiring the activity of "reinterpreting faith and life style diversely." Recalling the use of "accommodation" by Rogers and McKim to include the accommodation of revelation not only to the audience of the inspired writer, but also to the writer himself, Kraft stresses the human medium of inspiration: "The revelational information comes to us clothed in the perspectives of the biblical cultures."[18] And as an anthropologist, Kraft is acutely sensitive to the limitations of language in communication. He reasons that any communication from God to human beings must be limited by the imperfection of the medium. As far back as the time of Horace Bushnell, evangelicals have been reluctant to recognize any significant resistance of human language to the literally accurate communication of divine truth. Kraft, however, cannot ignore this, despite the inevitable relativization that results. He suggests that one can simply replace the inerrantists' model (imperfection is to scriptural languages as sin is to Christ [and thus impossible to admit]) with the model recommended here (imperfection is to scriptural languages as sin is to Spirit-led human beings). In the case of the latter model, both scriptural language and Spirit-led human beings are trustworthy, adequate, usable vehicles for God's working in the world, though neither is perfect.[19]

Since the mode of inspiration envisioned by Kraft, Dunn, and Goldingay seems to allow for a less immediate connection between God's truth and the human expression of it, the result would seem to be not an "inspired theology, providing doctrines," but rather "inspired theologizing, providing precedents or models." And such models may not always agree with one another. John Charlot, in his *New Testament Disunity*, explains that there are

> so many different pictures offered by the theologies of the New Testament that they could not, at least [not] all, be *pictures* of reality. Rather, they must be considered *models* that are partially useful in enabling one to be articulate about objects that are ultimately beyond one. Theologies, because they are, or use, models, cannot give one a picture of God.[20]

Such an understanding is implied in Dunn's discussion of the various Christologies in the New Testament. If one is incarnational and another is not, and both are equally legitimate for belief, then in what sense is either to be believed? Presumably as suggestive but not descriptive models of the reality of Christ. Dunn's sympathy for a less-than-literal understanding of biblical models is made more explicit in his essay on demythologizing in I. Howard Marshall (editor), *New Testament Interpretation*: "I do not mean of course that one must cling to the words [of the New Testament] themselves as though they were a sort of magic talisman. Rather one must always seek to rediscover afresh the reality of the love and faith which these words expressed, and then seek to reexpress that reality in language meaningful to one's own experiences and to one's neighbor."[21]

This shift toward understanding the religious language of scripture as models instead of descriptions of heavenly reality is just one of several instances observed already in the present study. The same broadening had begun to occur in the brief neo-evangelical flirtation with "conceptual inspiration." It was introduced again in the partial infallibilists' use of the "accommodation" concept to allow for a less direct correspondence between the divine meaning of God's acts and their human interpretations. If Goldingay, Dunn, and Kraft can adequately ground their view of diversity in the Bible, can they go on to justify the "canonical" function of the diverse biblical materials? Dunn draws the issue for evangelicals with acute clarity. He asks: "What continuing value has the canon? Since the New Testament is not a homogeneous collection of neatly complementary writings, can we any longer speak of 'the New Testament teaching' on this or that? . . . Since the New Testament writings do not speak with a united voice, where does that leave the authority of the New Testament?"[22]

From here, biblical (canonical) authority could go in either of two directions, both of which are anticipated in the writings of Kraft, Goldingay, and Dunn. It is not clear that the two options are compatible. One is the construal of the canon as an example of a process of theologizing to be carried on in the same manner. This theory has received clear treatment in Paul J. Achtemaier's *The Inspiration of Scripture*. (Achtemaier is a mainstream Protestant, not an "evangelical" in the sense assumed here. This fact will soon assume some importance.) The second option is to make the canon, with all its diversity, a more-or-less exclusive collection of possibilities, albeit rather disparate ones. Brief summaries of each position will clarify some of the implications of the "pluriform canon" schema with regard to hermeneutics.

AN OPEN-ENDED CANON

The first schema to be explored here is that whereby the canon provides the precedent for a *process* of theologizing, rather than normative *content* for theology. Achtemaier takes issue with what he calls the "prophetic model" of inspiration (which despite the similar nomenclature, is not to be confused with Goldingay's "prophetic mode" explained above). By this, Achtemaier refers to the traditional view that compared the production of biblical books to the production of inspired sermons by the Old Testament prophets. This model was misleading because so few of the biblical books were produced as "original autographs" at the hands of any one author. Instead, many were compilations, sometimes passing through many editorial hands before reaching final form. Of course this was precisely the essence of Beegle's criticism of the "inerrant autograph" notion years before. Accordingly, Achtemaier is led also to adopt Beegle's conclusion that inspiration would be better located in the whole process of tradition building and growth that culminated in the biblical books.[23]

And if one is to erase the line confining inspiration to the final canonical editions in one direction, can one avoid simultaneously letting inspiration escape in the other direction also? Sure enough, Achtemaier posits that "inspiration continues [in]to the reading and hearing of scripture" and into contemporary preaching as well.[24] For the record, Beegle had made the same connection: "In a secondary, derivative fashion, therefore, the revelation and inspiration of God's Spirit continues. Accordingly, from the standpoint of *theological interpretation* the canon has never been closed."[25] Among the "pluriform canonists," James Dunn also thinks that the process of inspiration continues:

> If the New Testament canon does not support the sole legitimacy of only one of the subsequent developments (Catholic orthodoxy), neither does it restrict legitimacy only to the developments which are actually enshrined within its pages. We must not absolutize the particular forms which Christianity took in the New Testament documents; we must not make the New Testament into law. The more we believe that the Spirit of God inspired the writers of the New Testament to speak the word of God to people of the . . . first century A.D., reinterpreting faith and life-style diversely to diverse circumstances, the more acceptance of the New Testament canon requires us to be open to the Spirit to reinterpret in similar or equivalent ways in the twentieth century.[26]

Charles Kraft is forthright:

> My focus on divine-human dynamics plus that on the unchanging method . . . and message of God (Mal. 3:6) lead me to attempt to

work the traditionally liberal concept of continuing revelation into an evangelical system. God has inspired and still inspires (some prefer to say "illumines") the whole Bible. We are to re-create the scripturally endorsed theologizing *process,* not simply to transmit the theological products of yesteryear.[27]

How might such continuing inspiration, such an "open canon," operate? Clearly, modern heirs of inspiration would follow in the trajectory set by the biblical writers. As Achtemaier sees it, such a procedure would basically be one of creatively "reinterpreting" the text of scripture so as to meet the needs of "ever-new" situations, since this is just what the biblical writers are imagined to have done:

> While the New Testament authors shared with their Jewish contemporaries a high reverence for the Old Testament writings as having their source in the will and words of God, they did not feel themselves bound to them in any literal sense. [Their uses of the Old Testament] all point to an almost sovereign disregard of the actual letter of that scripture. Clearly, what they regarded highly was the message, not the letter of that literature, and, above all, its character as a witness to Christ.[28]

What Achtemaier has in mind here is that set of tortuous exegetical contrivances whereby early Christians, Qumran sectarians, and others shamelessly read their own beliefs into Old Testament texts with little regard for any real contextual exegesis. For instance, one may be forgiven for wondering where the line is to be drawn between inspiration and imagination in the "exegesis" that produced the doctrine of resurrection from Exodus 3:6, or that suddenly made a singular out of the collective term "seed" in Genesis 12:7. Was baby Jesus' return from Egypt really foreseen by Hosea? "Sovereign freedom" is one way of putting it, but Achtemaier would likely choose different terms if he were to be asked about the skills of modern "interpreters" like Hal Lindsey. Achtemaier's cosmetic use of phrases like "reinterpreting traditions of the past, now recast to meet the new situation"[29] cannot disguise his own examples of New Testament exegesis of the Old Testament as anything but the same kind of gematria performed today by sectarian fundamentalists and cultists. Can he mean that this kind of "sovereign freedom" vis-à-vis the text should be today's paradigm? No, at least not intentionally; he is simply retrojecting onto the biblical writers his own liberal approach to scripture, whereby one is deemed "faithful" to the tradition if he merely "reacts to" it.[30] Thus, Achtemaier does unwittingly follow the lead of the biblical writers back into prescientific exegesis; he reads his own hermeneutics back into the text, mistaking it for the view of the ancient writers.

All this is especially ironic, since, even if Achtemaier realized the gap between the real exegetical tactics of the biblical writers and his own views, he still could not win his point. What he is doing, in effect, is to demythologize their hermeneutics, as if to say, "They practiced outrageous proof-texting; we cannot, so to get the same kind of flexibility from the text, we will reinterpret the text as the need arises, instead of actually interpreting it." Yet Achtemaier has already repudiated this sort of strategy, on the grounds that to retain the author's "intended meaning" is meaningless if one cannot accept the prescientific way he arrived at his point.[31] Actually, Achtemaier's illustrations of the "sovereign" "recasting" of the tradition often depict one writer misrepresenting the original text so as to reverse its sense completely and make it seem to support a different view, the writer's own. If this is to be the model for contemporary exegesis, whether in a literal or a demythologized "main intention" manner, the result is a model of canonicity whereby one is most faithful to the tradition insofar as he contradicts its plain meaning.

But there are versions of the "open-canon" model that are less beset with contradictions than Achtemaier's (for which, amazingly, some evangelicals have expressed some sympathy). J. Leslie Houlden, for example, claims: "Biblical authority can give us no explicit guidance. But the New Testament method may give us a hint . . . no firm instructions, but at least a feeling for the manner in which the question should be handled." Specifically, "the logic of their doctrinal work seems to be that each of them, from his own standpoint, with his own intellectual and religious formation and his own special pressures of circumstances, applied to all necessary matters the implications of a theism shaped and defined as a result of Jesus." According to Houlden, "all good Christian theology should adopt the same method."[32] This "trajectory" may be said to reach its culmination with the position of Robin Scroggs who frankly admits that "the New Testament and the creeds are no longer in any way authoritative or canonical for us."[33] Scripture's function is rather to raise questions that might never occur to us from contemporary culture, and to warn us of certain dead-ends of the past. In other words, the New Testament provides more in the way of questions and bad examples than of positive guidance. And the wheel turns finally back to Achtemaier, and with him to unreconstructed modernism: "The Bible is the result of the earnest search for God's will."[34] Herman Ridderbos sums up the dangers of this approach:

> So it would be a denial of the very nature of scripture if . . . we were to acknowledge scripture as only a human attempt to give expression to and interpretation of what some human writers long ago might, by way of their belief, have understood of the word of God; and in addition, we would [on this understanding] consider that our engagement to the Bible would consist only in having to do the same thing as they did.[35]

Ridderbos calls this a "perversion" of scripture, since it in effect removes any real divine authority, occasional claims to the contrary notwithstanding. The trouble with "open-canon" and "continuing inspiration" views is not so much that they elevate today's theologizing to the level of yesterday's. Just the opposite; the result is inevitably that yesterday's theologizing (that represented in the canon) is brought *down* to the level of today's. The whole question arose in the first place out of the perceived need for some norm by which to navigate in the present day. But it cannot help but be somewhat disappointing to take Achtemaier seriously and envision the "inspired" writers of the Bible as being on the same level as one's own half-educated local pastor.

Achtemaier's position, then, seems to locate "authority" in the biblical canon only in a very loose, and very Liberal, sense. Insofar as Dunn, Kraft, and Goldingay plot the same course, they will tend inevitably toward Liberalism themselves. Do they intend this?

A LIMITED RANGE

If the preceding model of canonical authority (or of the lack of it) was anticipated in the writings of the evangelical "pluriform canonists," so is the second model, that of the canon as a real limiting factor. Dunn talks about not only a "unifying center" but also a "circumference" determined by it. He says that "the New Testament can be said to function as canon by defining both the breadth and the boundaries of the word 'Christian.'" How does it do this? Dunn's answer is:

> The traditions of the New Testament have a normative authority which cannot be accorded to later church traditions . . . for the New Testament is the primary source for the original traditions whose interpretation and reinterpretation is the purpose of the dialogue. The New Testament is the initial statement (complex in itself) of the theme on which all that follow are but variations.[36]

Kraft also senses the need to impose some limits on further "inspiration:"

> The Bible . . . provides the "set radius" within which contemporary revelational encounters may occur and in terms of which all claims of divine revelation are evaluated. The range of allowable variation within which we work interpretationally and experientially is the biblical range . . . the inspired record of certain of God's previous interactions with human beings. God will not (we believe) contradict himself. We can therefore use an assuredly inspired collection of his revelations, often accompanied by inspired interpretations of them, as a measuring device against which to test and evaluate contemporary data.[37]

Kraft calls this schema the "tether model" of biblical authority, in that the canon understood this way allows considerable latitude and flexibility, but not *complete* freedom, since this would be the abdication of any guidance whatever. And the radius of the tether is set by inspiration; to recognize the presence of real and radical diversity within the canon need not militate against a belief in the Spirit's providential selection and preservation of (only) certain models from among the early Christians. (It has already been explained how Dunn, Kraft, and Goldingay provided, even if implicitly, an understanding of inspiration in terms of which significant theological disunity was allowable.)

How would the authority of a pluriform canon be applied? The key is that "*authority*" passes over into "*authorization*." Though Dunn warns that "the New Testament must not become law," there is an inevitable element of casuistry implied in the use of a real "rule of faith," even should it be visualized, as here, as a "rule of faiths." As Kraft puts it:

> The problem is to determine which contemporary understandings [of God and his practical will] fit within the scripturally allowed range and which fall outside. [Thus] our task is to discern whether or not there is an equivalence between items of contemporary behavior and belief and those recommended in the Bible. If contemporary behavior is functionally equivalent in meaning within the cultural context to what the Bible shows to have been acceptable (even though, perhaps, subideal) behavior in its cultural context, the measurement has proved positive. This may be called "dynamic equivalence revelation."[38]

Similarly, Goldingay reasons, "The church has to work out in each period how far it can face God's ideal in its own life, and what standard it can feasibly summon the world to."[39] Both Kraft and Goldingay are willing (because they think God is willing) to allow today any of the things allowed in biblical times if the circumstances are analogous, or if the hearts are similarly hard. For instance, Kraft legitimates the continuance of polygamy among African Christians whose culture is polygamous, since the Old Testament allowed the institution in a very similar culture. Goldingay implies that the Roman Catholic Church is justified in its conformity to New Testament "early Catholicism" even though this option forfeits some of the original spiritual dynamism of Pauline faith.

Dunn recognizes that most evangelical believers will flinch at the suggestion that they should admit differences in the Bible and then go ahead and choose the models that seem most appropriate to their situation. Yet his only response is to urge them to accept the fact that they are not so different from their forebears, since everyone "gerrymanders" (Walter Kaufmann) the Bible, like it or not.[40] Yet Dunn fails to come to grips with the reason for such alarm. Evangelicals have traditionally feared that the presence of contradictory "inspired" texts would make a decision between the two impossible. Both are authoritative in theory, but neither could be in fact, if they are contradictory. Must the donkey remain forever poised hungrily between the two haystacks? A possible escape suggests itself. Despite a doctrine of biblical authority held in common, evangelicals commonly tolerate quite a range of doctrinal latitude on various "secondary" doctrinal questions. One might legitimately believe in either Calvinism or Arminianism, pre- or post-tribulation eschatology, Pentecostalism or Dispensationalism, and so on, so long as either belief were sincerely thought to be drawn from the Bible. Even if one's view were argued against, he would never be accused of repudiating the authority of the Bible. What this meant was that even fundamentalists were not afraid of recognizing real ambiguity in God's word. In fact, if one is trying to decide between, say, predestination and free will, he is often advised to "line up the verses on each side of the question," and then decide.[41] And this by people who believe in the verbal inspiration of the Bible.

From this easy recognition of ambiguity in the canon, how big a step would it be to recognize real disagreement between biblical writers? It would seem not to be a very big step at all. The doctrinal questions listed above are all considered to be "nonessentials" (*ipso facto*, since they are not made clear in the Bible, which is after all supposed to be a *sufficient* guide to faith and practice). Could not even major doctrinal items over which biblical writers differed (e.g., Christology), be placed with as little difficulty into the same category of "important but nonessential" for orthodox belief? The theories of the pluriform canonists, Dunn, Goldingay, and Kraft, in reshuffling most of the cards in the evangelical deck, have reopened yet another question concerning biblical authority. Should it be the goal of a hermeneutic or model of biblical authority that, in order to be viable, it must provide unanimity of results when used properly? Of course, even the models that have sought this have never attained it, but should such a result be sought in the first place? Robert K. Johnston thinks so: "General consensus is the goal of that risky, communal process of theological interpretation." Johnston hopes to see "pluralism" give way ultimately to "unified opinion."[42] Yet why this should be so is neither self-evident nor explained by Johnston. By contrast, the view of James Dunn is that the canon of scripture "has a continuing function . . . in that it recognizes the validity of diversity; it canonizes very different expressions of Christianity."[43] This chapter may be concluded with the words of New Testament scholar E. F. Scott concerning scripture: "It is the authoritative book of our religion, not because it lays down a fixed doctrine to which all conform, but because it allows for a wide diversity of opinion."[44]

NOTES

1. Bright, *Authority of the Old Testament*, p. 131.

2. Stevick, *Beyond Fundamentalism*, p. 109.

3. John Goldingay, "Inspiration, Infallibility and Criticism," *Churchman* (January–March 1976): 14, 15.

4. James D. G. Dunn, *Unity and Diversity in the New Testament* (Philadelphia: Westminster Press, 1977), p. 376.

5. Kraft, *Christianity in Culture*, p. 230.

6. Charles Kraft's remarks at "Contextualization" conference at Barrytown, New York, April 18–20, 1980.

7. Dunn, *Unity and Diversity*, pp. 372, 381.

8. Goldingay, "Inspiration, Infallibility and Criticism," p. 14.

9. Kraft, *Christianity in Culture*, p. 237.

10. Goldingay, "Inspiration, Infallibility and Criticism," p. 14.

11. Kraft, *Christianity in Culture*, pp. 237, 187.

12. Goldingay, "Inspiration, Infallibility and Criticism," pp. 14, 15.

13. Dunn, *Unity and Diversity*, p. 380.

14. Clark H. Pinnock, "Can We Dispense with Chalcedon?" 1980, p. 9. (Mimeographed.)

15. Ibid.

16. Goldingay, "Inspiration, Infallibility and Criticism," p. 11.

17. Burtchaell, *Biblical Inspiration*, pp. 134–36; also see Pierre Benoit, *Aspects of Biblical Inspiration* (Chicago: Priory Press, 1965), pp. 36–43.

18. Kraft, *Christianity in Culture,* p. 248.

19. Ibid., p. 204.

20. Charlot, *New Testament Disunity*, p. 199.

21. James D. G. Dunn, "Demythologizing—The Problem of Myth in the New Testament," in *New Testament Interpretation*, ed. I. Howard Marshall (Grand Rapids: William B. Eerdmans Publishing Co., 1977), p. 301.

22. Dunn, *Unity and Diversity*, p. 374.

23. Paul J. Achtemaier, *The Inspiration of Scripture* (Philadelphia: Westminster Press, 1980), pp. 117, 133; Dewey M. Beegle, *The Inspiration of Scripture* (Philadelphia: Westminster Press, 1963), p. 27; and cf. Barr, *Bible in the Modern World,* pp. 130–31.

24. Achtemaier, *Inspiration of Scripture*, pp. 138, 143.

25. Dewey M. Beegle, *Scripture, Tradition, and Infallibility* (Grand Rapids: William B. Eerdmans Publishing Co., 1973), p. 308.

26. Dunn, *Unity and Diversity*, p. 281.

27. Kraft, *Christianity in Culture*, pp. 179, 205, 403.

28. Achtemaier, *Inspiration of Scripture*, p. 112.

29. Ibid., p. 128.

30. Ibid., p. 153.

31. Ibid., p. 101.

32. J. Leslie Houlden, *Patterns of Faith* (Philadelphia: Fortress Press, 1977), pp. 70, 71, 74.

33. Robin Scroggs, "Tradition, Freedom, and the Abyss," in *New Theology No. 8*, ed. Martin E. Marty and Dean G. Peerman (New York: Macmillan, 1971), 332–33.

34. Achtemaier, *Inspiration of Scripture*, p. 156.

35. Ridderbos, *Studies in Scripture*, p. 33.

36. Dunn, *Unity and Diversity*, pp. 379, 383.

37. Kraft, *Christianity in Culture*, pp. 187, 191.

38. Ibid., pp. 187–88

39. Goldingay, "Inspiration, Infallibility and Criticism," p. 15.

40. Dunn, *Unity and Diversity*, p. 375; also see Walter Kaufmann's interesting discussion of "gerrymandering the Bible," in *The Faith of a Heretic* (Garden City: Doubleday, 1963), pp. 109–16.

41. E.g., Gordon R. Lewis, *Decide for Yourself* (Downers Grove: Inter-Varsity Press, 1973); cf. the rival lists of texts at the conclusion of each chapter.

42. Johnston, *Evangelicals at an Impasse*, pp. 148, 154–55.

43. Dunn, *Unity and Diversity*, p. 376.

44. E. F. Scott, *The Varieties of New Testament Religion* (New York: Charles Scribner's Sons, 1946), p. vi.

Chapter 6

"IT AIN'T NECESSARILY SO"

Do Evangelicals Demythologize?

HERMENEUTICAL SAFEGUARDS

*T*he debate over biblical authority within evangelicalism has begun to focus on a new aspect of the question. The "battle for the Bible," it may be said, has moved to another front, that of hermeneutics. Two evangelical New Testament scholars, Gordon D. Fee and David M. Scholer, have sought to clarify things by indicating that "inerrancy" is a moot point in the face of larger questions of hermeneutics:

> We simply must be done with the nonsense that suggests that some evangelicals are "soft on scripture" because, for example, they believe in women's ministries in the church. . . . [This] is a hermeneutical question, and we will have differences here. But those differences are not questions of the authority of scripture. They are questions of interpretation, and have to do with our historical distance from the text and the whole question of cultural relativity. (Fee)[1]

> A clear distinction must be made and maintained between my formal premise that the scripture is the sufficient, truthful and authoritative Word of God and my finite attempts, prone to error, prejudice

153

and misunderstanding, to understand what in fact the scripture
intends to teach at any given point. Differences in interpretation,
especially when they relate to far-reaching issues such as theological
structures, hermeneutical methods and the relationship between the
culturally relative and trans-culturally normative, must not be so
quickly in evangelical circles identified or labeled as departure from
a "high view of scripture." (Scholer)[2]

Yet how clear is this "distinction"? Clear enough so that to deny it
would be "nonsense"? Some inerrantists do not think so. For them, the
two issues may be said to be technically distinct, but not separable as
seems to be implied by Fee and Scholer. This relation of inspiration
and interpretation was in fact crucial in the rift in the Lutheran Church,
Missouri Synod. Robert D. Preus declared that "hermeneutics, our
way of reading scripture, is not unrelated to our views of Biblical
inspiration and authority, but intimately associated with our attitude
toward scripture, its power, authority, and veracity."[3] Another conservative partisan in the Lutheran struggle, John Warwick Montgomery,
went on to explicate the nature of the connection seen:

> Scripture and its Christ do not give us an open concept of inspiration
> which we can fill in as the extra-biblical methodologies of our time
> appear to dictate. To the contrary, the total trust Jesus and the apos-
> tles displayed toward scripture entails a precise and controlled
> hermeneutic.[4]

The Lutheran dispute ended with the secession of the "moderates"
(or the modernists, depending on one's viewpoint). Among other tactics to exclude the *minim* was the adoption of a detailed hermeneutical
loyalty oath, "A Statement of Scriptural and Confessional Principles,"
which in Montgomery's words, "declares what will not be tolerated
hermeneutically . . . thereby preserving the doctrine of biblical
authority from 'adjustive interpretation.'"[5] Among the proscribed
theses were the limitation of scriptural infallibility to its salvific thrust,
any denial of traditional ascriptions of authorship, the recognition of

secondary material among the sayings attributed to Jesus, the denial of the historicity of any biblical events, and the cultural relativization of Paul's prohibition of women teachers.[6] At Montgomery's suggestion, an analogous statement of "built-in hermeneutic commitments" was adopted into the doctrinal platform of Melodyland School of Theology in 1976.[7] This action led eventually to the splitting of the institution in a replay of the earlier Concordia-Seminex rupture. This was particularly unfortunate since it forced to the surface doctrinal differences among an ecumenical faculty. Melodyland had been founded only a few years previously to give scholarly integrity to the interdenominational Charismatic Movement.

And in 1978, the International Council on Biblical Inerrancy drafted its "Chicago Statement on Biblical Inerrancy," which included a statement on "Infallibility, Inerrancy, [and] Interpretation."[8] This third document was not so strict in its guidelines as its predecessors, but the point was the same. Inerrancy must not be "fuzzified" (Montgomery) by any critical latitude in hermeneutics. The production of an actual "syllabus of errors" in hermeneutics was a rather astonishing phenomenon, occurring as it did among those Protestants whom one would think were most concerned to safeguard liberty of conscience in interpretation. Yet the development was neither unprecedented nor without a future. Strict inerrantists had sniffed out the danger of hermeneutical mischief at least as early as 1960, when J. Barton Payne published his essay "Hermeneutics as a Cloak for the Denial of Scripture."[9] In 1975, two publications by renowned inerrantists outlined slates of hermeneutical limitations required by the doctrine of inerrancy. In his booklet *No Final Conflict*, Francis A. Schaeffer set forth for the anxious scientific community a list of "the possible freedoms which the Bible gives us as we consider the cosmos. I will name seven," that is, seven options deemed by Schaeffer to comport with legitimate interpretations of Genesis 1.[10] J. I. Packer, in his article "Hermeneutics and Biblical Authority," sought to indicate how, in broad outline, "the principle of biblical authority underlies and controls evangelical hermeneutics."

Principally, this commits evangelicals never to admit any but apparent contradictions in the text.[11]

If the appearance of the hermeneutical creeds has not occurred *ex nihilo*, neither is it, in all probability, the end of the process. One may expect to see the gradual addition of such oaths of hermeneutical fealty onto institutions' doctrinal statements that have hitherto settled for requiring belief in inerrancy. Depending on how widespread such a movement becomes, one might next see suspicion cast on those individuals and institutions that maintain inerrancy but hesitate to adopt the creed, just as suspicion is already directed to those who merely affirm "infallibility." But an even more important aspect of these developments is the implied shift from *sola Scriptura* to an official requisite interpretation of the text by an ecclesiastical authority. This of course, would constitute a move in a decidedly "Catholic" direction. Actually, such a development has already occurred, and forms the subject of the next chapter. The balance of the present chapter, however, will explore the danger seen by inerrantists in the alleged "fuzzification" of biblical authority through hermeneutics.

The fundamental concern of strict inerrantists is that one may claim to believe that scripture is "inerrant" in some way such as that suggested by limited inerrantists, and then proceed to evacuate it of any historical veracity or directly applicable normativity in faith and practice. The first, as indicated in chapter 3 of the present work, is no imaginary danger, since limited inerrancy models have usually had no criterion enabling them to draw a line against complete dehistoricization. But what of the second fear? It will be argued here that this concern, too, is justified. However, it will also be argued that even traditional evangelical attempts at hermeneutics have often paralleled (sometimes in astonishing ways) the demythologizing program of Rudolf Bultmann. So, though it will be suggested that the fear of the strict inerrantists is in some measure justified, it will also become apparent that the movement toward Bultmann is proceeding on a trajectory set already by strict inerrantists themselves.

EVANGELICAL DEMYTHOLOGIZING

As is well known, Bultmann contended, "It is impossible to use electric light and the wireless and to avail ourselves of modern medical and surgical discoveries, and at the same time to believe in the New Testament world of spirits and miracles."[12] It is equally well known that evangelical theologians have risen up with one voice to counter this assertion; for do they not both live in the modern world *and* believe in the supernatural? Bultmann anticipated such a reaction: "We may *think* that we can manage it," but, it is implied, no one really *lives* as though he believed in the supernatural world of the New Testament, and actions speak louder than words. The following analysis will seek to demonstrate that, on several issues, evangelicals have unwittingly proven Bultmann at least partially correct. These issues concern doctrinal points that are rightly deemed secondary in their own right, but which have the important effect of bracketing off from present experience the supernatural elements to be expected if the biblical worldview were normative for today as evangelicals claim. Examples will make this claim clearer.

Evangelicals have tended to have something of a "love-hate" relationship with miracles. They have sought strenuously to vindicate belief in them against skeptics. Sometimes, as James Barr has shown with ruthless clarity, they have even unwittingly evacuated the miracle narratives of any supernatural element, making the text historically acceptable by analogy with well-established events that were similar in description to the biblical ones, but naturalistic in causation! (For instance, there *was* a "star" of Bethlehem, that is, the known conjunction of Saturn, Jupiter, and Mars in the constellation Pisces. But if this is what happened, poor Matthew was sadly mistaken in telling of a single star moving to hover over a stable.) Even the more sophisticated redefinition of miracles (as divine manipulations, not violations, of natural law) put forth by some apologists tends fatally in this direction, by making miracles into merely striking cases of providential "lucky breaks" of timing. But these expedients of desperate apologists really do not represent the actual belief in miracles held by most evangelicals; they merely do a poor job in defending that belief. The usual belief is that supernatural events (that is, with no antecedent cause in nature or history) occurred as recorded in the Bible.

Yet often, the same believers are far from enthusiastic at the prospect of miracles occurring today. In fact they almost surpass David Hume in their resistance to accept any contemporary report of a wonder. One reason for this might be that these "skeptics" hold an evidentialist posture vis-à-vis apologetics, whereby the truth of Christianity is imagined to depend upon the old "proofs from prophecy and miracle." Thus, if any other religion claims miraculous credentials, these must be proven counterfeit. Theoretically they might be real miracles, but produced by a "counterfeit" source, Satan disguising himself as an angel of light (2 Corinthians 11:14). But one only knows it is Satan behind the mask, and that the mask is on *his* face and not one's own, if one already knows that his own religion is the true one, and thus predicated upon true miracles. This circularity must be at least dimly suspected, so a different strategy is chosen. The rival's miracles never in fact occurred. With zeal befitting D. F. Strauss, B. B. Warfield, in his *Counterfeit Miracles*, applies critical scrutiny to the many pagan, medieval Catholic, and Pentecostal stories of miracles. None of them is valid.

But might not more miracles happen today, so further to authenticate Christianity? Additional proof certainly couldn't hurt, after all. And there *are* such claims to miracles among evangelicals themselves. But characteristically, Calvinists and Dispensationalists have repudiated them. Why? Because these wonders generally occur in the context of Pentecostal and Charismatic movements, where they accompany (and thus supposedly authenticate) "new revelations," utterances of prophecy and glossolalia. Though in general such "revelations" merely reinforce biblical injunctions or promises, often simply paraphrasing them, there is occasionally something qualitatively new, that is, heretical, such as the origin of Pentecostal Modalism (the "Oneness Doctrine").[13] And this is just what Reformed and Dispensationalist biblicists want to guard against. For them, the Bible is the sole locus of revelation, the only channel of grace. In this, their position comes strikingly close to the Muslim belief that the Koran is the only miracle of Islam. At any rate, the miracles and revelations of the enthusiasts must be rejected. The strategy here is to "prove" exegetically that the "sign (that is, miraculous) gifts" of the Spirit were limited by God's plan to the first century. Despite New Testament texts such as John 14:12 and 1 Corinthians 13:8-12, which certainly mandate miracles and revelations as the normal order of things for Christians, the anti-Pentecostal biblicists argue that 1 Corinthians 13:8 ("If there are tongues, they shall cease") means that miraculous phenomena were to last only through the "apostolic age," not till the Parousia.

"These gifts were not the possession of the primitive Church as such. . . . They were distinctly the authentication of the Apostles. Their function thus confined them to distinctively the Apostolic Church, and they necessarily passed away with it" (Warfield).[14] Walter Chantry takes the same position in *Signs of the Apostles*. Merrill F. Unger (*New Testament Teaching on Tongues*) and other Dispensationalists contend similarly that the "sign gifts" were purely "signs for the Jews" in the apostolic period, in accord with God's multicompartmentalized plan for the ages. Robert Gromacki (*The Modern Tongues Movement*) echoes many fundamentalists in the belief that revelatory experiences were only a temporary stopgap until the completion of the New Testament canon ("the perfect" in 1 Corinthians 13:10). But on all such strained readings, miracles must not occur after the apostolic period. Thus when he heard of a flood-tide of miracles during the charismatic "Indonesia Revival," much discussed by fundamentalists at the time, Dispensationalist George W. Peters of Dallas Theological Seminary traveled to Timor to investigate. He was able to discount most of the phenomena as exaggerations growing out of the non-Western and prescientific mentality of the Indonesians.[15] It does not occur to Peters that much of his analysis might apply equally to the early Christian church. But this is not the issue of concern here. The real point is that here is a large segment of evangelicalism wherein extensive efforts (exegetical and other) are spent in defense of the proposition that while the New Testament is supposedly normative for today, the miracles and revelations taken for granted there cannot be permitted today. Oral Roberts recalls his frustration in the ministry before discovering faith healing:

> How could I get up and preach about Jesus making the lame to walk, the dumb to talk, the deaf to hear, the blind to see, the leper to be cleansed, and the dead raised to life and then let it all be treated as something irrelevant to our life and time?[16]

For anyone claiming to believe that the worldview of the New Testament holds good today, this is a pertinent question.

A recent parallel to the irony just described grows out of studies by evangelical New Testament scholars of some of the rabbinic exegetical techniques employed in the New Testament. Some of these involved cultural and hermeneutical assumptions alien to the scientific exegesis practiced by the modern scholars themselves. For instance, like the Qumran exegetes, Paul sometimes claimed to find a "fuller sense" than that meaning intended by an Old Testament writer, allegedly referring to Christ. But if the Bible is normative, might it not be expected that what John Bright calls the "charismatic" exegesis of the early Christians might still be proper today? Richard N. Longenecker thinks not:

> I suggest that we should not attempt to reproduce their midrashic handling of the text, their allegorical explications, or much of their Jewish manner of argumentation. All this is strictly part of the cultural context through which the transcultural and eternal gospel was expressed.[17]

Gordon D. Fee agrees: "We cannot repeat the exegesis of the New Testament writers, because what they did at that point was inspired. In this case we know God's fuller meaning in the Old Testament because He revealed it to the New Testament writers." As for today, Fee warns:

"There is inherent danger in the concept of *sensus plenior* [fuller sense]. If indeed God intends something beyond what the human author intended—and I would certainly not deny that possibility—then who speaks for God? That is, who determines the deeper meaning God intends for us?"[18] Here, Fee (a Pentecostal, incidentally) recognizes the reality of inspired exegesis in the New Testament, but not for today simply because it would be unacceptable in practical terms—it would spring open Pandora's box for every enthusiasm and fanaticism to escape and bedevil scientific exegesis. It was good for ol' Moses (or in this case, ol' Paul), but it's not good enough for Fee. It is, however, good enough for Charismatic preacher Kenneth Copeland, roundly condemned by Fee for his unvarnished and triumphalistic materialism. Copeland, according to Fee's analysis, buttresses his get-rich-off-God theology with biblical interpretations derived from the Holy Spirit, that is, a *sensus plenior*. Fee warns that "he would do well to be careful about attributing to the Holy Spirit *that* bit of subjectivity."[19] No doubt Gamaliel would have issued Paul the same warning. Fee's concern is understandable, but what of the normativity of scripture for today?

A related doctrine held by many evangelicals concerns the inerrancy of the "original autographs" of scripture. Inspiration in that case guaranteed the inerrancy of the Bible only during the time of its composition, just as for Fee, inspiration guaranteed the validity of prescientific exegesis only by the biblical writers. Yet just as Fee does not press for the continuance of such techniques, but rather repudiates them, even so Warfield and his followers would never suggest that inerrancy extends beyond the original period to cover subsequent copies of biblical books. Indeed the whole point in the first place was to explain how the Bible might be explained as being inerrant, despite the absence of any demonstrably inerrant copies of it in our experience. So the Bible supposedly teaches its own inerrancy, but only in the long-gone "apostolic period," not today. Much different is the evaluation of the upholders of the "doctrine of preservation," who regard the Warfield apologetic as a sell-out to "unbelieving" textual criticism.

According to David Otis Fuller, Donald L. Brake, Jack T. Chick, and other disciples of Dean Burgon, the abandonment of inerrancy along with the autographs is a dangerous surrender in today's "battle . . . of Bibliology" (Brake).[20] Instead they affirm that inerrancy extends throughout church history, since if God troubled himself to inspire an inerrant Bible, he must have supervised its transmission or the original work would be in vain. To be consistent here, one would have to close one's eyes and pretend that no copyists ever erred. Not even the faith of the preservationists is so great. But they do go Warfield one better by positing a sort of doctrine of "indefectibility" of the textual tradition; the true reading of the text at every point still survives *somewhere* or other in the textual tradition but especially in large measure (need one add?) in the Byzantine text type.[21] Thus on their reading, inerrancy was not confined to the past but is alive and well in (a few) present-day Bibles.

There are other apologetics-motivated relegations of biblical truth from the present to the dim past. One of the most interesting is the explanation by "Scientific Creationists" of how, despite the results of radiometric dating techniques, the earth is merely six thousand years old. To dismiss the results of carbon-14 dating, creationists must challenge "uniformitarianism," the methodological assumption of geologists that the earth's age can be calculated with some probability only if natural processes (radioactive decay rates, erosion, and so on) are assumed to have operated always as they do now. Extrapolating back from such criteria, scientists reckon the earth to be between four and six billion years old. But Bishop Ussher's chronology of the Bible cannot accommodate such a count, so creationists maintain that "uniformitarianism" constitutes an unfair bias against miracles such as the Flood of Noah. If the Flood occurred, they insist, it would somehow have altered the subsequent rate of operation of these natural processes, giving a false impression of the earth's age.

Yet at the same time, Creation apologists need to affirm the regularity of the same "uniformitarian" natural processes in order to refute the theory of evolution! This is because of their (mis)understanding of the Second Law of Thermodynamics, the principle of entropy (inevitable randomization in a closed system). They believe that evolution would imply an increase of order in a closed system. Had entropy operated since the beginning in a uniformitarian manner, creationists claim, evolution could never have occurred. Of course, in order to use this argument, creationists must make the same uniformitarian assumption they will not grant to geologists. They conclude "that a principle of degeneration [entropy] has been superimposed on the original creation, which has also experienced one or more great physical catastrophes since the creation."[22] The upshot of it all is that creationists need to affirm the *present* uniformitarian operation of natural processes (especially entropy) *as well as* a period in the past when, instead, the direct creative acts of God operated, either preceding or interrupting natural processes. Creationists do not want to deny the *present* regularity of natural process. Like the old deists, creationists are content to have God merely winding the watch in a miraculous way, so that it may run with uninterrupted regularity henceforth.

However, there *are* fundamentalists who are not so content to live, so to speak, in the world of electric lights, radio, and entropy while reserving the prescientific worldview of Genesis for the primeval past. Flat-earthers ("Zetetic Astronomers") insist the Bible is right, and science is wrong, and that is that. "Scientifically" derived "evidence" to the contrary is simply falsified, according to these people. Flat-earth leader Wilbur Glenn Voliva once declared: "We are fundamentalists. We are the only *true* fundamentalists."[23]

Turning now to the area of psychology, it may be noted that evangelicals in this field have a particularly difficult time making room for biblical supernaturalism in present experience. This fact is evident in the matter of demons or evil spirits. Psychologist John White admits: "I can conceive of no demonic state which cannot be 'explained' by a non-demonic hypothesis. I can likewise conceive of no experiment to give conclusive support to demonic rather than parapsychological hypotheses."[24] In the same vein, Basil Jackson writes: "In all honesty, I have to say that I certainly believe in demon possession or demonization because the Bible teaches it. However I remain unconvinced that I have ever seen, or at least recognized, demonization in a patient with whom I was working."[25]

This absence of demons might seem a bit surprising (though who's complaining?) if one believes that the Bible's worldview is normative for today. How is this explained? A few evangelicals have suggested that "demon possession" was never anything other than psychotic disturbance, epilepsy, or multiple personality, that is, purely psychological. (This, in turn, is nothing but out-and-out demythologizing.) On the opposite end of the spectrum, extremist Pentecostals involved in the so-called "Deliverance Ministry" attribute (at least potentially) virtually every illness or problem to demons. Among them, exorcism assumes an importance proportional to that in Jesus' own ministry.[26] But it is between these two options that most "Bible-believing" evangelicals may be found. They either put the demons (and the whole problem) at arm's length by imagining that demon activity is quite real, but mainly among pagans on the mission field or Satanists in California, but never in the believer's own world of experience. Or they adopt the theory of William Menzies Alexander that "genuine demonic possession was a unique phenomenon in the history of the world; being confined indeed to the earlier portion of the ministry of our Lord. . . . There is but one explanation of the situation. The incarnation initiated the establishment of the kingdom of heaven upon earth. That determined a counter-movement among the powers of darkness."[27] In a maneuver analogous to that executed by Dispensationalists regarding glossolalia and miracles, Alexander has bracketed demonic activity to the "apostolic period," no doubt to the relief of White, Jackson, and others. Once again, a formula has been supplied whereby the New Testament, though it is supposed to be normative for today, is restricted in its embarrassing supernaturalism to the first century.

Finally, some attention must be paid to an even more important development among evangelical psychologists, having to do with conversion. The understanding of most rank-and-file evangelicals is certainly that an individual's conversion is literally a miracle—an operation of the Holy Spirit discontinuous with the ordinary chain of mundane cause and effect. Granted, a sermon or tract may have provided the *occasion*, but "God just reached down into my life!" By contrast, some evangelical psychologists have begun to admit that conversion is quite admissible to naturalistic causal explanation, and that the "supernatural" aspect of it must be redefined. In part, this change is probably due to their embracing of standard psychological methodology, wherein immanent causation, not otherworldly intervention, is the only scientifically calculable factor (recall the "surprise-free method" of sociologists in chapter 1). But one suspects that these psychologists have also felt the force of the challenge of William Sargant and others, who claim to be able to show the purely psychological roots of conversion. "When we find that the technique of 'saving' people at revival meetings follows the same pattern [as abreactive treatment of wartime patients] and depends on the same brain mechanisms, it is impossible not to wonder about the reality of the divine power supposedly responsible for the 'change.'"[28]

Charles Martin, Malcolm A. Jeeves, and others have responded to Sargant's challenge, to the effect that theological truth is of quite a different order than that of the facts of psychological causation. Thus, even if Sargant is right, one need not doubt that the supernatural is still involved, at least in some sense. Jeeves writes:

> Neither is the psychological account [of conversion] a competitor with the account which the person converted gives in his own personal and religious language. . . . The point is that within its own language system and at its own level, each account may be regarded as, at least in principle, *exhaustive* . . . but [not] *exclusive*. . . . Thus the personal account which refers to a personal encounter with God does not have to be "fitted in" to . . . the psychological . . . account. . . . In general, we find that the personal account of the event is much more concerned with the personal significance of the event than with particular psychological . . . mechanisms which may have been operative at the time.[29]

Thus conversion requires no miraculous intervention into the normal psychological process. There is an obvious and striking continuity between this understanding of conversion on the one hand, and Bultmann's "non-objectified" understanding of an act of God:

> In fact . . . a miracle in the sense of an action of God cannot be thought of as an event which happens on the level of secular (worldly) events. It is not visible, not capable of objective, scientific proof. . . . The thought of the action of God as [a] . . . transcendent action can be protected from misunderstanding only if it is not thought of as an action which happens between worldly actions or events, but as happening within them. . . . The action of God is hidden from every eye except the eye of faith (Bultmann).[30]

In "miracles" like the resurrection of Jesus, Bultmann says, no extraordinary events occurred, but God may still be said to have "acted" in the *significance* of events. Divine action did not interrupt or preempt the sequence of normal cause and effect. Jeeves has explained divine action in conversion in exactly the same terms, yet it is doubtful that he or his readers would be eager to join Bultmann in extrapolating such an understanding back into the time of the biblical miracles. By contrast, there are consistently supernaturalist evangelicals like Jay E. Adams, who has as little patience with scientific psychology as he does with Bultmann's theology. His rude biblicism is complete: "The issue resolves itself quite simply into this: if a principle is new to or different from those that are advocated in the scriptures, it is wrong; if it is not, it is unnecessary."[31] Accordingly, cure of neurosis is as simple as repenting of sin and claiming the miraculous power of God to overcome the problem. For instance, it is imagined to be a simple matter for a repentant homosexual to be "cured" by regeneration.

In all these instances, drawn from various areas of evangelical concern, it appears that, while the supernatural outlook of the Bible is affirmed as still normative, some rationale is offered whereby inconvenient or embarrassing aspects of biblical supernaturalism are bracketed off from the present. This was done with reference to miracles and prophetic gifts, charismatic biblical reinterpretation, the inerrancy of scripture, the direct and miraculous operation of nature, demon activity, and miraculous conversion. (Naturally, few individuals would consciously hold to *all* these formulations, though many evangelicals would likely embrace several of them simultaneously.) In each case, there were exceptions that proved the rule. Those groups (for example, Pentecostals, proof-texters, "preservationist" defenders of the *Textus Receptus*, flat-earth biblicists, demon exorcists, and know-nothing counselors) who *did* attempt to carry out biblical supernaturalism consistently have only demonstrated the repulsiveness of this alternative for most evangelicals, who readily recognize them as extremists and fanatics.

NEW HERMENEUTICAL MOVES

For mainstream evangelicals, the residual "supernatural" element of their faith would seem to be confined to aspects of the biblical message that do not touch life in any directly visible way; that is to say, the resulting belief system amounts in practice to an unspectacular adherence to ethics and practices derived from the Bible, and to *stories* of miracles recorded there. The evangelical also happens to believe the literal veracity of those stories, whereas Bultmann holds a different opinion. But where is the real difference? Both alike seek to follow Christ and take comfort and challenge from the providence of God seen by faith in events around them every day. But for both, the really supernatural element in the stories of the Bible is treated de facto as "a fairy story . . . about the sort of thing that often happened 'once upon a time,' but never does now and is not likely to" (Plato).[32]

The discussion will proceed to treat the recent hermeneutical measures taken by those evangelicals of whom inerrantists are suspicious. But first let it be noted that all of the preceding attempts to confine biblical supernaturalism to the long-gone world of the Bible have commonly been made by evangelicals who are well *within* the inerrancy camp. The fact that they did not emulate Bultmann's forth-right denial of supernatural events *in biblical times* has hidden from inerrantists the clear thrust of what they have long been doing to biblical authority. If evangelicals traditionally have de facto demythologized biblical authority, but done so unwittingly, are some of them now starting to do it intentionally? It is probably a bit more complex than that. The problem has to do with the cultural relativity of some elements of the Bible. Evangelicals have long had a feeling of uneasiness when they felt compelled to admit that an infallibly normative scripture nevertheless contained injunctions that were outdated and had to be disregarded. Usually such anxious decisions were prompted by biblical commands to cover one's head in church, wash one another's feet, greet one another with a kiss, shun jewelry and hair styling, and so on. Surely, evangelicals need not stifle themselves with such legalistic minutiae? Instinct has led most to conclude that the culture of the writer must have supplied some no longer existent reason for prohibiting or commanding these things. Yet, as Fee and Scholer pointed out, instinct was often not an articulate enough guide, with the result that factors such as tradition, convenience, and personal preference often arbitrated such "hermeneutical" decisions.[33] Both scholars, however, sought to sketch out rules of thumb for spotting the transcultural truth among its culturally relative expressions. Charles H. Kraft, too, has given some attention to this problem in his book *Christianity in Culture*, where he formulates an "ethno-linguistic" method of exegesis to be placed alongside the grammatico-historical method. All those attempts revolve around the interpreter's efforts to re-express a transcultural norm in contemporary cultural terms dynamically equivalent to those in the text. For instance, the wearing of veils or shunning of jewelry may be discounted in favor of modern ways of expressing the same values. This kind of hermeneutical experimentation would seem capable of arousing little controversy, though some evangelicals see even this sort of "relativization" of the text as a danger. Mennonite John C. Wenger warns, "We must resist every effort to introduce jewelry into our ranks. If we yield enough to allow wedding rings, for example, the camel will then have got his nose into the tent and it will likely only be a matter of time until every form of jewelry will be worn: finger rings, bracelets, lockets, necklaces, earrings, and so on. God give us the courage to speak out against jewelry and fashionable attire in obedience to the Word of God."[34] But if the "cultural relativization" of such texts as 1 Peter 3:3 is seen as the entrance of the camel's nose, the result of crowding its whole bulk into the tent might be a good deal more serious than wearing earrings.

From the willingness to dispense with the normativeness of "insignificant" texts like the ones in view above, it may not be a long journey to the position of those "biblical feminists" like Virginia Ramey Mollenkott, Letha Scanzoni, and Paul Jewett. They are willing to announce, "Gone, even, is the simplistic use of scripture." For "thoughtless obedience, even to a passage of scripture, can be disastrous in its effects in the moral life" (Mollenkott and Scanzoni).[35] This danger is due to a rather large gulf separating biblical culture from our own: "Because patriarchy is the cultural background of the scripture, it is absolutely basic to any feminist reading of the Bible that one cannot absolutize the culture in which the Bible was written."[36] This assertion has the ring of Bultmann about it. Bultmann himself asked rhetorically:

> Can Christian preaching expect modern man to accept the mythical view of the world as true? To do so would be both senseless and impossible. It would be senseless, because there is nothing specifically Christian in the mythical view of the world as such. It is simply the cosmology of a pre-scientific age.[37]

For "mythical," Mollenkott would substitute perhaps "patriarchal," but the main premise, as well as the resulting hermeneutic, is pretty much the same. The real difference, and it is an important one, is that Mollenkott and the feminists seem to have no interest in dispensing with biblical supernaturalism, as Bultmann does. But the scope of "deabsolutizing" is just as wide albeit on something of a different level.

In the last two chapters of the present work, it was shown that many evangelicals have come to regard the areas of disagreement in scripture as denoting *legitimate* differences of application and inter- pretation of the gospel by the biblical writers. Each such application was relativized via the concept of accommodation so it might be seen as relatively valid, though not absolutely. Still, each separate opinion was valid for its own purpose. Though the approach of Mollenkott, Jewett et al., is similar, there has been an important change. Their assumptions and method are closer to Bultmann's exegetical method of "content criticism" (*Sachkritik*). Now, Paul's thought, for example, is not only relativized but actually criticized as defective in part: "I would say concerning Paul's rationalization for the female submission which was standard in his culture: the passages are distorted by the human instrument, yet they are instructive in showing us an honest man in conflict with himself." This "distortion" indicates a "conflict between Paul's rabbinical background and his Christian insight."[38] Paul Jewett has made a similar assessment of Paul's position vis-à-vis women. Both agree that Paul's "rabbinic" strictures contradict the thrust of his own thought as expressed in Galatians 3:28, a charter of male-female equality. Both also accuse Paul of flying in the face of "the thrust of the whole Bible toward human justice and oneness in Christ."[39] So by comparing suspicious-sounding Pauline texts with the thrust of his own thought, and with that of scripture as a whole, the reader may "sift out which passages reflect human limitations and which passages reflect the will of God for all times and places."[40]

Insofar as one compares aspects of Pauline thought to the "central message" of scripture, one might as easily fall hermeneutically under the "partial infallibilist" rubric. But to revise Paul in the light of him- self is to engage in content criticism, just as Bultmann himself does in his discussion of Paul's list of resurrection witnesses in 1 Corinthians 15:5ff. (Paul is seen to be forced by Gnostic opponents into an apolo- getic for the resurrection that is both unconvincing and inconsistent with his understanding of the resurrection as invisible in human his- tory.)[41] Bultmann and Mollenkott are quite correct that content criticism is no arbitrary measure. Every literary critic, indeed every reader, performs this operation constantly when he or she discerns any inconsistency in a piece of literature.

What makes content criticism more controversial is its use in the service of a hermeneutical program necessitating the overthrow of the literature's cultural frame of reference. Mollenkott would seem to be advocating a reconstruction of Christian morality from the ground up. Such a reconstruction would be based on what the interpreter perceives as a basic moral stance implied, not by specific biblical moral injunctions, but rather by the theological meaning of the whole. The same procedure is already at work in the New Testament, as when, for instance, Paul counsels humility in the face of Christ's kenotic sacrifice for the world. But an interpreter sharing Mollenkott's perspective would not feel particularly bound to the biblical writer's own extrapolations of ethics from theology. As in the case of Paul, such biblical precedents might be "distorted" by who knows what influences. The question might well be asked just how one knows to draw the line between the ethics and the theology. Must not both be heavily influenced, even determined by their culture and worldview? This question remains merely implicit in Mollenkott's hermeneutical work, but it forces itself on the reader of Charles Kraft. In the preceding chapter, Kraft was discussed as one of the framers of the "pluriform canon" model. In that context, Kraft was concerned to show how the nature of the Bible allowed its varied reinterpretation in various cultures. The actual practice of such "dynamic equivalence theologizing" raises a whole new set of questions.

Kraft is an adherent of "contextualization" in missions and theology. By this term, some, for instance Bruce Nicholls, have intended something like a program of greater indigenization of Christianity in other cultures, or else a strategy for pre-evangelism in other cultures. Other theologians including John S. Mbiti have in view a program much wider in scope as well as more radical in nature.[42] Here contextualization is seen in terms of "remythologizing" the Christian gospel, its rearticulation in the religious concepts of new cultures. In his essay

"The Birth of Theology," Daniel von Allmen contends that the varie-
gated theology of the New Testament resulted from the same process
of contextualization as missionaries, teachers, and poets poured the
fluid faith into containers shaped by new cultural settings around the
Mediterranean. Kraft refers approvingly to Von Allmen's work,[43]
agreeing that the "dynamic equivalence theologizing" process advocated by Kraft himself is really no different than what the New Testament writers did. Kraft does not flinch from the implications of this
conception, allowing as it does a significant role for human theological creativity, both within and without the Bible:

> God apparently chooses to work in partnership *with* (not simply
> *through*) humans in theologizing (as in all other areas of life). He
> seems not to be very concerned with conformity, or with the abso-
> lute correctness of the conclusions reached. He seems to be more
> concerned with the *process* of theologizing and its appropriateness
> to a given individual or group.[44]

Kraft has given a rather controversial illustration. If African converts
have always believed in the survival of ancestors in the spirit-world,
may they not legitimately interpret a text like 1 Peter 3:19; 4:6 to give
hope that their pre-Christian ancestors are being offered a chance to
hear the gospel even now? The controversial nature of the suggestion
is due not so much to any assumption of Kraft's that the text literally
warrants such a belief; rather, what is disturbing to some is that it is
immaterial to Kraft whether the text "really" means this or not.
Remember, for Kraft, God is not so concerned about "absolute correctness" as he is with "appropriateness." Though most of Kraft's
critics may fear the possibility of syncretism opened up by his
"remythologization" program, a hidden implication is even more
interesting.

With his driving a wedge in between "correctness" and "appropriateness," has Kraft not provided a basis for demythologizing, that is,
the "contextualization" of the "supracultural" gospel in the forms of
the secular West? Let it be noted that Kraft himself has no intention of

rejecting biblical supernaturalism; he is happy "to affirm solidly both the historicity of the original events and the importance of that historicity to the purpose of God."[45] Yet Kraft also admits his willingness

> to employ terminology and concepts . . . [used] in other ways . . . [by] Bultmann and his followers [who] for example, seem to recognize that it is highly important for our contemporaries to understand and embrace the deeper meanings of the scriptures even at the expense of replacing the cultural forms in terms of which that content was originally expressed.[46]

Kraft is referring to Bultmann's "false scandal of mythology," because of which modern man never gets close enough to the real scandal of the cross to decide if he will accept it or reject it. Similarly, Kraft thinks, "To the members of Western culture the forms of Hebrew culture are perceived as so strange that they draw our attention to *themselves* rather than to the message of God and its effects."[47] In other words, Hebraic thought-forms become a false stumbling block. By contrast, Kraft feels that the Hellenistic thought-forms of the New Testament are more amenable to Western people.

But suppose Kraft were to conclude that for many Westerners, belief in the miraculous and the supernatural is simply not an option, whether in Hebrew or Greek thought-forms? It would seem to be consistent with his thought for him, despite his own faith in the historical miracles of the Bible, to give his blessing to Bultmann's demythologizing program as the "appropriate" albeit not "absolutely correct" contextualization of the gospel for modern Western people! Remember, for Kraft, all that is finally needed for salvation is faith "that God exists and will reward those who earnestly seek him" (Hebrews 11:6). More information *explaining* salvation is always helpful of course, but this rudimentary faith is salvifically adequate. Some people, even in today's world, are without the additional information (for example, the incarnation, atonement, and resurrection as the "how" of salvation). They are what might be termed "informationally B.C." And the communicator of the gospel may never be able to bring such a person to greater understanding. "The task of the Christian witness is to stimulate the receptors to faith on the basis of whatever knowledge they have, plus any information that the witness can helpfully communicate and that is accepted by the hearers."[48] Clearly implied here is the possibility of genuine "converts" who remain "informationally B.C.," even after having made the requisite decision of rudimentary saving faith as defined by Kraft. More is true than they are able to believe, but their belief (a genuine faith response to God) is adequate. Would not someone who believed in Bultmann's completely demythologized kerygma be in exactly the same (or at least a "dynamically equivalent") position? It seems difficult to deny that Kraft's general platform for cross-cultural contextualization makes room for the legitimacy of demythologizing even if one, like Kraft, is himself a supernaturalist evangelical.

Incidentally, though Kraft does, as has been said, maintain his own faith in the biblical history and miracles, it is interesting that his system would continue to work even if he decided to go the whole way and embrace a demythologized faith himself. For he already has adopted Bultmann's category of a revelation of *meaning* as a saving *event*. In his essay "Revelation in the New Testament," Bultmann explains that revelation in Christ includes the preaching of the saving event. Indeed the very preaching itself is part of the saving event, since as a bare fact of past history the cross of Christ is ambiguous in its meaning and its effect. Only as it is taken up into the kerygma is Christ's death experienced in its meaning as a saving act of God. A wedge is implicitly drawn between event and meaning since the "event" of the resurrection is not seen as literally having happened in history, but rather as consisting in the kerygmatic interpretation of the cross.[49] And now Kraft is willing to allow, "When God's messages are conveyed via new vehicles (whether new people, new languages, or new cultures) . . . such communication . . . involves new receptors and new meanings stimulated within their heads. These are new events in the stream of history." So "revelational meanings" are to be considered "new events in history."[50] If he felt the need to do so, it would seem a simple matter for Kraft, like

Bultmann himself, to relegate the biblical miracles as merely (a mythological) part of the particular cultural frame of reference into which God's revelation came once upon a time. This is not to imply that logic would *compel* Kraft to do this, but rather that nothing would logically stand in the way of his doing it.

Kraft has not in fact embraced demythologization, as simple as it would seem for him to do so, but other evangelicals have actually begun to explore the possibility. For instance, James D. G. Dunn does not reject miracles on principle as Bultmann does, but he does recognize the difficulty created by certain biblical narratives. For instance, a story like the ascension makes no sense at all unless heaven is really some kind of floor high above this one. Yuri Gagarin did not disprove God's existence as he claimed, but he did finally settle the question of the ascension. Dunn admits that the story is legendary and must be demythologized: "The process of demythologizing is therefore a dialectic between me in all my twentieth-century conditionedness and the faith of the first Christians in all its first-century conditionedness."[51] Donald G. Bloesch, too, admits the presence of "mythical and legendary elements in the scripture," even in the virgin birth narratives.[52] Yet, he opposes "Bultmann's call for demythologization."[53] Just what Bloesch intends by these hints is not clear. But what if Bloesch and other evangelicals did find themselves headed inevitably in a Bultmannian direction? Could it be adapted to become an evangelical position? In some ways, and not merely trivial ones, Bultmann's position is an "evangelical" position already, stressing as it does a radical decision for Christ and the abandonment of all worldly self-justification. As is well known, William Barclay once characterized Bultmann as the "most evangelical preacher" he had ever heard, and this observation is probably not merely metaphorical. Could his position be a viable one for non-inerrantist evangelicals to adopt?

ANOTHER LOOK AT BULTMANN

Traditionally, of course, evangelicals have flatly rejected Bultmann's gospel as "bad news," first of all because it dispenses with history in an "unbiblical" manner. It seems that limited inerrantists like Pinnock and Fuller could no longer raise this objection since their own hermeneutic leads to the same conclusion. They may not like the prospect but they would seem no longer to have grounds to declare it "unbiblical." But this is not the only objection offered by evangelicals. They have charged Bultmann with inconsistency. Hasn't he balked at pursuing his program to its logically inescapable conclusion—simple atheistic existentialism? On the one hand, why maintain "God" if everything else of a supernatural nature has been rejected as myth? On the other hand, why limit "authentic existence" as being available only through the kerygma of Christ? Cannot secular existentialists experience it, as in fact they presumably claim to do?

Several things might be said in response. First, Bultmann is hardly being inconsistent by retaining God in his system, since to demythologize is to reject only the *supernatural*, not the transcendent. A la Kant, God may well be (and for Bultmann, he *must* be) thought of as "transcendental" over the realm of phenomena, not stumbling around like Gulliver in the Lilliputian realm of particular phenomena. In fact, if God were active as one more worldly cause, it would be hard to see him as also transcending that realm, something which any theology presumably wants him to do.

Is Christ's kerygma superfluous in any existentialist framework? Not at all, because Bultmann is able to demonstrate the structural inadequacy of any existentialism apart from Christ. First, existentialism's own delineation of man's predicament of "inauthentic existence" implies the need for a transcendent reference point. If inauthenticity consists precisely in the reliance on worldly resources (including one's own) for security, then how could an atheist possibly reach authenticity as it were, by his own bootstraps? Such an attempt is by definition doomed to futility since it simply retreats again to the illusory sufficiency of one's own resources. Instead, one must consent to *be lifted* out of inauthenticity and into new authenticity. Someone else must do the saving. Bultmann says it is God, and the preaching of the kerygma of the risen Christ is the saving act.

But Bultmann is not out of the woods yet; why *Christ*? Why the kerygma, and not *any* object of religious faith? Can Bultmann justify this seemingly arbitrary claim? This is to ask, has Bultmann a theory of the atonement? That is, if he could explain *how* the kerygmatic Christ saves, then he could perhaps explain just why this, and no other preaching, saves. Bultmann's refusal is again a refusal to lapse into self-salvation, and thus into inauthenticity. For if salvation depended upon a theory of the atonement (as it seems to when it is claimed, "You must believe, or accept the fact that Christ died for your sins"), upon grasping a "plan of salvation," we would have something reminiscent of Gnosticism. But with sound instinct the apostle Paul had forbidden any notion of a saving gnosis, a magic formula. Such salvation would give grounds to "boast," because one's own intellectual resources enabled him to be saved. To *understand* a plan of salvation is to "master" it in both senses, and so to *achieve* it. Back to self-reliance and inauthenticity.

Thus disarmed of their usual objections to Bultmann, limited inerrantists might find a Bultmannian, an existentialist evangelicalism not only inevitable, but theologically palatable.

In retrospect, then, this chapter has indicated that strict inerrantists are indeed justified in seeing a real danger that the hermeneutics of some evangelicals will lead them far to the left. Yet it has appeared with equal clarity that this danger is very nearly as real even if one stays within the confines of every hermeneutical code formulated by inerrantists! In fact the newer hermeneutical paths to Bultmann almost seemed to be merely new versions of the traditional evangelical apologetics and hermeneutics designed to show that "things that you're liable to read in the Bible, ain't necessarily so," at least not for this dispensation.

NOTES

1. Gordon D. Fee, "Hermeneutics and Common Sense," in *Inerrancy and Common Sense*, p. 182.

2. David M. Scholer, "The Authority and Character of Scripture: A Brief Statement of Position," 1978, pp. 1–2. (Mimeographed.)

3. Robert D. Preus, "Biblical Hermeneutics and the Lutheran Church Today," *Crisis in Lutheran Theology*, 2 vols., ed. John Warwick Montgomery (Grand Rapids: Baker Book House, 1967), 2:82.

4. John Warwick Montgomery, *Faith Founded on Fact*, p. 223.

5. Ibid.

6. Ibid., p. 224.

7. For example, the Melodyland text included these provisions:

> The prime article of faith applicable to biblical interpretation is the attitude of Christ and His Apostles toward the scriptures. Their utter trust in scripture—in all it teaches—must govern the interpreter's practice, thus eliminating in principle any interpretation which sees the biblical texts as erroneous.
>
> Extra-biblical linguistic and cultural considerations must never decide the interpretation of a text.
>
> Not all literary forms are consistent with scriptural revelation. The interpreter must not appeal to destructive literary forms (such as mythology).

Montgomery. *Faith Founded on Fact*, pp. 225–26.

8. The relevant section of the Chicago Statement includes passages such as these:

> Apparent inconsistencies should not be ignored. Solution of them, when this can be convincingly achieved, will encourage our faith, and where for the present no convincing solution is at hand we shall honor God by trusting His assurance that His Word is true, despite these appearances, and by maintaining our confidence that one day they will be seen to have been illusions. Inasmuch as all scripture is

the product of a single divine mind, interpretation must stay within the bounds of the analogy of scripture and eschew hypotheses that would correct one Biblical passage by another. "Chicago Statement on Biblical Inerrancy," p. 9.

9. J. Barton Payne, "Hermeneutics as a Cloak for the Denial of Scripture," *Evangelical Theological Society Bulletin* 3 (Fall 1960): 93–100.

10. Schaeffer, *No Final Conflict*, pp. 25–36. The literal accuracy of the early chapters of Genesis is not negotiable for Schaeffer. If myth were recognized in the Bible at this point, Schaeffer fears, demythologizing the resurrection of Jesus would follow on its heels. And a suitably strict interpretation of the first chapters of Genesis would allow these seven options: (1) the "Omphalos" schema, whereby God created the earth with false signs of great age; (2) the "Gap" theory, postulating a primeval creation and destruction of an earth ruled by Satan and containing dinosaurs; (3) the "long day" expansion of the six "days" of creation; (4) "flood geology," whereby sedimentation is accounted for by Noah's flood; (5) the ambiguity of the word "kinds" in Genesis 1, somehow allowing for evolution across species boundaries; (6) the possibility that animals died peacefully and not by struggle before the fall of Adam (the point of this is not clear); and (7) the restriction of creation *ex nihilo* to only one of the words translated "create" in Genesis 1, so that the text need not be read as depicting the sun as "created" two days *after* the creation of "light."

11. Packer, "Hermeneutics and Biblical Authority," pp. 6–7.

12. Rudolf Bultmann, "New Testament and Mythology," in *Kerygma and Myth*, ed. Hans Werner Bartsch, trans. Reginald H. Fuller (New York: Harper & Row, 1961), p. 5.

13. See David Reed, "Aspects of the Origins of Oneness Pentecostalism," in *Aspects of Pentecostal-Charismatic Origins*, ed. Vinson Synan (Plainfield, NJ: Logos International, 1975), pp. 143–68.

14. Benjamin B. Warfield, *Counterfeit Miracles* (London: Banner of Truth Trust, 1972), p. 6.

15. George W. Peters, *Indonesia Revival: Focus on Timor* (Grand Rapids: Zondervan Publishing House, 1973), pp. 64–69.

16. Oral Roberts, *The Call* (New York: Avon Books, 1973), pp. 37–38.

17. Richard N. Longenecker, *Biblical Exegesis in the Apostolic Period* (Grand Rapids: William B. Eerdmans Publishing Co., 1974), p. 218.

18. Fee, "Hermeneutics and Common Sense," p. 181.

19. Gordon D. Fee, *The Disease of the Health and Wealth Gospels* (Costa Mesa: Word for Today, 1979), p. 5.

20. Donald L. Brake, "The Preservation of the Scriptures," in *Counterfeit or Genuine?* ed. David Otis Fuller (Grand Rapids: International Publications, 1975), p. 177.

21. John R. Rice, *Our Perfect Book the Bible* (Murfreesboro, TN: Sword of the Lord, 1958), p. 32; Brake, "Preservation," p. 181.

22. Boardman, Koontz, and Morris, *Science and Creation*, p. 29.

23. Martin Gardner, *Fads and Fallacies in the Name of Science* (New York: Dover Publications, 1957), p. 18; Robert J. Schadewald, "Equal Time for Flat-Earth Science," *Creation/Evolution* 3 (Winter 1981): 37–40.

24. John White, "Commentary on Psychological Observations on Demonism," in *Demon Possession*, ed. John Warwick Montgomery (Minneapolis: Bethany Fellowship, 1976), p. 253.

25. Basil Jackson, "Reflections on the Demonic: A Psychiatric Perspective," in Montgomery, ed., *Demon Possession*, p. 261.

26. Cf. Don Basham, *Deliver Us from Evil* (New York: Bantam Books, 1977); and Frank Hammond and Ida Mae Hammond, *Pigs in the Parlor* (Kirkwood, MO: Impact Books, 1973).

27. William Menzies Alexander, *Demonic Possession in the New Testament* (Grand Rapids: Baker Book House, 1980), pp. 247, 249.

28. William Sargant, *The Mind Possessed* (Baltimore: Penguin Books, 1975), p. 194.

29. Malcolm A. Jeeves, *Christianity and Psychology, the View Both Ways* (Downers Grove: InterVarsity Press, 1976), p. 141; cf. also *Scientific Psychology and Christian Belief* (London: InterVarsity Press, 1967), p. 13.

30. Rudolf Bultmann, *Jesus Christ and Mythology* (New York: Charles Scribner's Sons, 1958), pp. 61–62.

31. Jay E. Adams, *The Use of the Scriptures in Counseling* (Grand Rapids: Baker Book House, 1976), p. 6.

32. Plato, *The Republic*, trans. Desmond Lee (Baltimore: Penguin Books, 1974), p. 81.

33. Fee, "Hermeneutics and Common Sense," p. 173; David M. Scholer, "Cultural Relativity and Trans-Cultural Normative Authority in the New Testament: Some Basic Reflections," 1979, p. 2. (Mimeographed.)

34. John C. Wenger, *Basic Issues in Nonconformity* (Scottdale, PA: Mennonite Publishing House, 1951), p. 15.

35. Virginia Mollenkott and Letha Scanzoni, *Is the Homosexual My Neighbor?* (New York: Harper & Row, 1978), pp. 17, 18.

36. Virginia Mollenkott, *Women, Men, and the Bible* (New York: Abingdon Press, 1977), p. 91.

37. Bultmann, "New Testament and Mythology," p. 3.

38. Mollenkott, *Women, Men, and the Bible*, p. 104.

39. Ibid., p. 119.

40. Ibid., p. 118.

41. Rudolf Bultmann, *Theology of the New Testament*, 2 vols., trans. Kendrick Grobel (New York: Charles Scribner's Sons, 1951), 1:295.

42. Cf. John S. Mbiti, *New Testament Eschatology in an African Background* (London: SPCK, 1978); Shoki Coe, "Contextualizing Theology," pp. 19–24, in *Mission Trends No. 3*, ed. Gerald H. Anderson and Thomas F. Stransky (New York: Paulist Press and Grand Rapids: William B. Eerdmans Publishing Co., 1976); and Jung Young Lee, *The Theology of Change* (Maryknoll, NY: Orbis Books, 1979).

43. Kraft, *Christianity in Culture*, p. 295.

44. Ibid., pp. 311–12.

45. Ibid., p. 37.

46. Ibid., pp. 36–37.

47. Ibid., p. 227.

48. Ibid., p. 231.

49. Cf. Schubert M. Ogden, ed., *Existence and Faith, Shorter Writings of Rudolf Bultmann* (New York: World Publishing Co., 1964), pp. 78–79.

50. Kraft, *Christianity in Culture*, p. 178.

51. Dunn, "Demythologizing," p. 301.

52. Bloesch, *Essentials of Evangelical Theology*, 1:104–105.

53. Ibid., p. 78.

Chapter 7

THE ORTHODOXFORD OPTION

The Canon outside the Canon

ADOPTING A RULE OF FAITH

*T*he two preceding chapters indicated factors perceived by inerrantists as serious threats to biblical authority, to evangelical integrity itself. These factors had to do with exegesis and hermeneutics. The severity of the threat arises precisely from the gaping loopholes in evangelical epistemology revealed by these developments. For the fact is that the new, non-inerrantist evangelicals are exploring blind spots in the traditional stance. The pluriform canonists (and, albeit in less radical form, the limited inerrantists and partial infallibilists as well) have taken *sola Scriptura* and "literal interpretation" not more seriously, but in a different direction than the traditional inerrantists had done. If traditional dogma cannot limit the interpreter's honest exegetical judgment, who can tell him the text does not speak with many (somehow authoritative) voices? The hermeneutical "deabsolutizers" have similarly taken advantage of the fact that no doctrine of inspiration formally included a normative strategy for how biblical truth was to be applied to different cultures and worldviews.

183

In order to meet both challenges, that is, in order to stem the flood tide of exegetical and hermeneutical diversity beginning to pour through the crumbling dike, inerrantists have begun to resort to creedalism. As described above, several statements of hermeneutical guidelines have been adopted. This must seem something unexpected for avowed biblicists to do. What of *sola Scriptura*? Is dogma paramount, or is the Bible? The "hermeneutical creeds" are what might be called "half-way creeds" or "covert creeds" in that they flinch at explicitly dictating dogmas to be believed and never transgressed by interpreters. So the framers of such creeds sought to cover their tracks by putting the statements in the form of lists of guidelines for interpretation. The idea is that if the Bible is interpreted according to these fixed procedures, it must yield certain dogmas believed in tenaciously by evangelicals (or so it is fondly hoped). The questions now to be put to the text by the interpreter are "loaded questions," requiring certain answers, forbidding others. Using the covert creeds of the Lutheran Church, Missouri Synod; Melodyland; or the International Council on Biblical Inerrancy, one opens the Bible already confident of what he will find there. Naturally, no one is naive enough to be surprised at this, as if it had not always been clear that this was the case. But the new "creedal" strategy made the pretense of doing otherwise more difficult to maintain. The diversity of the newer evangelicals had called into question the assumption of traditionalists that unhindered exegesis, leaping the centuries in a single bound, would yield up evangelical theology full-blown; that "if they were consistent in reading the Bible 'from within' and receiving what its authors were concerned to teach, they would be led to the doctrine of scripture which we have expounded" (J. I. Packer).[1]

But another group of evangelicals has dropped the pretense altogether. They have moved toward overt creedalism. These are the scholars and church people involved in the "Orthodox Evangelical" and "New Oxford" movements, and the "Evangelical Orthodox Church," as well as several unattached individuals with an increasingly "catholic" flavor to their hermeneutics. These people, in other words, are seeking refuge from exegetical and hermeneutical chaos in the (hopefully) safe haven of a creedal "rule of faith," or a "canon outside the canon" of scripture. Already in reaction to the original generation of neo-evangelicals, fundamentalist Robert P. Lightner had grown suspicious, noting among them "a desire to place authority in the church and the creeds" instead of in the Bible alone.[2] James Dunn, in the same work wherein he delineates with inescapable clarity the biblical diversity so painful to evangelicals, also virtually predicted the new response:

> Indeed to argue that only one development within the New Testament is canonical is in fact to *deny* canonicity to the New Testament (where the elimination of elements unacceptable to later orthodoxy is far from complete) and actually shifts canonical authority to the great Church's *interpretation* of the New Testament writings from the late second century onwards—no longer a canon within the canon, but a *canon outside the canon.*[3]

Dunn was not alone in seeing the backlash to be produced by exegesis like his own. Others, driven altogether from conservative faith by the very same questions of biblical criticism, had also seen the handwriting on the wall. Southern Baptist Robert S. Alley warned:

> Although the implications of the critical method are not common knowledge, unexamined the method could drive much of Protestantism toward a more ritualistic and liturgically oriented emphasis. This would be no more than a replacement of biblical with ecclesiastical authority, an escape from the realities of the critical revolution.[4]

Ex-evangelical, now a Universalist, A. J. Mattill Jr., echoes precisely this assessment:

> Evangelical faith inevitably suffers if any other authority is placed over the Bible. Higher Criticism is destroying the Bible as the foundation of evangelical faith. Probably the only way one can honestly

and consistently study the Bible critically and remain relatively orthodox is by becoming "catholic" thereby accepting the teaching of the church as the final authority, regardless of what criticism may do to the Bible.[5]

Liberal theologian Gerhard Ebeling puts the dilemma in its most telling form:

Must we be ashamed of the history of modern Protestantism and confess: here the cause of Christianity has been betrayed, or at the very least men have been carelessly playing with fire? And must the conclusion be . . . the establishment of a final, absolute doctrinal authority, of an antimodernist oath and of an ecclesiastically authorized standard . . . theology?[6]

As Ebeling indicates, what is really at stake here is the admission that *sola Scriptura* was a mistake all along. Indeed, evangelical New Testament scholar J. Ramsey Michaels does admit that "*sola Scriptura* is more a slogan than a reality in the Protestant churches." He hastens to add that "I do not intend to make a negative judgment. Some sort of ordering principle is necessary if the church is to make the Bible an intelligible basis for its theology and life."[7]

And several other "evangelical" voices are to be heard calling explicitly for a canon outside the biblical text as well:

As the common insight of those who have been illumined by the Holy Spirit and seek to be the voice of the "holy catholic church," a confession should serve as a guide for the interpretation of scripture. (Morris Inch)[8]

Christian exegesis, it seems to me, must be rooted in the orthodox, Catholic tradition of the Church which recognized the canon in the first place. Such tradition has usually been designated the "rule of faith."[9] (David M. Scholer)

In the first place evangelicals should recognize that a doctrine of inerrancy is not a sufficient basis for authority; evangelicals should recognize that the key to interpreting scripture is the "rule of faith." (Robert E. Webber)[10]

As individuals we are simply not to decide for ourselves what the scriptures mean. . . . Thus we must stand squarely in the mainstream of the church of God regarding the interpretation of scripture.[11] (Peter E. Gillquist)

SOLA SCRIPTURA?

Where was the weak link in the traditional Protestant doctrine of *sola Scriptura*? Basically, it seems that weight had been placed on the Bible that it had not originally been intended to bear as part of its canonical function. In the period of consolidation against Gnostics and other troublesome competitors, the eventually prevailing "orthodox" or "catholic" Christians forged a three-linked chain with which to guard their charter beliefs. These three "canons" were the canonical guardians or formulators of the faith (the apostolic succession of bishops), the canonical formulation of faith made by them (the Apostles Creed), and the canonical writings believed to attest to the faith (the New Testament). The three work together. The bishops enforce the creed by pointing to the scriptures as "Exhibit A." They point to the creed as the rule for interpreting the scriptures. And they prevent an alien creed from so functioning, thus simultaneously preventing the scriptures from coming to the support of any other creed(s), Gnostic ones or Jewish ones. For instance, Tertullian proscribed the use of the text by heretics:

> I take my stand above all on this point: they are not to be admitted to any discussion of scripture at all. If the scriptures are to be their strong point . . . , we must first discover who are the rightful owners of the scriptures, in case anyone is given access to them without any kind of right to them.[12]

Centuries later, one of these "heretical" groups, led by Martin Luther, realized that this system allowed no room for those who did not agree with the ecclesiastical guardians of the creed and interpreters of the text, which is of course what the system was designed to do! So the system had to go. Both other pillars of the faith were kicked away, leaving the weight of the world of religion on the shoulders of the Bible, a puzzled Atlas, ill-prepared for the job.

> The preponderance, it is true, which the opposition to the Catholic understanding of revelation now accorded exclusively to scripture had at once the result that this sole surviving foundation amid the great collapse of authorities was . . . safeguarded also in theory, i.e., an unassailable realm *sui generis*, . . . and the doctrine of verbal inspiration received an intensification and fundamental significance that were hitherto unknown.[13] (Ebeling)

For the scripture began more closely to resemble Pandora's box. With no authoritative interpreter or interpretation, anyone could open the covers of the Book and out would fly a cloud of exegetical evils. If no one is the pope, everyone is the pope; except of course the Bible (contra Karl Barth's "paper pope"), since it must suffer in mute silence. The Magisterial Reformers, of course, lost no time in trying to jump on top and force the lid closed. They did this by drawing up their own confessions, which claimed merely to set forth systematically what the Bible said "perspicuously" if unsystematically. So it remained *Scriptura* but not so *sola*.

This embarrassment was easily ignored and forgotten until some exegetes began again to realize just what *sola* meant. Semler, Gabler, Eichhorn, Von Hoffman, and others in the eighteenth and nineteenth centuries founded the "Biblical Theology" method (not to be confused with the "Biblical Theology Movement" of the twentieth century, associated with neoorthodoxy and discussed in chapter 4 of this work). They noisily rattled the chain of *sola Scriptura* against the conscience of Protestantism. "For the historical approach excludes at all events any idea of a canon which implies the hermeneutical rule that without distinction and in all its parts the canon is of equal authority and [that] discrepancies and contradictions within it are excluded in principle"[14] (Ebeling).

ECCLESIASTICAL AUTHORITY

Today, non-inerrantists like Dunn and Kraft have also dared to notice the lack of one-to-one correspondence between scripture and traditional evangelical orthodoxy. In reaction, as already noted, some want to remain biblicists, but they do so with less plausibility, since their covert creeds tacitly admit that the Bible cannot be trusted to speak impromptu to the exegete. Other evangelicals have given up, as Alley, Mattill, and Ebeling predicted they would. They have turned to the church, either to tell them what the Bible says, or to tell them what to believe should critical studies garble the voice of the Bible.

In this move, there seem to be two stages. As one might expect from would-be-ecclesiasticists from an evangelical background, we find a sort of "biblicism of the Early Church." Evangelicals had always invoked the exemplary "Early Church" against which to measure their own supposedly feeble efforts and dedication. This model they found *in scripture*, so that it actually functioned as one more part of scripture. Now it seems as if the new ecclesiastical evangelicals have simply pulled the same Early Church out of the text and extended it through the second-century church of the "Apostolic Fathers." Now they have in effect placed the text inside of, or under the authority of, the Early Church. Or to put it another way, the Early Church is pictured as a kind of authoritative interpretation of the New Testament, making good the regrettable lapses of the text in not providing a clear and unified picture of church organization, liturgy, theology, sacraments, and so on. The Early Church, then, functions for these evangelicals as an authoritative commentary on the New Testament. Webber writes confidently:

> Because of the faithful witness of the second-century church, we are
> able to see that there is a "tradition within the tradition," a "canon
> within the canon." This is the rule of faith (standardized in the Apos-
> tles Creed) which clarifies the essential biblical framework which
> the church proclaims, believes, guards, and passes on.[15]

But Webber seems to be talking about an idealized "Early Church
of faith" such as has always been used as a warrant, sort of a "Donation of Constantine" for whichever theology or group presents their
particular version of the Early Church.[16] The second-century church
was not necessarily the "bride without blemish" envisioned by
Webber. He seems to be picturing this pristine church as unanimous in
doctrine and polity, holding its ground against the encroachment of
heresies, as in the Matthean parable of the wheat and the tares. But the
researches of other church historians like Walter Bauer (*Orthodoxy
and Heresy in Earliest Christianity*, actually, in second-century Christianity, but this is precisely the period Webber is interested in), suggest
another picture. In this version, the Early Church was like unto a field
in which a man scattered various kinds of seeds. Each seed bore a different plant, and after a while one plant was able to choke out some of
the others and stigmatize the rest as tares. In other words, historical-
critical exegesis of early Christian literature reveals exactly the same
troublesome diversity in the Early Church as it does in the New Testament! So the whole problem has merely been moved back one step.

A related attempt to seek a canon outside the canon is that pursued
by the signers of the 1977 "Chicago Call," the self-designated
"Orthodox Evangelicals." Here the appeal is not to the Early Church
per se, but instead to "the creed" (singular), which "sets the direction
and perimeters of our endeavor."[17] It is imagined that there is a unified
history of dogma and biblical interpretation. But, as David F. Wells
indicates, there is and never has been such unity. The creed is referred
to by the Chicago Callers in the singular as "it," but "Only those who
are historical neophytes would imagine that the thousands of creeds
and confessions which are extant represent a solid and undivided testimony as to the meaning of scripture."[18]

The problem is that these evangelicals cannot bring themselves to identify any particular church or creed that will be the canon outside the canon. There is no such generic Early Church or creed such as they invoke in general terms. No, the ecclesiastical solution will only work, if at all, if these evangelicals are willing to name a church/creed, to the authority of which they will yield. Real ecclesiasticists have no trouble seeing this. For example, Luis-Alonso Schokel, a Roman Catholic sympathetic to biblical criticism, explains why a definite church authority must be chosen: "First, there must be a body of men who can with authority interpret the sense of the sacred text and set the limits of tolerance within which personal variations will remain authentic. . . . We call this body the magisterium."[19] In other words, for there to be an interpretive rule of faith, like Webber et al. want, there must be a group of authoritative interpreters who will apply the rule of faith to the scripture. And this is to restore the original threefold canon of bishops, creed, and text. The threefold cord was not easily broken (Ecclesiastes 4:12), and it may not be so easy for evangelicals to mend it. Webber and his fellow Orthodox evangelicals may be less than ready to go the whole way (at least they may have been reluctant in 1977), but others are seemingly quite enthusiastic. These evangelicals may be found in the ranks of the Evangelical Orthodox Church and the New Oxford Movement.

Both of these groups contain individuals disillusioned with standard American evangelicalism (though the New Oxford group also includes Anglo-Catholics who are affronted by recent liberalizing moves in the Episcopal Church). The platforms of the two movements are virtually identical. The Evangelical Orthodox Church's manifesto is Peter E. Gillquist's *The Physical Side of Being Spiritual*, together with the Evangelical Orthodox Church newspaper, *Again*. The voice of the New Oxford Movement is to be heard in issues of *The New Oxford Review*. Basically, evangelical Christianity, having been tried, is found woefully wanting in its myopic ignorance of church history, its view of the church as a mere voluntary association like a Moose Lodge, its scorn of the human aspect of scripture and normative ecclesiastical interpretation, its arrogant theological parochialism, its bare-bones, exclusively cerebral worship, and its superficial spirituality. In contrast, both groups reemphasize ecclesiastical, sacramental, and ecumenical understandings of Christianity. The chief difference between the two groups is that the New Oxonians apparently serve as a bridge for passing over to Roman Catholicism, while the evangelical Orthodox at length negotiated their own absorption by the Antiochene Orthodox Church. Thomas Howard, who early on fled the sectarian Bible Protestant Church for the incense-perfumed halls of Anglicanism, finally followed in Cardinal Newman's footsteps. For years he had mused, "I would be one of those people for whom the big question is whether I'm not morally obligated to become a Roman Catholic."[20] Howard found Romanist claims to be "almost inevitable." Completely inevitable, as it turned out.

Michael O'Laughlin of the Evangelical Orthodox Church recounts the change in attitude towards *sola Scriptura* among members of his flock: "Most of us held the idea . . . that God's Word was the only guide to faith and practice, and that that which the Bible fails to mention had little importance for the committed Christian. How wrong we were!"[21] The alternative? "The Gospel cannot be fully comprehended outside of the timeless Church . . . Standing within the tradition of the Church is necessary to properly interpret scripture."[22] Exegesis remains important in Evangelical Orthodoxy, but, as Gillquist puts it, "We don't care about biblical criticism."[23] By contrast, Robert E. Webber remains jealous for the exegete's critical freedom. As far as he is concerned, the traditional evangelical position "has been disastrous. It has practically closed the door to an intelligent discussion of the origin of scripture."[24] Yet the positions of Gillquist and Webber are not actually so far apart. Gillquist recoils from the confusing diversity of doctrine emerging from *sola Scriptura* Protestantism, even from that quarter professing inerrancy. Higher criticism would only add another log to the fire. Normative ecclesiastical interpretation will end this hermeneutical diversity. Webber wants critical freedom to recognize the work of Dunn or others like him, but ecclesiastical normativity will protect him from the possible ill effects of such exegesis in a way that *sola Scriptura* Protestantism could never do. For the results of exegesis are no longer even supposed to be *immediately* authoritative.

Is this "Orthodoxford option" the direction for non-inerrantists *en bloc* to follow? No, A. J. Mattill is probably on the right track in his judgment that "for many, if not most, evangelicals the church cannot be the standard of truth, for the church itself has spawned too many errors."[25] Orthodoxford evangelicals seem almost to be gazing at their beloved, the Church, with love-struck infatuation. Are they confusing the projected eschatological "radiant church, without stain or wrinkle or any other blemish, but holy and blameless" (Ephesians 5:27) with its sometimes dubious counterpart here below? Before the union is consummated, perhaps another look at the fiancé would be in order. And such a glimpse of domestic life in an Ecclesiastical/evangelical "mixed marriage" is available in the Catholic Charismatic Renewal. There one can observe various tensions between popular "born-again" zeal and more staid clergy not trained in such a tradition, between creedal, sacramental theology and new, hard-to-rationalize experiences with the Holy Spirit. For example, how will these evangelicals reconcile their belief in justification by grace through faith with the sacramental and synergistic understandings of their new church homes? And what will be the meaning of a "personal relationship with Christ" in such a context—the mark of salvation itself? Or merely one more devotional idiom, comparable to the Sacred Heart cult or the "Jesus Prayer"?

Clearly, then, more issues beside that of scripture are involved in the evangelical exodus now underway into Catholicism and orthodoxy. But those considering such a move primarily as an answer to the exegetical-hermeneutical question had better realize that this is not the only question to which they would be accepting an "answer." And if they do not wish to go so far, is there any viable stopping-point in the middle? The "biblicism of the Early Church" and the covert creedalism of the Lutheran Church, Missouri Synod; Melodyland; and the International Council on Biblical Inerrancy do not seem to provide campsites that are long habitable. Poised at Kadesh-Barnea, will such evangelicals press on into the Ecclesiastical Promised Land? Or will they return to the fleshpots of inerrancy? Or perhaps just continue to wander in the wilderness?

NOTES

1. Packer, *'Fundamentalism,'* p. 152.
2. Lightner, *Neoevangelicalism Today*, p. 78.
3. Dunn, *Unity and Diversity*, p. 380.
4. Robert S. Alley, *Revolt against the Faithful: A Biblical Case for Inspiration as Encounter* (New York: J. B. Lippincott Co., 1970), p. 61.
5. Mattill, "Bible and the Battle of Faith," p. 57.
6. Gerhard Ebeling, "Significance of the Critical Historical Method," in *Word and Faith*, trans. James W. Leitch (Philadelphia: Fortress Press, 1963), p. 51.
7. J. Ramsey Michaels, "Scripture, Tradition, and Biblical Scholarship," *Reformed Journal* (May–June 1970): 14, 16.
8. Morris Inch, "A Call to Creedal Identity," in *The Orthodox Evangelicals*, ed. Robert Webber and Donald G. Bloesch (New York: Thomas Nelson, 1978), p. 13.
9. Scholer, "Authority and Character of Scripture," p. 2.
10. Robert E. Webber, *Common Roots: A Call to Evangelical Maturity* (Grand Rapids: Zondervan Publishing House, 1978), p. 125.
11. Peter E. Gillquist, *The Physical Side of Being Spiritual* (Grand Rapids: Zondervan Publishing House, 1979), p. 79.
12. Tertullian, "Prescriptions against Heretics," in *Early Latin Theology*, ed. and trans. S. L. Greenslade (Philadelphia: Westminster Press, 1956), p. 41.
13. Ebeling, *Word and Faith*, p. 32.
14. Ibid., pp. 92–93.
15. Webber, *Common Roots*, p. 125; Robert Webber, "Historic Models of Social Responsibility," paper delivered to the evangelicals for Social Concern Workshop, September 1975. Webber uses the norm of the Early Church, specifically the writings of the Apostolic Fathers and others, to endorse

"catholic" views of ecclesiology, sacraments, scripture and tradition, and church authority. In his paper "Historic Models of Social Responsibility," he presses the Fathers into service for the formulation of a contemporary evangelical social ethic.

16. Robert L. Wilken, *The Myth of Christian Beginnings* (Garden City: Doubleday, 1972).

17. Webber and Bloesch, eds., *Orthodox Evangelicals*, p. 85.

18. David F. Wells, "Reservations about Catholic Renewal in Evangelicalism," in *Orthodox Evangelicals*, ed. Webber and Bloesch, p. 216.

19. Luis-Alonso Schokel, *The Inspired Word* (New York: Herder & Herder, 1965), p. 277; cf. also Jean Levie, *The Bible, Word of God in Words of Men* (New York: P. J. Kenedy & Sons, 1961), pp. 276, 277, 301; and Benoit, *Aspects of Biblical Inspiration,* p. 35.

20. Robert E. Webber, "On the Implications of the Incarnation: A Critique of Popular Evangelical Christianity," *New Oxford Review*, October 1979, pp. 6–10.

21. Kenneth L. Woodward, "Today's Oxford Movement," *Newsweek*, January 12, 1981, p. 80.

22. Michael O'Laughlin, "Scripture and Tradition," *Again* 2 (July–September 1979): 14.

23. Quoted in Bruce Wollenberg, "The Evangelical Orthodox Church: A Preliminary Appraisal," paper presented at American Academy of Religion, Western Regional Meeting, Berkeley, CA, March 27–29, 1980, p. 16. (Mimeographed.)

24. Webber, "Implications of the Incarnation," p. 8.

25. Mattill, "Bible and Battle of Faith," p. 57.

CONCLUSION

Onward to Post-Evangelicalism

SELF-FULFILLING PROPHETS

*I*n the first chapter of the present work, it was asked whether there was any substance to Harold Lindsell's charge that a new fundamentalist-modernist controversy is building. It seemed that this perception was largely accurate. Subsequent chapters have indicated several points at which non-inerrantist evangelicals are indeed tending in a leftward direction. Sometimes this shift is inadvertent, as in the case of the limited inerrantists, whose attempt is basically one of preservation, trying to safeguard basic evangelical theology by roping off revelational assertions from the area of critical debate. Instead, certain unnoticed tension points allow much more leftward drift than they intend. Others, like the hermeneutical "deabsolutizers," actually intend to clear space for real creativity and pluralism in evangelical theology. In the case of Charles H. Kraft, his openness implicitly allows for Bultmannian demythologizing. So there are definite, traceable ways in which non-inerrantist evangelicals are moving in a "modernist" direction.

But in another equally important sense, the prediction of Lindsell, Schaeffer, and others is a self-fulfilling prophecy. Their opponents are being cast by definition as "modernists" since the sole criterion for such a characterization is the rejection of "inerrancy." So one may do considerably less than embrace Bultmann to be anathema in Lindsellian eyes. On the other hand, it should be remembered that Lindsell's "non-inerrancy = modernism" criterion is not entirely arbitrary. It does reflect the reality of the original controversy, when the initial deviation that led to all the others was in fact the dispensing with inerrancy in favor of biblical criticism. And the present study has demonstrated that, true to the prediction, many non-inerrantists have gone on to more liberal positions, or at least to positions with more liberal implications. And in making such a shift in position, the non-inerrantists may have fulfilled a prophecy of their own.

Beginning with the neo-evangelicals' call for dialogue with Liberal and neoorthodox theologians, the interest in at least some type of peaceful coexistence has never died in neo-evangelical and Young evangelical circles. Non-inerrantist evangelicals have expressed increased interest in real interaction, even cross-fertilization, between evangelicals and the various mainstream Liberal, neoorthodox, and Catholic theological camps. John Scanzoni speaks for his compatriots: they "want to enter into genuine dialogue with all Christians, believing that they themselves can learn and change, as well as help other Christians to learn and change."[1] It is plain that mainstream Christians are often quite happy to accept such invitations, but leftward developments such as those considered in this study lead one to wonder whether the non-inerrantists themselves are not in effect *becoming* the mainstream "dialogue-partners" they asked for. As partial infallibilists like Jack Rogers adopt *Heilsgeschichte* methodology and inch farther into their denominational mainstream; as hermeneutical deabsolutizers like Kraft and Mollenkott adopt more flexible, open-ended approaches to biblical and modern worldviews; as pluriform canonists like Dunn consistently adopt the historical-critical method; and as "Orthodoxford" evangelicals move into Catholic and Orthodox communions one is moved to ask on which side of an "evangelical/Mainstream dialogue" they are placing themselves. Are they asking Ecumenical, or evangelical, Christians to dialogue with them? Paul Tillich once warned regarding interfaith exchanges that both parties must begin by *believing their own religion.* Real dialogue between representatives of different viewpoints "presupposes that each of them is able to represent his own religious basis with conviction, so that the dialogue is a serious confrontation."[2] Instead, one wonders whether in proposing dialogue, the non-inerrantist Young evangelicals are not really exploring new options for themselves, a mirror-image of the earlier neo-evangelical desire for dialogue as a covert platform for evangelizing and refuting Liberals. If this description is accurate, then it may be that non-inerrantists should no longer deny Lindsell's claim. Would it not be more conducive to the dialogue they seek if they accepted Lindsell's claim so as better to define the two sides of the dialogue?

The theological and hermeneutical divergence of the non-inerrantists separates them not only from traditional strict inerrantists, but also increasingly from one another. This fact seems to cast doubt not only on the possibility of a hermeneutical united front for evangelicals, but even on its desirability. Hermeneutical unity is a long-standing goal among evangelicals. It is presupposed by the frequent remarks on how ironic it is for evangelicals to insist on inerrancy as the shield for correct theology, when in fact inerrantists are divided over every conceivable doctrine. For example, Calvinists and Arminians alike hold to inerrancy, despite the one's belief in predestination and the other's adamant repudiation of it.[3] Pre- and post-tribulationists agree that biblical teaching on eschatology is inerrant, but as to what that teaching is, they cannot reach agreement.[4] There is even diversity over Trinitarianism. Most hold to the doctrine, but the Arian Jehovah's Witnesses, the Dynamic Monarchian followers of Victor Paul Wierwille's "The Way International," binitarian Worldwide Church of God members, and Sabellian United Pentecostals are ranged against it, all with inerrant proof-texts (or disproof-texts) at the ready. Armstrong's Church of God gladly enlisted on Lindsell's side in the Battle for the Bible.[5] Whether he sent them a 4-F notice is unknown. The concern for a hermeneutic that might ensure uniform results is really, one suspects, an apologetic concern for the "perspicuity of scripture," the notion that, not only is the Bible the book of divine truth, but its readers must be able to *find* that truth in it. If they constantly come up with different readings, then the claim that the Bible presents us with divine truth becomes irrelevant—the revelation is there, but impossible to find with certainty.

J. I. Packer expresses this concern when he damns neoorthodox and *Heilsgeschichte* hermeneutics for their "subjectivism." Robert K. Johnston voices the same concern in his *Evangelicals at an Impasse*. There he articulately documents wide hermeneutical disagreement on several issues including feminism and homosexuality. He is concerned that such cacophony invites outsiders to disregard the evangelical claim for "biblical authority" in ethics and theology. For, without a clear hermeneutic for all to use, how can the "authority of the Bible" be seen as superior to Liberal approaches to religious authority and theological methodology? So Johnston calls for "unified opinion."[6] Peter Toon issues a similar challenge in his *The Development of Doctrine in the Church*: "The logic of the evangelical commitment to an inspired, written Word of God is that there should be, [at least] in [any single] culture and language, a general agreement by evangelicals regarding its doctrinal meaning."[7] Yet what Johnston's own study shows, and what the present work also makes plain, is that the hermeneutical diversity of evangelicals themselves is at least as great as that among other Christians. Furthermore, many of the newer models of hermeneutics employed by evangelicals are parallel to, or actually derive from, hermeneutical models used by Liberals, neoorthodox, and Catholics. So it would seem that there is no longer any "distinctly evangelical" appeal to the Bible being made among non-inerrantist evangelicals. (It would even be possible to argue that strict inerrantists have no real uniqueness, since their unprincipled harmonization technique commits them to an unacknowledged but de facto canon-within-the-canon approach like Käsemann's, wherein one text silences another.) In the face of this variety, one receives an odd feeling of déjà vu. Johnston's attempt to paper over the cracks in his desired "united front" are ironically reminiscent of Lindsell's frantic efforts to harmonize all the contradictions of the Bible.

POST-EVANGELICAL DISTINCTIVES

The thrust of the present work has been to map out the hermeneutical diversity so bemoaned by Johnston. In the process it has become unavoidably clear that the disunity among evangelicals is much greater, and runs much deeper, than Johnston seems to realize. It has turned out that the non-inerrancy wing of contemporary evangelicalism was comprised of five diverse parties, each with a distinctive hermeneutical platform, despite some overlap. First, limited inerrantists saw the problem with scripture primarily in terms of justifying the theological infallibility of texts despite the presence of minor factual errors. In spite of surface differences, major limited inerrantists including Daniel P. Fuller, Clark H. Pinnock, Harry R. Boer, and Henry P. Hamaan tended to make factual statements negotiable, while theological/ethical material remained normative. Second, partial infallibilists were concerned not simply with factual inaccuracies, but with disunity within the theological/ethical material. The strategy of Jack Rogers, Donald G. Bloesch, G. C. Berkouwer, George E. Ladd, and Richard J. Coleman was to make such diverse material peripheral to a normative "central message," the story of God's "mighty acts" in which he reveals himself. Third, pluriform canonists drew attention to serious disunity at the very heart of the "central message," and proceeded to make the whole extent of the canon normative again, but in a new sense. James D. G. Dunn, John Goldingay, and Charles H. Kraft reconceptualized the "authority of scripture" to mean the authorization by scripture of any of several theological options contained within its "tether." Fourth, cultural deabsolutizers agreed that whether or not there is troublesome discord within the canon, there can be no monolithic uniformity in the application of biblical truth to diverse cultures today. Charles H. Kraft (also active in this area of the debate), Paul K. Jewett, and Virginia Ramey Mollenkott called for the deabsolutizing of the first-century cultural assumptions of the New Testament, and the contextualization of the gospel today. Fifth, the "Orthodox evangelicals" reacted to the alarming diversity issuing from both exegesis and hermeneutics, by taking refuge in ecclesiastical and creedal authority. Peter Gillquist, Robert Webber, and others involved in the Evangelical Orthodox Church and the New Oxford Movement declared their willingness to interpret scripture under Church authority.

Along with this surprising degree of pluralism, it appeared that as they grew apart, non-inerrantists did so by proceeding in directions already marked out by other, non-evangelical, theologians. The attempt to limit inerrancy tended logically, though probably not intentionally, in the direction of Bultmann's sundering of revelation from concrete historical facts. The circumscription of the "central message" inevitably made the peripheral area surrounding the kerygma negotiable in authority, reducing the direct usefulness of the text for systematic theology in a manner reminiscent of the older Biblical Theology Movement. The recognition of radical diversity throughout the extent of the canon produced a model capable of moving in either of two fairly Liberal directions. The first paralleled that of Paul J. Achtemaier, wherein the canon is basically a springboard for speculation. The second resembled the view of John Charlot, wherein the canon enshrines a limited but diverse number of theological models that however are taken to speak of God only in a highly indirect manner. The program of deabsolutizing and contextualizing was reminiscent of Bultmann's twin hermeneutics of demythologizing and content criticism. In fact, this approach could lead to demythologizing as a legitimate form of contextual adaptation, even if one did not reject the supernatural on principle. Finally, the advocates of ecclesiastical authority were self-consciously and avowedly heading in a Roman Catholic and/or Eastern Orthodox direction. Insofar as these logical and programmatic tendencies come to be followed, it will be fair to say that Lindsell's prediction was largely correct: non-inerrantists are moving out of evangelicalism into modernism (or Catholicism).

If there is after all no distinctive evangelical approach to the authority of the Bible, then perhaps it is time to question "the assumption that it is important for evangelicals to maintain a separate and distinct identity within the Christian church. . . . [This is] a possibility which deserves more consideration than it has received. . . . [Evangelicals] might safely . . . concentrate on . . . more general Christian goals . . . thus losing themselves in the larger body of Christ" (J. Ramsey Michaels).[8] As long as it is happening anyway, it behooves evangelicals to consider just where they are headed and what difference their evangelical background should make. It might be suggested that as non-inerrantists move into the ecclesiastical/theological mainstream, they should drop the attempt to maintain a distinctive evangelical theology or hermeneutic. Despite their move from traditional evangelicalism, the various non-inerrantists will never put evangelicalism completely behind them, nor should they. Their past involvement makes them "post-evangelicals" (Richard Quebedeaux, Dave Tomlinson), not, strictly speaking, "Ex-evangelicals." True, if they continued to claim to be evangelicals pure and simple, Lindsell would be justified in suspecting that the wool is being pulled over someone's eyes. Yet if they *denied* they were evangelicals in some sense, one would have to suspect they were hiding something. So they are *post*-evangelicals, going beyond, yet tied to, their religious background. They can interact creatively with it and draw on its resources for their further theological work. What would be the distinctive features of post-evangelicalism?

RELIGIOUS STYLE

First, it would be possible to speak of a surviving "evangelical style" that would color post-evangelical contributions to any new theological context. David W. Aiken surmises: "*How* one believes one's religion may be at least as important as *what* one believes. Perhaps 'evangelical,' then, refers to a way of believing Christianity rather than to a specification of any particular doctrinal content."[9] Richard J. Mouw supplies some of the specifics:

What, finally, does the evangelical label come to? For many of us, it comes down to the fact that there are basic elements in the evangelical understanding of the Christian message and life style that we cherish and do not find adequately treated in nonevangelical Christian groups: the sense that Christianity is a *message* (although it is surely more than this) that must be verbally articulated to those who do not profess Jesus Christ as Savior and Lord of one's life; a set of basic *attitudes* toward the Holy scriptures, which are typified by certain devotional patterns and regular references in Christian discussion to what "the Bible says."[10]

Though this is hardly the place to enter into a full-scale discussion of Mouw's list, a brief exploration of it would help explain the present suggestion about an "evangelical style."

Mouw is keenly aware that no form of evangelical Christianity can afford to dispense with evangelistic zeal. Yet would not the move of some non-inerrantists in some of the directions traced out above mean the end of evangelism? For instance, what about those evangelicals moving in a Catholic direction, and away from a Donatistic "believers' church" model? What of those like Bill Lane Doulos, for whom shoulder-to-shoulder activism with non-evangelical Christians has erased the theological boundaries that once separated the sheep from the goats? In short, the traditional concern to encourage others to begin a pietistic "personal relationship with Christ" would seem problematical, if other "once-born" Christians are seen to be safely within the fold already. Would this mean that the "born-again experience" would no longer be important, no longer part of Mouw's "message to be articulated"? Not necessarily. Instead, one need only return to the way in which revivalistic or pietistic language originally functioned. In the context of the evangelical Revivals and German Pietism, a "crisis experience" denoted not salvation, but *renewal* for those already regarded as saved (and in fact this is exactly how "personal evangelism" operates in the Catholic Charismatic Renewal).

Bearing witness to one's intensely personal experience of Christ would still have a place in a Post-evangelical's "religious style," even if bearing such witness were no longer a matter of eternal life or death. This would be equally true even should the Post-evangelical embrace some version of the doctrine of universal salvation. One might still testify to his faith in Christ's gospel to believers in other religions. Of course the post-evangelical Christian should be equally open to rejoicing in the testimony of the Buddhist or the Jew. But Christianity would still be a "message to be articulated" to outsiders.

Mouw's second feature to be preserved in any new synthesis is the conception of piety as a "personal relationship with Christ," as has been anticipated in the discussion of evangelism. Suppose post-evangelicals moved in a Bultmannian direction, so that Jesus were no longer believed to have personally survived death in a literal fashion. Would it be nonsensical to continue to talk about having a "personal relationship" with Christ? No, all that would be necessary is that, again, the revivalistic origin of this kind of terminology be recalled. In that context, preachers exhorted their complacent Christian hearers not to be satisfied with an intellectual assent to beliefs about Christ. Instead they should make their relationship (or commitment) to him a personal (or existential) one. The emphasis, then, was on the personally felt quality of one's faith, not on the confusing question of whether Jesus Christ is epistemologically available to the individual believer in such a way that latter may have interpersonal communication with him. Even so, post-evangelicals, who imagine Jesus to be "alive" for faith today in a less literal sense, may refocus the "personal" element on the believers' side of the relationship, not on Christ's side. In other words, "I have a personal relationship with Christ" would mean "I take my commitment to Christ very seriously, very personally." "Personal savior" pietism would still hold its place in a post-evangelical style. Even arch-modernist Harry Emerson Fosdick could confess Jesus as "not alone a religious and ethical teacher, but a personal savior whom to meet, with whom to fall in love, by whom . . . to be empowered."[11]

What of post-evangelical attitudes toward the Bible, Mouw's last hallmark? How can evangelical veneration of scripture accommodate the thoroughgoing biblical criticism and relativization implied in some of the theories considered in previous chapters? Are not Dunn, Kraft,

Fuller et al. impiously daring to criticize the Word of God, rather than humbly allowing God's Word to criticize them? This charge has often been leveled at biblical critics,[12] though no one seemed to notice the equivocation in the use of "criticism," or the fact that notorious critics like Bultmann, Ebeling, and Fuchs themselves employed the same dialectic implied in this charge. They, too, claimed that the exegete must allow himself to be questioned and interpreted by the text.[13] The point, of course, is that biblical "criticism" is simply the effort to interpret scripture carefully, and all the more carefully since one wants to understand it precisely in order better to obey it. The new departure in the kind of criticism traditionally damned by evangelicals like Harold Lindsell is that negative judgments regarding historical narratives in scripture are not deemed incompatible with reverence for scripture. The question of whether such historical criticism is compatible with the theological authority of the Bible has already been treated in earlier chapters. Here it will suffice to note that the "stylistic" element of reverent, even devotional, faith is quite compatible with biblical criticism. An excellent example of such an approach may be found in Walter Wink's *The Bible in Human Transformation*. Wink's approach is actually reminiscent of Inter-Varsity Bible discussion booklets. He encourages readers of the Bible to put themselves in the place of the Pharisee or the Publican of Luke 18:9–14.[14] Yet in order to do this, one by no means need adopt a literalist view of biblical historicity. Wink cautions his readers early on:

> Throughout the essay I have assumed the victory of the critical consciousness, even though vast reserves of pre-critical mentality remain on our continent. I am especially concerned that these arguments not be seized upon by reactionary dogmatists and used against those who still struggle for freedom of inquiry and an empirical method.

Instead of giving aid and comfort to fundamentalism, Wink believes that, since "the terms of the modernist-fundamentalist debate were mistaken from the start, it is I hope not irresponsible to turn my back on that conflict and try to take a step in a different direction."[15] It is just such a positive new departure that Post-evangelicals intend as they apply biblical criticism in a reverent spirit.

Post-evangelicals would find themselves working with a distinctive slate of theological concerns, left over from their evangelical past. They would continue to be concerned with many of the same questions, even if they have become dissatisfied with the traditional evangelical answers. Such questions could be seen as a set of axes along which Post-evangelicals are moving on their way out of evangelicalism, as they adopt or formulate new positions relative to the same issues. The old "fundamentals of the faith" (doctrinal items like the atonement, the incarnation, the resurrection, miracles, eschatology, and so on) would be fundamentals. But now they would be fundamental *questions* rather than fundamental affirmations. They would comprise an agenda for inquiry instead of a creed.

Among other things, the continuing centrality of these items for Post-evangelicals would mean that any theological modification would attempt, if possible, to reinterpret them rather than to jettison them. This is an important distinction. Clark H. Pinnock has correctly noted that Bultmann's suggestion to demythologize scripture was nothing new, at least insofar as earlier Liberals had advocated non-supernaturalist forms of theology.[16] But Bultmann's program was significantly new in another sense. He criticized Harnack for rejecting New Testament myth as mere "husk," whereas Bultmann saw that myth was rather the very language of the kerygma itself.[17] Similarly, Tillich even hesitated at the use of the word "demythologizing" since it unintentionally invited the very abuse it was meant to avoid—the simple subtraction of the mythical element. By contrast, Tillich opted for "deliteralization," recognizing the irreplaceability of myth for religious speech.[18] Bultmann and Tillich realized that any new theological paradigm must try to "save the appearances" of traditional doctrine. New models, for instance nonsupernaturalist ones, must make sense of as much as possible of the data accommodated by the traditional model, which must now be replaced because of its inability to deal with new and troublesome data. (In the case of the traditional theological model, the anomalous data include the impact of biblical criticism and the encounter with world religions.)

Tillich is willing to reject occasional biblical symbols, such as the virgin birth, as inadequate, or even heretical,[19] but on the whole, he and Bultmann want to make new sense of the traditional categories such as incarnation, atonement, resurrection, and so on. Perhaps surprisingly, several other theologians have not shown similar caution. Many seem content to focus on one particular aspect of Christian theology and to leave the rest aside. For instance, David R. Griffin, in his *A Process Christology*, freely admits that his model finds no particular utility in the doctrine of the resurrection. It really adds nothing to his Christology, based as it is on his view of Jesus' self-consciousness.[20] To take another example from the realm of Christology, John B. Cobb Jr.'s Process Christology allows for "a full recognition of the variety of structures of existence among which that of Jesus is one and that of Gautama, for example, is another."[21] Here Jesus seems to have become one of many prophets or revealers through whom "God spoke at many times and in various ways" (Hebrews 1:1), rather than a definitive redeemer. John Hick's Christology has arrived at a similar destination.[22] The same is true of several Christologies proposed in the context of Jewish-Christian dialogue, wherein Jesus becomes a "new Abraham" or a prophet of Israel to the Gentiles, rather like Jonah sent to Nineveh.[23] Post-evangelicals would seek to continue to answer the question of what it means, for example, for Jesus to be a redeemer as well as a revealer or prophet. If they came to conclude that the questions were wrong-headed to begin with, and that given items of historic Christian faith should simply be subtracted, this conclusion should not be feared, but they should probably then admit to being Non-evangelicals pure and simple. The continuity with the evangelical past would have been lost.

AN EVANGELICAL METHOD

A particularly evangelical agenda of issues would not be the only basis for continuity with their past as non-inerrantists move along their various hermeneutical paths to new positions. For if no one hermeneutic unites them as evangelicals, perhaps a different sort of theological method would provide them a common identity as Post-evangelicals. Such a new method would really require little more than making explicit the logic of much traditional evangelical thinking. Theological discussions often open with questions like "Can evangelical theology accommodate so-and-so view?" rather than "Does the Bible teach so-and-so view?" Evangelical categories are implicitly assumed to have their own integrity and viability independent of their roots in biblical texts. The importance of this distinction can be seen with a few examples chosen at random. First, one might draw attention to the category of "bibliocentrism." This, of course, is the basis for the ongoing "battle for the Bible." All parties have in common the assumption that evangelical theology must be Bible-centered. The discussion is really about how much critical and hermeneutical flexibility can be allowed before this bibliocentrism is lost. To be sure, various writers judge particular doctrines of biblical authority as insufficiently "biblical," but this begs the question since the nature of biblical authorization for theological statements is itself the point at issue. The real question underlying it all is whether the Bible will remain central, or whether some other factor (perhaps present-day experience, Church authority, or human reason) will predominate.

A second controlling rubric is that of "appropriation." An individual must respond in faith, claiming for himself God's promises. This understanding underlies debates in several distinct doctrinal fields. The discussion (usually negative) of universal salvation turns on whether the sinner must consciously appropriate Christ's redemption in order for it to be effective. The debate over limited (or "definite") atonement is concerned with the same issue, since if the atonement's effectiveness precedes its appropriation, then such appropriation must be equally *God's* (predestined) action on behalf of the believer. Again, the questions of "entire sanctification," the "subsequence" of the Baptism of the Holy Spirit to salvation, and the continuing need for "deliverance" from demons, are all versions of the same issue: must God's saving and sanctifying grace be consciously appropriated at a given point in time, or is it automatically effective? And again, all these issues are as often debated on the question of logical consistency as on that of biblical proof-texts.

Another crucial category for evangelical thinking is that of God's direct or indirect sovereignty in the world. Would God be a liar if the Bible he inspired were found not to be inerrant? One answers "yes" only if he believes that there is a direct, one-for-one, identification between the words of the Bible and those of God. Is the decision to accept Christ as one's savior predestined by God, or a natural human option? This depends on whether one regards God's authorship of salvation to be so direct and comprehensive as to include even one's appropriation of it. Why must evangelicals oppose the thesis of *The Myth of God Incarnate*? According to George Carey, for God to have sent someone other than himself to redeem us would mean that he did not really save us himself.[24] (The same logic might also lead one to espouse Patripassianism, but that is another issue.) In all these instances, the question is debated on the basis of what seems more consistent with God's sovereignty, however the particular theologian conceives of it.

A final example concerns the uniqueness of Christ as the way of salvation. Evangelical discussions of "the final destiny of the heathen" proceed primarily from what the various writers see as the logical implications of Christ's exclusive centrality. Some (J. Oswald Sanders, Richard Wolff) reason that "unreached" pagans are damned, since for whatever reason, they have never "called upon the name of the Lord."[25] Others (Charles H. Kraft, Neal Punt) hold out hope for a special dispensation of mercy for those who have not heard, since one need only hold that Christ is the exclusive basis for salvation, not that only those who are consciously aware of this fact will be saved.[26] In both cases, theologians have the same texts in mind (John 14:6; Acts 4:12, and so on), but they extrapolate from these passages in diverse ways.

With all four of the categories summarized here, the implicit assumption is that doctrinal positions may be accepted, not, strictly speaking, if they conform to biblical texts, but rather if they fall within the confines of broad theological categories that admittedly did first arise from biblical texts but now stand on their own coherence and utility. The upshot of all this is that, since the Bible is not the sole source of theological assertions for any variety of evangelicalism anyway, if non-inerrantists became aware of severe difficulties in their inherited biblicism (as they have done), their theological method (logical deduction from general categories) need not change appreciably. It is especially interesting that conservative apologists have often appealed to just this kind of justification for evangelical belief. Since outsiders could not be expected to accept the Bible as authoritative, some other warrant had to be adduced. J. Gresham Machen appealed to the continuity of evangelicalism with the historic shape and inner logic of traditional Christianity. If one had to identify the genuine heir of historic Christianity, which claimant, evangelicalism or modernism, would be recognizable by family resemblance? Francis A. Schaeffer employed a presuppositionalist argument, contending that life's depth and richness are illusory apart from the presuppositions of traditional Christianity. The approach bears more than a passing resemblance to Kant's moral argument for God, though Schaeffer tried to press a good deal more out of it. Whether Schaeffer is deemed successful or not, the point is that he, as Machen did, is trying to establish evangelical categories of faith not on the basis of biblical texts, but rather on the bases of continuity with historic definitions and the common experiences of humanity.[28]

If Post-evangelicals found that their traditional appeal to the Bible became impossible, warrants like those adduced by Machen and Schaeffer would still be available to ground their theological categories. As a matter of fact, non-inerrantists might find their strongest defense against Lindsell's accusations in the kind of argument outlined here. Lindsell warns that only the doctrine of inerrancy safeguards evangelical belief from eroding into modernism. Non-inerrantists might reply that there are other distinct safeguards for the evangelical system. Yet the argument of the present work has tended to support Lindsell's charges. Why is this? While the simple denial of inerrancy need not in and of itself lead to modernism, it developed that particular elements in the hermeneutical options pursued by various non-inerrantists were in fact leading them logically to Liberal (or Catholic) positions. The similarities between the new non-inerrantist positions and those of non-evangelical thinkers have already been discussed and need not be repeated here.

This concluding chapter has suggested that many hallmarks of evangelical Christianity could be preserved recognizably in one form or another in any of several theological contexts, some farther removed from traditional evangelicalism than others. This observation is double-edged in significance. On the one hand, it has shown that even though many non-inerrantists do in fact seem to be moving out of evangelicalism as inerrantists predicted they would, this movement is due to factors more complex than the simple rejection of inerrancy. One's identity as an evangelical depends on more than one's view of inerrancy. It also entails a distinctive style, agenda, and set of categories. The way in which all these function and interact will determine how evangelical one's faith is. For instance, if the agenda of "fundamentals" is more one of questions than of propositions, one is more Post-evangelical.

On the other hand, since important elements of evangelical Christianity (even in a Post-evangelical form) are compatible with several kinds of theological content and hermeneutical approach, non-evangelical Christians should direct more attention to the intra-evangelical debate. Non-inerrantists are exploring the possibilities of Liberal and Catholic hermeneutical methods in creative new contexts. Liberals and Catholics may stand to learn something about their own approaches, borrowed here. And if the non-inerrantists continue in a Post-evangelical direction, they may become new brothers and sisters in non-evangelical communions. They can breathe new life into these bodies, and bring new perspectives to them. This has already begun to happen on the popular level with the penetration of Catholic and Mainstream Protestant Churches by the Charismatic Movement. Now an analogous penetration may occur on the level of theology and leadership with the shift toward Post-evangelicalism. So all in all, the crisis of biblical authority has shown a surprising breadth in the factors requisite to evangelical identity, in the range of options espoused by non-inerrantists, and in the potential significance of the issues for the Christian community at large.

NOTES

1. John Scanzoni, "Resurgent Fundamentalism: Marching Backward into the '80s?" *Christian Century*, September 10–17, 1980, p. 849.

2. Paul Tillich, *Christianity and the Encounter of World Religions* (New York: Columbia University Press, 1964), p. 62.

3. J. I. Packer, *Evangelism and the Sovereignty of God* (Downers Grove: InterVarsity Press, 1973); Roger T. Forster and V. Paul Marston, *God's Strategy in Human History* (Wheaton, IL: Tyndale House Publishers, 1974).

4. John F. Walvoord, *The Blessed Hope and the Tribulation* (Grand Rapids: Zondervan Publishing House, 1979); Robert H. Gundry, *The Church and the Tribulation* (Grand Rapids: Zondervan Publishing House, 1979).

5. Non-Trinitarian inerrantist writings include *Is the Bible Really the Word of God?* (New York: Watchtower Bible and Tract Society of New York, 1969); Robert C. Boraker, "The Holy Bible—Is It Reliable?" *Plain Truth*, September 1980, pp. 18–19, 45 (the reference to Lindsell occurs on p. 18); Victor Paul Wierwille, *Jesus Christ Is Not God* (New Knoxville, OH: American Christian Press, 1975).

6. Johnston, *Evangelicals at an Impasse*, p. 149.

7. Peter Toon, *The Development of Doctrine in the Church* (Grand Rapids: William B. Eerdmans Publishing Co., 1979), p. 125.

8. J. Ramsey Michaels, "Inerrancy or Verbal Inspiration?" p. 52.

9. David W. Aiken, "What Is an 'Evangelical'?" 1979, p. 1. (Mimeographed.)

10. Richard J. Mouw, "New Alignments: Hartford and the Future of

Evangelicalism," in *Against the World for the World*, ed. Peter L. Berger and Richard John Neuhaus (New York: Seabury Press, 1976), pp. 109–10.

11. Fosdick, *Modern Use of the Bible*, p. 231.

12. Packer, '*Fundamentalism*,' pp. 153, 157–58; Rice, *Our Perfect Book the Bible*, p. 22.

13. Bultmann, "Is Exegesis without Presuppositions Possible?" p. 296; Paul J. Achtemaier, *An Introduction to the New Hermeneutic* (Philadelphia: Westminster Press, 1969), p. 100.

14. Walter Wink, *The Bible in Human Transformation* (Philadelphia: Fortress Press, 1977).

15. Ibid., p. iv.

16. Clark H. Pinnock, "Evangelical Theology: Conservative and Contemporary," *Christianity Today*, January 5, 1979, pp. 23–29.

17. Bultmann, "New Testament and Mythology," pp. 12–13.

18. Paul Tillich, *Dynamics of Faith* (New York: Harper & Row, 1958), pp. 50–53.

19. Paul Tillich, *Theology of Culture* (New York: Oxford University Press, 1977), p. 66.

20. David R. Griffin, *A Process Christology* (Philadelphia: Westminster Press, 1973), p. 12. "Christian faith (as I understand it) is possible apart from belief in Jesus' resurrection in particular and life beyond bodily death in general, and because of the widespread skepticism regarding these additional beliefs, they should be presented as optional, whereas the present essay focuses on what I consider essential elements of Christian faith."

21. John B. Cobb Jr., *Christ in a Pluralistic Age* (Philadelphia: Westminster Press, 1975), p. 169.

22. John Hick, ed., *The Myth of God Incarnate* (Philadelphia: Westminster Press, 1977), pp. 179–84.

23. Michael E. McGarry, *Christology after Auschwitz* (New York: Paulist Press, 1977), pp. 72–103; John T. Pawlikowski, *What Are They Saying About Christian-Jewish Relations?* (New York: Paulist Press, 1980), pp. 33–48.

24. George Carey, *God Incarnate* (Downers Grove: InterVarsity Press, 1978), pp. 48–49.

25. J. Oswald Sanders, *How Lost Are the Heathen?* (Chicago: Moody Press, 1972); Richard Wolff, *The Final Destiny of the Heathen* (Lincoln, NE: Back to the Bible Publishers, 1961).

26. Kraft, *Christianity in Culture*; Neal Punt, *Unconditional Good News* (Grand Rapids: William B. Eerdmans Publishing Co., 1980).

27. J. Gresham Machen, *Christianity and Liberalism* (Grand Rapids: William B. Eerdmans Publishing Co., 1923).

28. Francis A. Schaeffer, *The God Who Is There* (Downers Grove: Inter-Varsity Press, 1974).

CLARK H. PINNOCK

Conservative and Contemporary

*A*s everyone now recognizes, evangelical theology in North America is in the midst of an exciting ferment. And just as the previous generation produced formative thinkers like Carl F. H. Henry, Bernard Ramm, and E. J. Carnell to take the baton from Warfield, Hodge, and Machen, so today new voices have arisen to lead evangelical theology into perhaps its most challenging era yet. It may be too early to spot Carl F. H. Henry's successor as the dean of evangelical theologians, since the contributions of, for example, Jack Rogers, Donald G. Bloesch, and Donald W. Dayton are all so important. But it would not be surprising to see the name of Clark H. Pinnock rise to the top. Part of the reason for this is Pinnock's own theological pilgrimage. His roots in evangelical, even fundamentalist, pietism give him credentials that cannot be gainsaid. And as the movement has grown and developed in the last decades, Pinnock has been there in the thick of it, a participant-observer who has come to see both that the voice of evangelical Christianity needs urgently to be sounded in the modern world, and that it has little chance of being heard and heeded unless it speaks in the idiom and to the concerns of "modernity." It will be our object here to plot out Pinnock's theological development, and to critique it where this may help us to understand it better. For to understand Pinnock's theology may well be to understand the evangelical theology of the coming generation.

PERIOD I: DEFENDING BIBLICAL AUTHORITY

Clark Pinnock's theological development may readily be divided into three periods, the first of which began, naturally enough, with his evangelical conversion:

> I was raised in a liberal Baptist church. It had forgotten both the truth and the reality of God pretty much. It was a bore. Fortunately, I had a Bible-believing grandma and a like-minded Sunday School teacher at the church who led me to know Christ. I received further help from Youth for Christ in Toronto and the Canadian Keswick Bible Conference one summer. . . . So I was introduced to God in the context of the fundamentalist portraiture of the Gospel. It alerted me to the fact that there are a lot of modernists out there who had vacated the house of authority and sold our birthright for a mess of relevant pottage. I sensed early on that this was wrong-headed and dangerous, and never really came to see it differently.[1]

Indeed he never did. This experience contains the germ that would grow into Pinnock's whole system of theology. Though there have been many twists and turns along the way, the trajectory was already crystal clear.

At age twenty-three, Pinnock completed his BA with honors in Ancient Near Eastern Studies at the University of Toronto and shortly began the PhD program at Manchester University, studying the New Testament under evangelical New Testament scholar and apologist F. F. Bruce. Completing his dissertation on Pauline pneumatology in 1963, Pinnock continued his association with Bruce for two years as an Assistant Lecturer in New Testament Studies. During the same period he was in close correspondence with apologist Francis A. Schaeffer and worked for a while at Schaeffer's retreat for troubled and doubting intellectual youth at L'Abri in Huemoz, Switzerland. The influence of both men on the content and style of Pinnock's own subsequent apologetics and theology was great. In 1965, Pinnock accepted a position teaching the New Testament at New Orleans Theological Seminary, a Southern Baptist school. There he began in earnest his career as a shaper of American evangelical thought.

Pinnock decided early on that his mission was to promote the soundness and success of evangelism by defending the evangelical message from unbelieving skepticism, Christian synergism, and theological relativism. In his early booklet *Evangelism and Truth*, his agenda is set forth concisely:

> Evangelism is the declaration of a specific *message*. It is not holding meetings, or getting results. It is communication of the good news. Therefore, *evangelism and truth are inseparable*. Biblical evangelism requires divine truth; divine truth requires revelation in language; revelation in language requires the deposit of infallible scripture. As soon as confidence is weakened in the integrity of our source material, evangelism is weakened to a corresponding degree.[2]

In the same work, he explains that Calvinism is just as foundational to biblical evangelism, since any other (that is, Arminian) view would imply that sinners could in some measure deserve to be saved or aid in their own salvation, and in neither case would salvation be by grace alone. Also, says the early Pinnock, "our constant prayers for God to *save* the lost, not just to *help* them to be saved, imply that the divine choice alone is operative."[3]

So the first priority of the early Pinnock is the gospel of evangelical conversion, and his goal is to do his best to promote an accurate presentation of it and to gain a fair hearing for it. Here we see the beginning of Pinnock's concern with biblical inerrancy as a safeguard for religious epistemology, for apologetics as the necessary phase of "pre-evangelism," and for polemics against both liberal theologians who dissolve and obscure the saving message in the "acid bath" of relativism and non-inerrantist evangelicals who have let down the barriers against such relativism. We must briefly examine Pinnock's early work in these areas.

Pinnock's exposure to Francis Schaeffer and his work with students at L'Abri made further apologetics work, both in print and in person as he lectured on many campuses, inevitable. Two early books, *Set Forth Your Case* (1967) and *Live Now, Brother!* (published in 1972 and reprinted in 1976 as *Are There any Answers?*) were dedicated to clearing away intellectual obstacles to conversion. The second was really a shorter tract version of the first, echoing Francis Schaeffer's *The God Who Is There* and its précis *Escape from Reason*. In both books Schaeffer's influence is everywhere obvious. Everywhere the reader turns, Schaefferisms confront him; in *Set Forth Your Case* we find: "pre-evangelism" (p. 19), "the 'upper-story' pattern in contemporary theology" (p. 20), "a divided field of knowledge" (p. 21), "the line of despair" (p. 48), "moral motions" (p. 52), "time-space history" (p. 68), "infinite personal God" (p. 109), and "paneverythingism" (p. 117). The gist of the Schaefferian apologetic is that humanism, with its focus on human ability, and scientism, with its "naturalistic presuppositions," have combined to spawn a mechanistic worldview with no room for God, who is the only possible source for authentic meaning and value. Humanity is seen as the futile, chance product of blind and irrational forces; our only possible fate is final destruction, and our only consistent attitude must be nihilism and despair. Pinnock, following Schaeffer, rapidly proof-texts representatives of modern art, culture, theater, film, existentialist philosophy, and neoorthodox theology to show how all alike have come to the brink of this chasm of nihilism only to flinch and make a desperate "upper-story leap" into an irrational and imaginary zone of meaning, transcending despair by an arbitrary act of will. By contrast, the Christian gospel answers all the questions and supplies an epistemological and metaphysical basis for meaning and value. Believers can breathe easy.

Thus far, Schaeffer. But Pinnock goes on to supplement this "cultural apologetics" with a more traditional "evidentialist" defense derived almost as completely from John Warwick Montgomery. It would be wonderful to believe that the Christian answer was true, but what makes belief in it any more than another irrational "upper-story leap"? "The beauty of the gospel in the avalanche of competing religious claims is precisely the possibility we have of checking it out historically and factually."[4] Pinnock follows Montgomery in seeing in the recent philosophical discussions of the verifiability and falsifiability criteria an opportunity for a new hearing for classical apologetics. Analytic philosophers had suggested that an "assertion" is in fact meaningless if it is untestable in principle. If a claim is compatible with any and every state of affairs, it is no real claim, that is, that things are *this* way or *that* way. Pinnock and Montgomery believe that traditional Christianity passes the test admirably, while liberal and neoorthodox theologies fail tragically. It is not only arbitrary to accept a religious claim in the absence of evidence; the claim itself is mere gibberish if it is not even susceptible to proof or disproof, as liberalism is not but conservatism is.

In setting forth his case Pinnock maintains that the four gospels are unimpeachable sources written by eyewitnesses or their secretaries. From these accurate sources we can know that Jesus "time and again" claimed both to be God incarnate and that his own resurrection would vindicate that assertion.[5] The resurrection, in turn, is vastly more probable than the alternatives (for example, the Swoon Theory, the Wrong Tomb Theory, the Hallucination Theory) and so must be accepted as the only sufficient explanation for the rise of Christianity and the dynamic transformation of the hitherto-cowardly disciples. Once we know this, we know that Jesus was in fact divine and thus an infallible oracle. Jesus endorsed the Old Testament as the inerrant Word of God and endorsed the New Testament in advance as more of the same by investing the apostles with his own authority and promising them the Holy Spirit. Thus the Bible is added to Jesus as another infallible oracle.

Having arrived at this point, Pinnock, with Montgomery, thinks to have established a plausible basis for believing in an inerrant Bible and the Christian truth-claims that arise from it. So no one need hesitate to accept the gospel for fear of having to make a sacrifice of the intellect. Apologetics, like Abraham's ram caught in the thicket, makes this unnecessary.

If the historical evidence for the resurrection makes Christian faith plausible, it also makes belief in inerrancy inevitable. Pinnock proceeds from general apologetics to inerrancy apologetics in two books, *A Defense of Biblical Infallibility* (given as a lecture in 1966, published in 1967) and the much more substantial *Biblical Revelation: The Foundation of Christian Theology* (1971). In these two volumes, Pinnock follows the traditional Warfield line. Though we arrive at faith in Christ by an inductive approach to the evidence, once we have done so, we must adopt Christ's own view of biblical inerrancy, and henceforward treat the relevant evidence *de*ductively. Biblical texts may appear to be in error or in contradiction to one another, but these "phenomena of scripture" are misleading. It may be that further study will clear them up, or we may assume textual corruption or harmonize one passage with the other by seeking in it some less obvious but more orthodox interpretation. Following Montgomery's lead, Pinnock denies that this procedure *is* deductive. Rather, it is "inductive inerrancy."[6] How so? Because we inductively accumulate information about what Jesus says of scripture and what scripture says of itself. This operation informs us just what kind of book we are dealing with so we can arrive at an appropriate way of interpreting it—in this case it turns out to be a divinely inspired book that cannot teach error. So it would be just as foolish to read a difficulty as an error as it would be to read a phone directory listing as if it were a cookbook recipe.

The implications of all this for biblical criticism are clear: "Complete critical freedom is purchased at the price of Christian faith."[7] Much historical criticism is seen to employ "naturalistic methodology" and "antisupernatural bias."[8] If we admitted error to exist in the Bible as "negative criticism" proposes, then we would betray Reformation Christianity by subjecting common Bible readers to the papal domination of a new clerical elite of biblical critics who must pronounce on what in the Bible is valid and what is not.[9]

Pinnock knows that some well-meaning scholars seek to reconcile the presence of biblical errors with the fact of divine inspiration, but he is none too sympathetic. Some would suggest that the liability to err is allowed by the parallel between the inspiration of the Bible and the incarnation of Christ. But Pinnock reasons that if the incarnate Word could be free from sin, the inscripturated Word could, and must be, free from error.[10] Others, like E. J. Carnell, had suggested that the inspired text might contain errors taken over by the writer from fallible sources. (Carnell had in mind especially the inflated figures of the Chronicler.) But Pinnock, aware that this would make the Bible a mere inerrant record of errors, doesn't see why the divine-human conflu- ence of inspiration wouldn't have included the careful choosing and checking of sources.[11]

The reader of Pinnock's early works on inerrancy may be sur- prised to note his condemnation of "the fundamentalist tendency to overbelief in the matter of inspiration."[12] Given the argument thus far, what could this possibly mean? There is no need, Pinnock assures us, to join Harry Rimmer and other fundamentalists in twisting the text to make it seem to anticipate modern science. No, let us admit that the biblical writers expressed themselves in prescientific terms. But this does not compromise inerrancy. "Infallibility is obviously restricted to the intended assertions of scripture."[13] "Such [prescientific] references are incidental to the teachings intended. We need to ask what is being asserted in this passage."[14] As he will later put it, the Bible may be said to contain errors but not to teach any.[15]

Pinnock is also willing to recognize that certain literary forms and genres of a less than strictly factual nature may be employed in the Bible, and that when they are, inerrancy is not imperiled. For instance, on this basis, an inerrantist may question "whether the serpent really spoke, because it cannot be established without doubt that the writer intends simple literalism."[16] "Figurative, symbolic, and even mytholog- ical language is employed in scripture as the subject matter and literary form require."[17] Yet some "deceitful" literary forms are ruled out: legend, midrash, etiology, and pseudonymity. "Fragment hypotheses" whereby works like Ephesians, the Pastorals, or 2 Peter may have been worked up from the notes of Paul or Peter by a disciple would not be out of the question, but Pinnock dismisses them as "wholly speculative."[18]

As we will see, it is quite true that Pinnock will move beyond his early thinking on inerrancy, but it usually goes unnoticed that even in his early period, he has a rather more flexible approach to the difficulties in the text than did Warfield or Pinnock's own mentor Schaeffer. But Pinnock was at one with Warfield in warning that to deny the doctrine of inerrancy would be to shred the seamless garment of biblical teaching. If Christ, who taught inerrancy, was wrong at that point, where else might he have been mistaken? And if the Bible erred here (for example, the duration of Pekah's reign), how can we be sure it does not err there (for example, God has justified us by his grace)?

This all-or-nothing stance explains why the early Pinnock regards inerrancy as theologically central. "Denial of it brings into serious jeopardy the entire epistemological base of Christianity."[19] Why? "Without the propositional revelation in scripture, theology is an impossible endeavor."[20] Pinnock echoes John Warwick Montgomery in seeing theological method as theory-building wherein the best paradigm is the one that fits most of the biblical data. "The exegesis of scripture thus has *absolute priority* over all systems. Systems which fail to fit the data are to be dismantled. A faulty theological system is one which cannot satisfy the biblical evidence."[21] It is probably no caricature to suggest that the early Pinnock sees theology as a vast jigsaw puzzle, with Bible verses (assertions) as the pieces. The fewer left out when the puzzle is finished, the more correct the theology. Thus one must know whether all the pieces belong in this puzzle. If some do not (if some assertions are not inerrant) we have no hope of ever getting the puzzle right.

One observation needs to be made regarding Pinnock's whole apologetic approach. Though motivated by the same gospel zeal that makes him express his faith in a Calvinist framework, as we have seen, his apologetics is distinctly un-Calvinistic, as he himself seems aware. Pinnock notes that the Warfield approach to inerrancy apologetics is rejected by Cornelius Van Til because it appeals to unregenerate sinners as if anything short of the miraculous electing grace of God could open their eyes to the truth of the Bible. It is "an Arminian view of the defense of scripture."[22] Pinnock sides with Warfield against Van Til because he fears that the *a priorist* "believe it or not" approach of Van

Til would fail to meet the "verifiability" test. Yet his *is* an Arminian view of apologetics, as can be seen from Pinnock's own *Set Forth Your Case*. In this work Pinnock repeatedly claims that sinners are so captivated by bad faith and "the noetic effects of the Fall" that they cannot fairly consider evidence unless the miraculous intervention of the Spirit enables them to do so.[23] He sees apologetics, in fact, as dispelling pseudoproblems manufactured not by the evidence but by "naturalistic presuppositions" and "anti-supernaturalist biases." But if this is the case, why address the difficulties at all? Why not simply demand that the unbeliever drop the pretense and repent? Then the smokescreen of pseudoproblems should dissipate by itself. But Pinnock's whole mode of argumentation tacitly assumes that his skeptical readers are interested in the truth, can evaluate arguments, and might even grudgingly acknowledge the strength of the Christian case. The sinner *can* do something toward his own salvation, as Arminians claim: he can of himself listen and consider the gospel. We will see that this perhaps small variation from the Calvinistic framework is only the first step in what will eventually amount to a wholesale repudiation of Calvinism by Pinnock, one that will have dramatic implications for his whole theology.

Once the early Pinnock has completed his apologetical stronghold, he sallies forth from it in polemical sorties against liberal theologians and compromising, non-inerrantist evangelicals. Pinnock holds out no hope for liberal and neoorthodox theologians. He sees them simply as tragic examples of theology gone off course and shipwrecked. He tells the sad tale of their rejection of biblical authority and consequent slide into relativism and anthropocentric, solipsistic speculation: "Like Roman Catholics at the time of the Reformation, and like Paul's Galatian opponents, liberal theologians have substituted a human religion for the divine Word, good views for good news."[24]

Whatever one thinks of Pinnock's evaluations of liberal and neoorthodox theology, it is evident from the discussion in *Biblical Revelation* that he has read many important theologians in depth and with understanding. Unlike many conservatives, he is not content to

reject them simply for not being conservative. Rather he is able to criticize them for what they *say*, not for what they do *not*. He is able to
sniff out and label important ambiguities and often-overlooked contradictions. But for all his study of non-evangelical thinkers, Pinnock
seeks to engage not them, but his fellow evangelicals. He seems to
regard the liberals and neoorthodox only as warnings. He points to
them and exhorts his fellow Bible believers, "Remember Lot's wife!"
If we yield up inerrancy, there is no guarantee we will not end up as
lost souls like Macquarrie or Ogden or Kaufman or Altizer. Just as
their talk of demythologized symbols and "suprahistorical" acts of
God is unverifiable and meaningless, a non-inerrantist evangelicalism
would be starting down the same path: "Their position would be
meaningless, for it would imply that belief in infallibility would not be
affected by errors in scripture."[25]

In his earliest writings, Pinnock does more than exhort, however.
In *A New Reformation* (1968), he urges, even demands, that the
denominational hierarchy of the Southern Baptist Convention move to
purge the seminaries of non-inerrantist professors.[26] Later Pinnock
will moderate this zeal, once he comes to see that the issues are not so
clear-cut after all.

All items on Pinnock's agenda in this first period proceed from
and cohere in one central concern: the possibility of evangelical conversion and piety is endangered by the loss of inerrancy, which leads
to relativistic liberal theology. "Liberal theology robs the church of its
only valid knowledge of redemption."[27] "Doubts and perplexities have
discouraged the faithful" because of this theology.[28] With liberal theology "there is absolutely no way to challenge the non-Christian to
receive Jesus Christ."[29] It becomes "impossible to defend the gospel"
in apologetics.[30] "At stake is the very possibility of knowing and
preaching the gospel."[31] In short, liberal theology will produce more
churches like the one in which Pinnock grew up, *despite* whose ministry Pinnock managed to hear the gospel and be converted. Thus Pinnock's whole theological and apologetical structure is built on the
foundation of piety. The best view of biblical authority is that which

safeguards and promotes evangelism. The right theology is that which is consistent with evangelical conversion and the bliss of spiritual certainty. Even his Calvinism is based on the logic of the experience of grace and prayer for the salvation of souls.

None of this may be bad, but it is certainly ironic, because it implies that Pinnock's own theology is profoundly, even fundamentally, *experience centered*. And this would seem to smack of the very liberal subjectivity so vilified in his early works. "Both the older Liberalism and the newer existential theologies are basically pietistic, experience theologies."[32] Note the similarity of Pinnock's own theology to that of Schleiermacher as Pinnock himself later describes it:

> Schleiermacher, the father of modern theology, reared as a pietist, connected revelation to the experiences of the heart. We experience the feeling of absolute dependence, and this gives rise to the idea of God on whom we depend. . . . The main point is that revelation leads to doctrinal formulations out of religious communion.[33]

Perhaps the main reason Pinnock himself fails to see this striking parallel is that he skews Schleiermacher's emphasis on religious experience as the epistemological norm. Pinnock seems to think Schleiermacher viewed "God-consciousness" or the "feeling of absolute dependence" as the *object* of theology rather than as simply the *medium* of our knowledge of God, the real object of all theology. Is it not clear that for Pinnock, too, piety is the criterion for proper theology? His own theological epistemology, then, is more "liberal" than he imagines.

As Pinnock's theology begins to evolve and develop in the second and third periods, we will be able to see that it does so along four trajectories. First, he moves further and further away from Calvinism. Second, he moves from a defense of biblical authority in a formal sense to a greater application of it in a material sense. Third, religious experience continues to shape his theology as both source and criterion. Fourth, he seeks to forge a "post-liberal" theology, learning from theological liberalism, and not simply rejecting it.

PERIOD II: OBEYING BIBLICAL AUTHORITY

Various experiences in the 1960s prompted Clark Pinnock into a period of rethinking and intellectual ferment. Papers and books resulted from it, and they cover, roughly, the early and mid-1970s from 1971 to about 1977. In this period some items are added to his theological agenda, and his thinking about others changes radically. We have already previewed four trajectories along which his thought will be seen changing during this time, but we must note as well that as each focus of his thought changes, it has a noticeable impact on most of the others. This is perhaps the mark of a truly systematic thinker.

Pinnock recounts a spiritual experience that, like his conversion, was to shape his theological concerns profoundly. "It happened to me in 1967 in New Orleans. I was a young theologian, heavily into intellectual reflection as I am now, but feeling a lack of reality and power which comes from an unbalanced life. Although Paul plainly says we should use both mind and spirit, theologians generally exercise only the mind." One night after church, Pinnock and his wife Dorothy were invited to a home fellowship and prayer meeting. "As the meeting began, it was obvious that God was very real and much loved by these people." The enthusiastic testimonies and fervent, believing prayers convinced Pinnock that "these people were alive unto God, as Paul says." The result: "I was touched by God that night. I glimpsed the dimension of the Spirit which the New Testament describes but is so often absent in churches today. The Bible came alive to me in this and other respects. Being a Christian became an exciting adventure instead of a drag. I was filled with the Spirit."[34]

Pinnock began to interpret this experience biblically and theologically. The results were published in a series of papers in *Christianity Today* and Theological Students Fellowship mailings including "Truce Proposals for the Tongues Controversy"[35] and "An Evangelical Theology of the Charismatic Movement."[36] In previous writings, Pinnock had expressed only suspicion of the Charismatic Renewal, as in *Set Forth Your Case*, published the very year of his own charismatic experience, where he faults glossolalia as simply one more irrational "upper-story leap." "The dramatic rise of occurrences of tongue-speaking fits into this picture, too. Release from anxiety can be obtained by letting the mind go free to the accompaniment of soft babblings from the throat." He warns of "the extreme dangers implicit in the movement, simply because of its wider context, the widespread retreat from all rational controls."[37] In *Biblical Revelation*, written three years later, Pinnock is still wary, though in light of his experience, less negative: "To deny the very possibility of private revelation would be to imply that God is now silent. However, a check there must be on such things. Religious experience or private revelation more often than not corresponds to the mind-set of the recipient."[38]

That said, Pinnock goes on in his writings of this second period to endorse charismatic spirituality, defending Charismatics and Pentecostals from the charge that their "Tongues Movement" is unbiblical. Pinnock suggests that the controversial phrase "Baptism in the Holy Spirit" ought not to be the cause for disputing, since, first, it really refers more to an experience than to a (new) doctrine and, second, the use of the phrase in Acts is broader than non-Pentecostals have been willing to admit, referring not exclusively to initial regeneration but also to subsequent "fillings" with the Spirit.

Pinnock then leaves the defensive posture for attack. He argues that mainstream evangelicals have been quenching the Spirit, and that they dare not ignore the more spectacular charismatic gifts like tongues and prophecy since these gifts are perfectly *biblical*. We see here evidence of a shift that characterizes Pinnock's theological widening and deepening in this second period: having defended the authority of scripture formally, he now presses home the actual material stipulations of the authoritative Bible. What right have "Bible-believing" evangelicals to embrace familiar gifts like teaching and administration yet reject and spurn stranger gifts like tongues and revelations? "Although they are not entirely consistent, evangelicals tend not to be open to the entire range [of gifts in the New Testament]. They are open to A-P, let us say, but not gifts Q-Z."[39]

This new emphasis on charismatic spirituality will influence other areas, as we will see, but it is also important to note that we see here the beginnings of Pinnock's new role as an agent of reconciliation among evangelicals, as he seeks to weld them into a united front to present to the outside world of secular humanists and theological liberals.

A second new area to which Pinnock directs his attention is that of political and social concerns. Again, it is seen as a question of the material authority of the Bible. "Evangelicals have in recent years been rather more inclined to defend the gospel than practice it."[40] Of course Pinnock here describes his own transition, which occurred, apparently, during his tenure at Trinity Evangelical Divinity School from 1969 to 1974. While there, he participated in the discussions which led to the founding of *Post-American* (later *Sojourners*). Before, he had regarded radical politics ("A strident cry for political revolution") as a misguided attempt to correct a problem curable in truth only by widespread conversion, the traditional apolitical fundamentalist line. "In the last analysis, neither racism nor war nor pollution is the deepest problem but rather [man] himself. Modifying the system will not deal with hate and self-centeredness and greed. Something more is needed."[41] Not only would leftist politics be inadequate to solve our problems; it would make them much worse, for "Socialism or collectivism is the political system of humanism. . . . The current move toward collectivism in America is based on a humanistic view of man, his nature and problems, and we may all live to regret it." In fact, in the first period, Pinnock was advocating an agenda identical to that of today's "New Christian Right," opposing "secular humanism," homosexuality, the teaching of evolution as propaganda for atheism, and so on, and supporting the establishment of private Christian schools and prayer in public schools.[42]

What a difference in this second period! As one of the contributing editors of *Sojourners*, he has come to embrace pacifism and to reject Capitalism and the right to private property.[43] He would actually vote for Communist candidates, seeing in Maoist revolutionaries true partisans for the Kingdom of God.[44] Yet, despite all this, Pinnock never came to see political action as an excuse to neglect evangelism: "We are most definitely in favor of quantitative evangelization and are opposed to its being substituted by or changed into the struggle for social justice."[45] Neither is he willing to allow the demands of radical discipleship to harden into a new legalism that would obscure the gospel of Galatians. Rather, he argues, radical obedience to Jesus should be seen precisely as an outgrowth of salvation by grace alone.[46] Having become a political radical, Pinnock still has no desire to become one of those theological liberals creating their own speculative man-centered gospels.

Far from being a denial of the biblical authority he had defended vociferously, his newly radical stance stems directly from the authority of scripture. "It is not even possible to be doctrinally sound without being ethically responsive because the Word of God clearly demands costly discipleship of us. . . . I am socially concerned because I am a biblical Christian, not in spite of it."[47]

> How is it, in light of Jesus' teaching about money, that church members do not have more of a conscience about materialism, and how is it, in view of Jesus' teaching about non-violence, that the churches have not included instruction in nonviolent action on the educational agenda? Even in Christian ethical theory it has often seemed as if the norms of Jesus are all of them negotiable to the reasonable demands of our own judgment.[48]

But if socially conservative evangelicals reject biblical authority materially, Pinnock is still alive to the danger of radical theologians rejecting it formally. Against the Liberation theologians, Pinnock warns his readers not to make the Bible's liberation themes a canon within the canon in order to deny other aspects of biblical teaching, or to elevate Marxist social analysis to a "second source of revelation."[49] However, as we will see, the emphasis on practical obedience to the Bible over abstract preoccupation with theories of inspiration does seem to have moved Pinnock to relax his position a bit with regard to inerrancy.[50]

During the 1970s many evangelicals were becoming interested in either the Charismatic Movement or *Sojourners*-type radicalism, but few were involved in both. Pinnock, of course, was one of those few. And here again we can see his concern to mediate and reconcile. In his "The Acts Connection," he shows how any genuine outpouring of the Spirit must result in a social radicalism such as we find in Acts 4:32–35. In his "An Evangelical Theology of Human Liberation," he urges that every "Christian community that has been convicted by the Spirit to be socially concerned should move in the direction of becoming charismatically renewed as well so that its mission of servanthood in the world might be in the power and under the direction of the Spirit."[51]

Pinnock, along with the rest of the "radical evangelicals," has basically opted for an Anabaptist understanding of discipleship, ethics, and the state. In doing so, Pinnock has taken another step away from the Calvinist worldview. He rejects not only the historic Calvinist belief in the state as a Christian commonwealth with its "Christ the Transformer of Culture" model, but also specific Calvinist doctrines, such as perseverance. His new view of radical discipleship makes him suspicious of the "cheap notion of eternal security" with which lukewarm American evangelicals love to comfort themselves.[52] Also, his embracing of the Pauline doctrine of the Principalities and Powers (as politically interpreted by Hendrikus Berkhof in *Christ and the Powers* and John Howard Yoder in *The Politics of Jesus*) inclines him less toward a Calvinist doctrine of individual depravity and more in the direction of an environmentalist view of sin.[53]

For these and other reasons, in this period Pinnock completely repudiates Calvinism and becomes a full-fledged Arminian. In large measure, this theological revolution is yet another result of taking the actual texts of the infallible Bible with appropriate seriousness. For, at least as Pinnock reads it, the Bible speaks loudly and clearly of a genuinely contingent and open-ended history and of really free human will, neither being under the constraints of divine predestination. For Pinnock, the Bible clearly speaks of God's will to save all humanity, not just some imagined supralapsarian elect. There is no sense in sacrificing the law of excluded middle (something his mentor Francis Schaeffer warned him against sufficiently)[54] to hold both free will and complete determinism together. Pinnock sees Calvinism capturing the dynamic and compassionate God of the Bible in alien categories of bloodless metaphysical abstraction.[55]

What of his former objections to synergism? He now sees that to reach out with the empty hands of faith to grasp God's grace is no meritorious act whereby one might think to earn God's grace.[56] But what of the experience of piety, wherein one knows all is of God and no credit is due oneself? Be that as it may, experience now inclines Pinnock in a. different direction, because equally undeniable is the intuitive knowledge that we are free: "When faced with a decision, we *know* with a subjective certainty that we can take one of the two or more alternatives before us."[57] Note again how Pinnock, like the subjectivistic liberals he criticizes, uses human consciousness as a source of theological knowledge. Similarly, Arminianism is to be preferred and Calvinism to be rejected because the former is now deemed more consistent with the assurance of salvation and the practice of evangelism than is the latter. "On [the doctrine of free will] hangs, we believe, the validity of the universal offer of the gospel, and the possibility of Christian assurance. If we do not know that God loves all sinners, we do not know that he loves us, and we do not know that he loves those to whom we take the gospel."[58] Ironically, it is these very factors that once made Calvinism attractive to Pinnock: Calvinism was the consistent implication of pious prayer and God's sovereign offer of grace. Now, on second thought, "It is hard to see on the basis of [Calvinism] how the gospel can be preached at all."[59] In a later work Pinnock writes of Calvinism, "This is the kind of theology that makes atheists."[60] Theology, again, is a function of piety.

Pinnock's zeal for apologetics seems to have taken a back seat to other, newer interests in this period, but it is still present, influencing other areas of his thought and being influenced by them. For instance, apologetics has added its vote to Pinnock's rejection of Calvinism: he has decided it would be inconsistent to use the "free will defense" in one's apologetics if one were going to deny genuine human freedom in one's theology.[61]

Several articles devoted to apologetics appeared in this period. A series of them appearing in *His* magazine from October 1976 through April 1977 were collected, revised, and expanded as *Reason Enough: A Case for Christian Faith* (1980). The other important piece was a critical review of Francis Schaeffer's *How Shall We Then Live?*, which appeared in *Sojourners*, July 1977. It was titled "Schaefferism as a World-View" and seems at first glance to be a decisive break with his old master. But on closer inspection we find that most of Pinnock's criticisms of Schaeffer have nothing to do with apologetics. He faults him for too sketchy a grasp of the artistic and intellectual history he pretends to analyze and criticizes him for not holding an Anabaptist view of the state. He also rejects Schaeffer's views of inerrancy, a topic to which we will presently return. But Pinnock's only serious criticism of Schaefferian apologetics is that it is essentially existentialist and pragmatic; it tries to show that one needs meaning and that Christianity can give meaning, so one ought to believe in Christianity. Pinnock points out that Schaeffer is really inviting his readers to make an "upper-story leap" like those made by the liberal theologians and existentialists he criticizes. But this insight represents no break with Schaeffer. Pinnock must already have seen this flaw back when he wrote *Set Forth Your Case*; there he supplemented Schaeffer's presuppositionalist apologetics (the first half of the book) with John Warwick Montgomery's evidentialist approach (the second half) in order to show how Christian faith was a step of faith, not a leap of faith.

Both presuppositionalist and evidentialist arguments return in *Reason Enough*, essentially unchanged. He repeats two of Schaeffer's main points, that humanism cannot justify meaning and value, and that intelligent life cannot be the product merely of unintelligent nature. What is new in *Reason Enough* is the addition of emphases garnered from Pinnock's own growth during the second period. For example, we see his Arminianism in his stress that God gives us freedom to believe or not to believe and his willingness to grant that at least some doubts are genuine, not the result of bad faith or total depravity.[62] There are separate chapters on how the religious experiences of humanity (Christian and non-Christian) count as evidence for God's existence. In the early period, Pinnock would never have said this; under Montgomery's influence, he liked to denigrate subjective religious experiences as indistinguishable from mere indigestion unless one had an inerrant Bible to distinguish true from false.[63] We may infer it is Pinnock's discovery of charismatic spirituality that led him to this change. Similarly, his *Sojourners* experience suggests to him the propriety of a chapter on the social achievements of Christianity throughout history as an argument for faith. At the same time, his commitment to radical discipleship leads Pinnock to warn the reader to count the cost. Are you now convinced Christianity is true? Not so fast! Are you prepared for the life of costly discipleship conversion will entail? This aspect is conspicuous by its absence in most works of apologetics. We have noted Pinnock's objection to Schaeffer, that the mere desirability of believing something is not adequate grounds for believing in it. In "Inspiration and Authority: A Truce Proposal for the Evangelicals," Pinnock levels this charge again, this time focusing on the question of biblical inerrancy. He admits that the inerrancy doctrine stems more from the needs of apologetics than from the logic of inspiration. He connects Schaeffer explicitly with this charge and objects that one cannot properly derive theology from the needs of apologetics. "That in a nutshell is what liberal theology has always done."[64] We have suggested that Pinnock himself has always done the same, and at least in the case of inerrancy, he has finally come to see it this way himself. Commenting on his earliest writings on this subject, he admits, "A few years ago, I claimed that the Bible taught total inerrancy because I hoped that it did—I wanted it to. How else would it be possible to maintain a firm stand against religious liberalism unless one held firmly to total inerrancy?"[65]

In this second period, Pinnock begins to reexamine the doctrine of biblical infallibility. And though one might think that he will be careful to bracket the needs of apologetics, having learned his lesson, this is not entirely the case. Perhaps through his work in the Theological Students Fellowship, Pinnock has become aware that the inerrancy doctrine, instead of preserving and protecting evangelical faith, may actually endanger it! Pinnock, for example, commends Stephen T. Davis's anti-inerrancy polemic *The Debate About the Bible* for its "pastoral service to those who are troubled with marginal difficulties in the Bible but are deeply committed to the evangelical faith. The theory of perfect error-lessness when pressed can leave such persons stranded with nothing to hold on to if a single point however minute stands in any doubt. . . . Finding nowhere to stand outside strict inerrancy, they cease to stand at all"[66] and bolt to liberal theology! So strict inerrancy having proved impractical, it's back to the drawing board.

We have already seen that even in the earliest period Pinnock by no means held to the strictest possible version of inerrancy and took pains to distance himself from those who did, for example, apologist Harry Rimmer. He was already drawing a strategic line, like Charles Hodge, between the assumptions and the assertions of the biblical writer and admitting that ancient literary genres could accommodate prescientific, nonliteral, and even mythic language. In the writings of his second period, Pinnock makes no fundamental shift, but he does loosen up his stance a bit, accepting some ideas he had rejected previously. For instance, he now sees how his understanding of only the writer's "intended assertion" being inerrant could accommodate Carnell's suggestion that biblical "writers may have copied erroneous source material without bothering (or knowing) to correct it. It is entirely proper to ask with Carnell what the purpose of the Chronicler was in recording the public genealogies."[67] He admits Dewey M. Beegle's point that it is meaningless to appeal to Jesus' belief in biblical infallibility and then to claim that only the original autograph copies were error-free, since Jesus made no such distinction, regarding the then-available copies as infallible.[68] Most surprising of all, he now admits that if one qualifies inerrancy according to intended assertions, "one could fairly say that the Bible contains errors but teaches none."[69] Recall how in *Biblical Revelation* he said that any evangelical "position would be meaningless" if it implied "that belief in infallibility would not be affected by errors in scripture."[70]

Despite these shifts to the left, Pinnock remains quite hesitant to accept many of the conclusions of what he calls "negative biblical criticism." For instance, he thinks M. Kuitert has gone too far in accepting the view that the Acts of Elisha in 2 Kings are a cycle of legends.[71]

Pinnock is also careful to define his position over against other evangelicals who have sought to modify inerrancy but have gone farther than him. For instance, he rejects Daniel P. Fuller's suggestion that inerrancy be restricted to "revelational" matters, leaving historical and scientific assertions up for grabs. Pinnock sees it as "an unwarrantable and arbitrary move" to take the "macropurpose" of scripture (to instruct in matters of salvation, faith, and practice) and set it up as a canon within the canon. Pinnock prefers his own view since it at least allows that all *assertions* on whatever subject are inerrant, though incidental *assumptions* may not be.[72] (In fact Pinnock's view is not so different from Fuller's since it is of course troublesome *factual*, not *theological*, assumptions that Pinnock wishes to exempt from inerrancy.) He also resists the attempt of Paul K. Jewett and Virginia Mollenkott to use the main thrust of Pauline teaching on women attested in Galatians 3:28 in order to bracket his chauvinistic statements in the Pastoral Epistles as residual rabbinism. This, too, Pinnock sees as a canon within the canon, and a manipulation of scripture according to human whim.[73]

Pinnock's view is hardly as far to the left as one could go, but it is certainly dubious whether one ought to continue to consider him an "inerrantist" of any kind. He himself questions whether the word is still serviceable. In his "Inspiration and Authority: A Truce Proposal," he suggests that since the same rubric covers J. I. Packer's view (which resembles his own) and Francis Schaeffer's stricter view, it is purely a matter of (misleading) semantics whether one calls oneself an "inerrantist" or not.[74] This he points out in hopes of stopping the destructive fight raging over the term in the wake of Harold Lindsell's *The Battle for the Bible*. "No term is worth battling over with these results."[75]

In his review of James Barr's *Fundamentalism*, Pinnock suggests that inerrancy is so fraught with conceptual and hermeneutical difficulties that it might be best to retire the term.[76] In a pair of essays in *Christianity Today* and *Theology Today*, he speculates what shape a new, admittedly non-inerrantist evangelical understanding of inspiration might take. He admits that the sort of qualified, nuanced form of inerrantism he espouses may be little more than a halfway house on the way to such a position.[77] Clearly, Pinnock is charting the prospects for his own further development, which we will take up in our third section.

In his early writings, Pinnock saw inerrancy as all important as a bulwark against the devastating tide of theological liberalism. If he has become more critical of inerrancy in this second period, he has also become a bit less hostile toward theological liberals. He still warns theological students to beware of liberalism. To be attracted to it would be the seduction of the devil, and to embrace it would be apostasy and damnation! The only way to avoid this is to combine study with an active piety.[78] He is still talking about the evangelical obligation to "refute" and "answer" liberal formulations such as Process Theology. But there is a new note. Pinnock realizes there is much to learn from liberal and neoorthodox theology after all. He comes to be an enthusiastic partisan of Karl Barth and Wolfhart Pannenberg, seeing both men as more like Daniel Fuller—essentially orthodox, but with a few defective views here and there. And even other, less acceptable liberals he now acknowledges to be "some of the most creative Christian thinkers the church has ever known."[79]

In fact, in the second period, we find Pinnock's own theological vocabulary almost bare of the once-familiar jargon of Schaeffer and Montgomery. These are replaced by concepts borrowed from Schubert Ogden, John A. T. Robinson, David Tracy, Langdon Gilkey, and others. He is enthusiastic in his praise of Hans Küng and can bring himself to critique Küng's *On Being a Christian* only with manifest reluctance. He acknowledges his indebtedness to Gordon Kaufman's "historicist" theology in his new, non-Calvinist view of the historical process. Eventually, Process Theology's criticisms of classical theism move Pinnock to a startling reformulation of his doctrine of God, but this last must be deferred to our third section.

What accounts for such a change? We have seen how in this period Pinnock has sought to be a reconciler in various intra-evangelical disputes. But his ecumenical sympathies do not extend as far as linking hands with liberals. He still, as we have seen just above, considers them the enemy. In fact the reason he wants so badly to halt the "battle for the Bible" that he himself once helped to foment (in *A New Reformation*) is so evangelicals can present a united front against the threatening foe of liberal theology: "What seems so unfortunate about the 'inerrancy debate' today . . . is that it has to be taking place between evangelical scholars, pitting one against another, rather than between the whole evangelical coalition and those who are *bona fide* opponents of biblical authority such as Barr, Nineham or Evans."[80]

The clue to his ambivalent attitude is to be found in his 1971 essay "Prospects for Systematic Theology." There he suggests the need for "an evangelical alternative" to "the present theological ferment" that "will be clearly seen to be, not preliberal (as if we wished to pretend that nothing of importance had happened in theology since Luther or Calvin!), but postliberal, a proposal which self-consciously turns away from the deficiencies of liberal thought. and aligns itself in a fresh way with the historic faith of the church."[81] Prior to this essay that opens his second period, Pinnock's approach to theology had in effect been to "pretend" that nothing important (nothing good, anyway) *had* happened since the Reformation. But once he decided to listen to his opponents, he did find that much had happened that needed to be taken into account.

The influence on Pinnock (at admittedly secondary points) by the likes of Pannenberg, Gilkey, Küng, and Ogden is a sign of the "postliberal" character of his emerging theology. But more significant is the fact that in the second period he no longer makes biblical inerrancy (even the modified or nuanced variety) the watershed between "Christianity and Liberalism" (Machen). In essays including "Evangelical Theology: Conservative and Contemporary" and "Where Is North American Theology Going?" Pinnock suggests a new shibboleth.

"Classical Christians," whether evangelicals, Roman Catholics, or Eastern Orthodox, are united in accepting certain "didactic thought models"[82] contained in scripture as binding upon Christians. They agree on "the time-honored assumption that the concepts of Christian revelation were normative categories whose truth was binding upon Christian thinkers."[83] These concepts would include the personality of God, the temporal fall of humanity, the saving merit of the death of Jesus, his bodily resurrection, and his second coming. In other words, classical Christians believe "there is rational truth-content in revelation, and not merely existentially significant symbols."[84] On the other side are theological liberals like Bultmann, Tillich, Gilkey, Kaufman, and Tracy, who employ a hermeneutic of demythologizing or deliteralizing and so dissolve the factual realities underlying the symbols.

This new criterion for orthodoxy represents an important strategic shift for Pinnock. He is no longer in a position to offer his doctrine of inspiration as the criterion for dividing the orthodox sheep from the modernist goats because his nuanced doctrine of inerrancy by itself would not prevent anyone from sliding over into the Bultmannian camp. Pinnock has always faulted Bultmann's existentialist hermeneutic whereby the resurrection preaching may impart authentic existence even if the resurrection did not actually happen. Pinnock protests, "Before a redemptive fact can be existentially meaningful, it must first be a fact."[85] Yet his own willingness to accept a biblical writer's intended assertion without his factual assumptions seems to be the same procedure on a smaller scale. This view of "inerrancy" could open the door to Bultmann, and Pinnock seems to be uneasily aware of this irony. So instead of strict inerrancy (which he has come to reject) or nuanced inerrancy (which would not logically prohibit demythologizing), he sets forth normative scriptural "didactic thought models" or "concepts" or "categories." The doctrine of scripture no longer has to play the role of Atlas, upholding the whole weight of orthodoxy on its sagging shoulders.

As the references to Bultmann and demythologizing might imply, the single greatest hurdle in the path of Pinnock's postliberal reconstruction is biblical criticism. So far he has been unwilling to deal seriously with it. In his early writings he saw higher criticism as simply an unbelieving attack on scripture, producing "pseudoproblems" with its "anti-supernatural bias." Despite his having earned a PhD in New Testament studies, he reveals an acquaintance with biblical criticism such as one might derive third- or fourth-hand by reading evangelical apologetics. He glibly dismisses form-criticism and the JEDP hypothesis of the Pentateuch. Even in the second period, he seems to feel that the worst problem inerrancy has to face is the presence of individual difficulties and inaccuracies here and there. Granted, he comes to believe strict inerrantism is not even up to such a mild challenge, but he never seems to glimpse the magnitude of the challenge posed to any evangelical view of scripture by the historical-critical method. Of course, Pinnock does finally wrestle with biblical criticism, and this struggle ushers in the third major period of his theological development.

PERIOD III: RETHINKING BIBLICAL AUTHORITY

The centerpiece of Clark Pinnock's "postliberal" theology is a new understanding of scripture for "post-critical believers."[86] This new view of inspiration was anticipated in a 1980 paper, "The Inspiration and Interpretation of the Bible" and set forth full-blown in "This Treasure in Earthen Vessels" (a draft written in 1981) and *The Scripture Principle* (1984), the second being a completely rewritten version of the first, really a second book on the same themes.

Pinnock admits that in an age of biblical criticism (which, despite its practitioners' tendency to ignore the divine dimension of scripture, has discovered innumerable important things), the traditional Hodge-Warfield doctrine of "divine-human confluence" will not pass muster. With its double-think claim that every word was chosen both by God and by the human writers, the theory is in effect no different from the older dictation view. The older view at least had the merit of being coherent, however implausible it might seem, but the "confluence" view is self-contradictory and makes no better sense of the phenomena of the text.

Perhaps it is time for a fresh reexamination of the Bible's claims for itself. If it does in fact teach either dictation or confluence, we are in trouble if we wish to be critically honest with the text. But if it does not, we may dismiss the pseudoproblems over which evangelical apologists have for so long exercised themselves. Clearly Pinnock suspects that the traditional evangelical understanding of scripture has been imposed on it from above by anxious theologians. It is time for a truly inductive theology of inspiration "from below."[87]

In his 1963 anti-inerrancy polemic *The Inspiration of Scripture*, Dewey M. Beegle suggested that the Bible's claims for its own inspiration (for example, 2 Timothy 3:15–16) should be defined and understood in light of the "phenomena" of scripture, those historical difficulties in the text uncovered by criticism. If we approached the definition of inspiration this way, reasoned Beegle, we would never wind up troubling ourselves with belief in inerrancy. The early Pinnock joined other inerrancy militants in repudiating this whole procedure, insisting that instead we ought to deduce the implications of inspiration from the idea itself (that is, what would "God-breathed" seem to us to imply?) and then reinterpret any apparent difficulties in the text in the light of this definition.

Pinnock now has more sympathy for Beegle's idea: he does not want to let an abstraction like inerrancy control our reading of the text. But he goes Beegle one better: "The deductive tendency that would see inerrancy as a necessary corollary of inspiration works against honestly facing up to the data [even] in the case of the claims themselves."[88] Perhaps even Warfield will prove to have been guilty of "fundamentalist overbelief" in this matter of inspiration.

First, Pinnock admits that it is even a bit misleading (certainly question begging) to ask after what scripture teaches about "itself," as if it were known from the outset to be one united and harmonious whole in which a claim made in one text would apply to all other texts. If Jeremiah claims to speak the word of the Lord, is he also referring to Chronicles? So we have to approach it text by text and face the fact that some portions of the Bible "claim" nothing for themselves.

He notes that the strong claims of the Hebrew Prophets were intended to apply to their spoken oracles, not (in the nature of the case) to the later written texts containing them. For the most part we know nothing of these later transcribers and compilers. We are told that Jeremiah dictated his oracles to Baruch, but even this is not said to have been inspired. So Pinnock rules out the model of inspiration that would make the biblical writers prophets with pen in hand. Texts seem to claim inspiration, when they do, in different ways. Especially in regard to the Psalms, a claim for inspiration becomes a delicate business. On the whole, regarding the Old Testament, Pinnock concludes, "Many texts express the Word of God, but some are content to perform lowlier tasks, such as giving utterance to a spiritual struggle or expressing an honest doubt."[89]

When he comes to Jesus' view of scripture, Pinnock seems to have profited from James Barr's discussion of how traditional apologetics treats this question. We are always assured by J. I. Packer and others, Barr says in *Fundamentalism*, that Jesus fully shared the rabbinic view of scripture current in his day, and that he humbly submitted his life and ministry to the letter of its teaching at every point. Barr calls this nonsense, rejecting the implied notion of Jesus as a biblicist, as if he had had a daily "Quiet Time" with scripture Union study booklet in hand. His use of scripture was hardly traditional. Jesus saw scripture as fulfilled in his career and that of John the Baptist where the literalist Pharisees could not. He rejected divorce by pitting one Pentateuchal passage against another.

Pinnock agrees that Jesus' (and the early church's) use of scripture was more dynamic than that of his contemporaries, and that we have no right to isolate Jesus' statements about scriptural authority from the context of his charismatic hermeneutic. Again, he agrees with Beegle in denying that Jesus could be cited to support Warfield's view that only the autographs were inerrant, since Jesus extolled the authority of the errant copies extant in his day.[90] Yet, surprisingly, Pinnock does retain the standard apologetic that Jesus "preauthenticated the New Testament canon as the scripture of the church" when he invested the Twelve with his authority (Matthew 10:40) and promised them the guidance of the Spirit of Truth (John 16:13).[91] Critical problems notwithstanding, if Jesus actually said these things, he said them to the Twelve, not to Paul, Mark, Luke, James, Jude, and the writer to the Hebrews.

But Pinnock departs again from apologetical orthodoxy when he points out that the "prophetic model" of inspiration presupposed by Warfield scarcely comports with many features of Paul's letters (for example, 1 Corinthians 1: 14–16; 2 Timothy 4: 13) or with Paul's own intentions. For often Paul reasons and appeals as if he does not want to be a legalistic master but rather a partner in dialogue or a colleague in seeking the truth. When Paul persuades and advises, it is arbitrary for a doctrine of inspiration to make him command and dictate.

What blanket statements the New Testament does seem to make about scripture cannot be pressed to refer to the whole canon; at least we cannot pretend the writers intended any such reference. (Of course, once one accepts the whole canon on other grounds, it is reasonable to apply what the New Testament writers say of the Old Testament to the New as well, but we can only use such proof-texts in a limited way if we are asking what the Bible claims about "itself.") In many texts wherein New Testament writers speak of the word of God" (for example, Hebrews 4:12; 1 Peter 1:23), they do not mean the scriptures, but rather the gospel message (1 Peter 1:25), so these texts must be left aside. Second Peter 1:20–21 refers to spoken prophecy, not to written scriptures, so it, too, must be bracketed. At last, Pinnock considers the lone witness of 2 Timothy 3:15–16. Surprisingly, he now agrees with Daniel P. Fuller, whom he once sought to refute at this point, that this passage authorizes us to speak only of salvific truth relating to faith and practice. It does not imply inerrancy on other matters.[92]

Once Pinnock defended his refusal to recognize scriptural errors as an inductive procedure, or at least as legitimately deductive, because it was only a matter of appropriate hermeneutics. If the author explains he has written a gardening book, one does not expect to find recipes in it; if the author explains he has written a divinely inspired book, one does not expect to find errors in it. Now, ironically, he employs the same notion to explain why inerrantism is no longer mandated: "The interpreting of any book depends upon the kind of book it is," and 2 Timothy 3:16 tells us it is a book of faith and practice, not of science and history.[93]

His conclusion? "The Bible does not give us a doctrine of its own inspiration and authority that answers all the various questions we might like to ask. Its witness on this subject is unsystematic and somewhat fragmentary and enables us to reach important but modest conclusions."[94]

What model of inspiration would be most appropriate given both the phenomena and the newly understood claims of scripture? Here is Pinnock's greatest departure from his earlier thinking and from evangelical orthodoxy. Though he does not actually use the term, it is clear that he has adopted the theory of "concomitant inspiration" proposed by Jesuit theologians in the seventeenth century. According to this view of inspiration, God simply supervised the writers of scripture, making sure that all went well and that the result was an adequate scripture. Actually, the Catholic thinkers proposed that the superintending Spirit protected the writers from all error, but they qualified inerrancy in much the same way as Pinnock now does.

Pinnock sets forth his view of concomitant inspiration in statements like these: "God did not negate the gift of freedom when he inspired the Bible but worked alongside human beings in order to achieve by wisdom and patience the goal of a Bible that expresses his will for our salvation."[95] "God exercises a significant but not determining influence over people writing scripture so that the result is really their script and also what he delights in. It requires me to see inspiration more as persuasion and less as coercion."[96] Similarly, Jacques Bonfriere had written, "The Holy Spirit acts concomitantly, not by dictating or inbreathing, but as one keeps an eye on another while he is writing, to keep him from slipping into errors."[97]

Equally important is the question of literary genre. Pinnock, of course, has always realized this, even in his earliest apologetics for inerrancy. So there is nothing new in principle here. The new thing is that he is now willing to accept many genres he regarded as destructive and deceitful before. "I think it is excessively deductive to declare what literary forms the Bible may or may not have in it. How are we in a position to say that?"[98] Even the presence of legend and fiction would not be tantamount to error: "Inerrancy simply means that the Bible can be trusted in what it teaches and affirms. The inerrant truth of a parable is of course parabolic, and the inerrant truth of a fable is fabulous. If Matthew gives us some fictional midrash, then it is inerrant according to the demands of this genre. All this means is that inerrancy is relative to the intention of the text. If it could be shown that the Chronicler inflates some of the numbers he uses for his didactic purpose, he would be completely within his rights and not at variance with inerrancy."[99] He once explicitly rejected such genres as midrash as incompatible with inspiration. Pinnock still feels that out-and-out forgery would be incompatible with the truthfulness to be expected of scripture, so he looks more kindly upon the suggestion that 2 Peter, the Pastorals, and Ephesians might have been worked up by disciples of Peter and Paul from Petrine and Pauline notes and fragments, a proposal he once disdainfully dismissed as "speculative."[100]

But, it might be asked, what would it mean to believe the intended teaching of a passage that makes its point in a fictional manner? An instructive example might be Matthew's midrashic expansion (14:22–33) of Mark's story of Jesus walking on the sea (6:45–51). Matthew makes Peter, too, walk on the water, only to begin to sink when he takes his eyes off Jesus. The inerrant assertion of Matthew's midrash is not that Peter walked on the waves, but that we ought to keep our eyes fixed on Jesus in the midst of life's tossing sea of trouble. The same inerrant assertion is made using a different genre by the writer of Hebrews (12:1–2).

In other words, Pinnock qualifies the inerrancy of each text's assertion in the light of the salvific/paraenetic intention of scripture as a whole (its "macropurpose") as we find it set forth in 2 Timothy

3:15–16.[101] Again we notice a decided shift toward the position of Daniel P. Fuller, even toward that of Jack Rogers and G. C. Berkouwer who see the central gospel message of salvation as the locus of scriptural infallibility. "The authority of the Bible in faith and practice" is the important thing, as in the Fuller Theological Seminary credo. "The Bible will seem reliable enough in terms of its soteric purpose, and the perplexing features on its margins [these are almost Beegle's very words] will not strike fear into our hearts and minds."[102]

Where Pinnock would differ from evangelicals to the left of him hermeneutically, such as Paul K. Jewett and Virginia Mollenkott, is that while he allows scripture's salvific macropurpose to subsume factual errors, he will not use the macropurpose to trim away apparently aberrant assertions vis-à-vis faith and practice, as when Jewett uses Galatians 3:28 to lop off 1 Timothy 2:12. All texts' salvific/didactic assertions must be upheld. And this is to say that Pinnock further qualifies the inerrancy of assertions *canonically.*

What does Pinnock suggest we do when we encounter divergent theological views in the text? "I would not want to deny that belief in inspiration supplies a hermeneutical guideline for me and makes me tend to deny the reality of apparent contradictions."[103] Why? Because, as in his earliest period, he feels that "if contradiction exists our doctrine of scripture is overthrown."[104] Yet Pinnock claims to have finished with deductive text twisting. Instead of harmonizing the divergences, explaining them *away*, pretending as fundamentalists have always done that they do not differ, he attempts to explain why they do in fact differ. "There is something to be learned from their not fitting neatly."[105] Apparently following the lead of James D. G. Dunn, Pinnock is willing to "look for the underlying unity beneath every case of surface contradictions."[106] In other words, it may be that Paul's and James's truly different ways of relating faith, works, and justification are divergent theologizings stemming from the same basic gospel, but called forth by different circumstances. Had their theologizing been prompted by the same set of circumstances, perhaps they would have said the same thing. So some of the difficulty is obviated, but there is no denial that their resultant doctrines do differ. We must listen and learn from both and try to penetrate to that ur-gospel both began with.

Another way of understanding diversity within the canon is to arrange the different writers (or different works by one writer) along a timeline of progressive revelation. This is taken for granted in the case of the Old Testament. Applied to the New Testament, it would allow us to see that, for example, Mark's Christology is not the same as John's more advanced incarnational doctrine because not as much of the truth had yet been revealed to Mark. So Mark's Christology is true as far as it goes, or, to borrow a phrase from Francis Schaeffer, it is true but not exhaustively true. (Pinnock gives less attention to this notion in *The Scripture Principle* than in "This Treasure in Earthen Vessels," so he may have become less pleased with it. In fact, he is subtly less inclined to see diversity in the canon in the second book, but there seems to be no major change of mind.)

Mark's Christological assertions, to pursue this example, would be read in the first instance for what Mark himself meant by them, but one must also read Mark as part of the canon that also includes John, and thus as part of a progressive revelation process that leads ultimately to the doctrine of incarnation. This would mean, for example, that one cannot adopt Mark's Christology and reject John's. John's includes Mark's; Mark's points forward to John's, just as Isaiah 7:14, which originally predicted the birth of a child in Isaiah's lifetime, points forward to a secondary fulfillment in Jesus' birth centuries later. We might then speak of a kind of "canonical *sensus plenior*" whereby each text has its own meaning according to authorial intent, plus another sense charismatically superimposed on it by virtue of its presence alongside other texts in a canon. The Old Testament is fulfilled in the New Testament; the individual New Testament books are "fulfilled" in the New Testament canon.

Surprisingly, we find the seeds of this model implicit back in *Biblical Revelation*: "For inspiration is here predicated of the writing itself, not of the writers or of the ideas which made it up. . . . What the scriptures record is God-breathed, not what the writers may have thought, or what we think they thought."[107] Pinnock's point was simply to fend off the liberal "inspired man" model on the one hand and the fundamentalist "overbelief" that regards even the writer's assumptions and not just his assertions as inerrant, on the other. But once stated, this notion can be applied in a new context, that of diversity, and we get the result that the inspired canonical meaning of a text is not necessarily identical with original authorial intent. This observation leads us (really it has already led us) to consider the hermeneutic that results from Pinnock's new understanding of inspiration and biblical diversity.

Gone is Pinnock's old understanding of theology as a biblical jigsaw puzzle. "God's Word is most likely to be heard when we take the historical context of texts seriously and when we heed the inner canonical dialogue. We are likely to miss it when we pick out isolated texts without regard for their setting and look at them all as of equal significance, to be harmonized into some rational system of our own making."[108] We would, however, be bound by the "normative concepts" and "didactic thought models" yielded by the final stage of revelation in the canon, for example, John's Christology, Paul's soteriology.

When it comes to decision making and applying the Bible ethically and ecclesiastically, and otherwise practically, the Bible is not to be viewed as a legalistic instruction manual, but rather as a place to stand and listen for God's voice. We examine the rich diversity of biblical views on an issue, for example, Paul's praise of celibacy in 1 Corinthians 7 versus the Song of Solomon's celebration of sex. We seek the Spirit's guidance to decide which biblical text is most appropriate, always keeping the other(s) in mind for perspective's sake. Pinnock shows the influence of Brevard Childs at this point.

How is the biblical Christian to apply the scripture to issues of belief and lifestyle that have arisen in the many centuries since the closing of the canon? Here Pinnock seems equally influenced by the thinking of Paul J. Achtemaier (*The Inspiration of Scripture*) and Charles H. Kraft (*Christianity in Culture*) on the one hand, and by his pietistic background and charismatic experience on the other. Historical-critical study has disclosed that the biblical writers interpreted the scriptural texts in ways that often disregarded or even reversed the original authorial intent. Remember, Pinnock has said that we are not entitled to the New Testament doctrine of scripture unless we also adopt the New Testament hermeneutic of scripture. Instead of jettisoning both, as much modern scholarship does, Pinnock wants to retain both. Not the very same, for example, rabbinic, techniques, but the same *kind* of thing.

Pinnock has seen believers experience "existential encounters" with the text where the Spirit seems to speak to their situation through the words of a single verse taken out of context. For instance, at L'Abri, Pinnock and other staff used to see their retreat center in the Alps as a kind of fulfillment of Micah 4:1–2: "And peoples shall flow to it . . . and say, 'Come, let us go up to the mountain of the Lord.'" Obviously Micah did not have this in mind, but somehow it did seem that God spoke through the text anew. This is a common experience among pious Bible readers, and Pinnock sees the practice as the legitimate continuation of the process of reinterpretation and multilevel exegesis we see in the Bible itself. Or a different kind of example: Matthew recasts Mark's teaching on divorce to update it for his situation. Might the Spirit lead us to further reinterpretation on the same question today?

Realizing the danger of subjectivity thus introduced into hermeneutics (what a departure from *Biblical Revelation*!), Pinnock hastens to add that it is not simply the *practice* of reinterpretation that is our canonical norm (an impression one might carry away from a reading of Achtemaier), but the canonical content as well. No "*sensus plenior*" may legitimately contradict the author's literal intent, and further developments and reapplications must be "dynamically equivalent" to some one of the original options attested in the canon. The canon forms a "tether" (Kraft) that defines the range and limits of our flexibility and creativity. We should allow no less freedom than the canon does in its diversity, but we must not allow greater diversity than it does either. For example, all writers who mention it seem to condemn world-negating Gnosticism, so a Gnostic posture or its equivalent would be unscriptural. Dangers remain, to be sure, but Pinnock has learned from the Charismatic Movement not to stifle the Spirit's freedom to speak for fear that someone will abuse it.

Though the theology of scripture has always been Clark Pinnock's leading interest, it has never been his only one, as we have seen. Even so, in this third period, he has given his attention to other theological matters. In his wide study of liberal theologians, he has often come to see the validity of their questions, if not of their answers. This was certainly true with Liberation Theology, and more recently Process Theology has helped shape his agenda. Pinnock has come to see the force of Process theologians' critique of classical theism. He has come to agree with them that the God of the philosophers (abstract, unchanging, atemporal, impassive) is simply not the God of the Bible (living, acting, involved in history, loving). But Process theism's finite and changing God is in his own way no less abstract and unbiblical. So what is Pinnock's third alternative? "A biblical, and therefore neo-classical theism." Pinnock wants to take the authoritative scripture at its word when it describes God as a living, loving, hating, repenting person who makes threats and promises and waits to see what will happen. If we believe in the God of Israel and the Father of Jesus Christ we must simply reject the divine attributes of aseity, atemporality, omniscience, and immutability. To impose these philosophically derived abstractions onto biblical theism would be no less arbitrary and deductive than to impose a modern standard of historical accuracy on the biblical text. With regard to theism itself no less than the idea of inspiration, Pinnock wants to let the texts speak with their own voice.

It is not difficult to see that in this major shift, Pinnock is moving farther along the same trajectory he followed when he rejected Calvinism. The God of eternal decrees is one with the God of timeless awareness. After all, Calvin himself employed the notion of "accommodation" to explain away biblical anthropomorphisms. Pinnock first rejected predestination, now he rejects foreknowledge.

It should be noted that his rejection of the Warfield "divine-human confluence" model of inspiration, too, may be seen as a stage of his systematic purging out of Calvinism. To say that the Bible is simultaneously the spontaneous work of man yet also verbally inspired by God "stems from the Calvinistic orthodoxy underlying so much of the modern [evangelical] movement. The theology of a Warfield or a Packer, which posits a firm divine control over everything that happens in the world, is very well suited to explain a verbally inspired Bible." But surely many Arminian, Dispensationalist, and other evangelicals hold to verbal inspiration without embracing Calvinism? Yes, but they simply "do not think systematically and limit their Calvinism to this one subject."[109] "Cleanse out the old leaven that you may be a new lump" (1 Corinthians 5:7).

Apologetics does not play quite the same role in Pinnock's thinking in this third period that it did in the earlier two. He writes no books on apologetics, but apologetical concerns still influence him at several points. In his earlier books he was much concerned with whether or not theological claims could be verified or falsified. He clung tenaciously to inerrancy for the shield it afforded against the unfalsifiable vagueness of liberal subjectivism. Yet now the tables have turned. "The category of inerrancy as used today . . . is unfalsifiable,"[110] as can readily be seen from the death of a thousand qualifications it dies, for example, in the Chicago Statement on Biblical Inerrancy.

Yet verifiability is still important, though for Pinnock it no longer hinges on strict inerrancy, and apologetics is still called for.[111] Were he to write another book of apologetics, chances are his arguments would be about the same. In *The Scripture Principle* he alludes to his earlier defenses of the historical factuality of Jesus' resurrection.[112] But he understands the nature of apologetical arguments differently. As implied in the title *Set Forth Your Case*, he used to see it as a matter of proving a case in a legal fashion. This is true even of the less strident *Reason Enough*, where he compares his arguments to "points in a lawyer's presentation which are adduced to convince a judge and jury."[113] But in *The Scripture Principle* he more modestly claims that "belief in the truth of the Bible and the gospel is rationally preferred over not believing in it, because it economically explains some important data."[114] This language reflects that of Thomas Kuhn (*The Struc-*

ture of Scientific Revolutions) and his discussion of paradigms and implies a softer and subtler kind of convincement, where no definitive proof is possible but where one explanatory paradigm is provisionally adopted as more workable and comprehensive than others.

Concomitant with his recognition of the tentativeness of the assent rational argumentation can produce, we find Pinnock acknowledging that real conviction of the gospel can only finally come from the Holy Spirit: "God's working in the human heart in response to faith is . . . the main cause of faith."[115] "While still wary of fideism, I understand better what scholars like Daane, Berkouwer, Rogers, Bloesch, Barth, Wink, and Grounds have been trying to tell conservatives like me who have an overly rationalist bent."[116] He admits, "Now I'm halfway between where I used to be and the Reformed fideists."[117] How ironic that when he was a Calvinist and a stricter inerrantist, he accepted the "happy inconsistency" of Warfield's "Arminian" approach to apologetics, and now that he has repudiated Warfield's Calvinism and his predestinarian model of inspiration, he has moved more in the direction of Reformed apologetics!

Apologetics has not only served as the defense of Pinnock's theology; it has sometimes been one of the sources of it as well. This is no less true in the third period. "From whence comes our belief in the Bible? Not really from impartial consideration of the evidence, but because in our experience it has been able to . . . introduce [us] to a saving and transforming knowledge of Christ."[118] Similarly, Process theism is to be rejected because its God is inadequate to "evangelical experience" and "religious needs."[119] Is not Pinnock, like Schleiermacher, extrapolating theology from the consciousness of piety?

Though his rejection of both verbal inspiration and classical theism may seem dramatic enough, perhaps the most startling recent mutation in Pinnock's thought has been his political about-face. In the early period he was anticommunist; in the middle period he became a radical pacifist and socialist; after that he embraced a militant neoconservatism that is in fact difficult to distinguish from the stance of the so-called New Christian Right. Pinnock came to find himself in complete agreement with Michael Novak and others who have been baptized in the "Spirit of Democratic Capitalism."[120] He now supports a vigorous free-market economy, a strong military defense of the West against communism, and the Christian reclamation of Canadian (and presumably American) society. He even opposes the teaching of evolutionist propaganda in the public schools. This new conservatism is in evidence even in *The Scripture Principle* where Pinnock dispels the pseudoproblems presented to the modern Western reader by Old Testament laws mandating death for the adulterer and the incorrigible child. The offense is one taken, not given, says Pinnock. It is only our overly lenient humanist sentimentality that makes us fault God's Word for what is really only proper severity![121]

However else one might seek to account for this change, it is most important to see it as having everything to do with his early Schaefferian apologetics, as odd as this may sound at first.

In *Set Forth Your Case*, as we have seen, Pinnock, like Schaeffer, saw Western Civilization allowing its biblical foundations to be eroded by the creeping decay of secular humanism. A basic contradiction ran throughout Schaeffer's own books at this point, and it was repeated, as might be expected, in those of his protégé Pinnock. Schaeffer and Pinnock called for a "cultural apologetics" as a necessary stage of "pre-evangelism" before it would be possible to "speak the Christian message into the Twentieth Century." The idea was that our contemporaries needed to be told the bad news of how their secular and humanistic presuppositions could not justify meaning, love, or hope metaphysically and epistemologically. Only then would they realize their need for the good news of Jesus Christ.

This all assumes that most contemporary men and women have bought into secular humanism. Yet Schaeffer and Pinnock documented their thesis of cultural decline by proof-texting an elite of luminaries from the fields of philosophy, art, theater, music, film, and so on. This rarified atmosphere is hardly what most Western citizens breathe. Had Schaeffer and Pinnock made the same error of which they and other apologists had always accused Bultmann: taking an antisupernaturalist clique of intellectuals and hastily generalizing them as "modern man"?

Apparently so, yet at other times, the apologists seemed to realize otherwise and warned that the real danger was that such a conspiratorial clique would erode Western Society from the top down unless stopped. "One of the best kept secrets from the public at large in the twentieth century has been the death of hope and the loss of the human" entailed in nihilistic humanism.[122] Humanists, however, are trying to spread the "secret" knowledge through a program of "brainwashing" by teaching evolutionism in the public schools. "One can only conclude that the ruling intelligentsia have some motive for pushing this myth and converting our people to it. The motive is not difficult to discern. For the myth allows secular man to retain his autonomy."[123]

Which is it? Is naturalistic humanism a pandemic malaise of a "post-Christian society," so pervasive that pre-evangelism is necessary before evangelism can even begin? Or is it the perverse ideology of a nefarious coterie of Illuminati who must be stopped? Toward the end of his life, Francis Schaeffer resolved the contradiction in favor of the conspiracy version and began to write books like *A Christian Manifesto*, which actually advocated the overthrow of the humanistic American government by the Christian people should it become necessary, as he feared it soon might. Pinnock has now resolved the tension the same way, though he is not the extremist militant Schaeffer became. So now, instead of presenting a cultural apologetics, the same concerns motivate him to urge political action (for example, in *The Untapped Power of Sheer Christianity*, 1985).

Incidentally, it may be interesting to note how Pinnock's eschatology changed with his politics. In his first period, while a Calvinist, he embraced Amillennialism (the whole period between the first and second advents of Christ, while he reigns at God's right hand, constitutes the Millennium). In his second period, he embraced the pessimism usually associated with premillennialism (things will only get worse till Christ returns to set things right), without actually adopting that doctrine. In fact, at this time he roundly condemned the fundamentalist preoccupation with chart making and date setting as a distraction from social discipleship. We must be socially involved, Pinnock reasoned, but not over optimistically. The "Christ the Transformer of Culture"[124] model seemed to him to take insufficient account of the continuing activity of the demonic Powers until the Parousia (Second Coming). Yet in his third period, Pinnock again closed ranks with Schaeffer, returning to a Calvinist model of the state as "Christendom," and, appropriate to his agenda of "re-Christianization," he adopted Postmillennial eschatology (Christ's return caps off his people's triumph in realizing the kingdom of God on earth).[125]

If the early militancy Pinnock displayed against secular humanists in *Set Forth Your Case* has returned, what about his early vehemence against the liberal-leaning theologians whom he wanted expelled from evangelical seminaries? In light of *The Scripture Principle*, it is obvious that the Pinnock of the 1980s would have been a prime target for the Pinnock of the 1960s! Still, today's Pinnock is as dead set against liberal theology, whatever positive lessons he may have learned from it, as he ever was. Remember that he wanted to unify the evangelical ranks precisely in order to make a concerted assault on the Bible-denying modernists! He minces no words: "The cornerstone of liberal theology is the rejection of scriptural authority."[126] He imputes morally dubious motives to theological liberals: "But when it comes right down to it, there is only one reason for the rejection of content in revelation: the idea that the Bible has a right to limit human freedom of thought and action is a hated idea that must be crushed and eliminated. . . . Conversion is what is needed." Liberal theology is still viewed as a denial of the gospel of grace, a scheme of salvation by human wisdom and achievement.[127]

Opposition to liberalism in theology is one with the struggle to eject secular humanists from their positions of national influence, for, "Liberal theology is essentially a synthesis of Christian thought and modern humanism in one form or another."[128] In a paper given before a meeting of Canadian Baptists, Pinnock called for the formulation of a new confession that would effectively debar theological liberals from ordination.[129] Soon thereafter, he himself wrote and published such a document.[130] As far as purging seminaries, he seems to feel that the most practical solution is an "agreement [between liberals and conservatives] to work side by side avoiding conflict . . . although it hardly satisfies one's concern for truth."[131]

So here is Clark H. Pinnock, conservative and contemporary, some would say too conservative in his politics, others would say too contemporary in his views of the Bible. How can he move so noticeably to the left in one area and to the right in another? If we may attempt to harmonize this "apparent contradiction," it must surely be that, as with scripture, Pinnock wants to avoid deductively imposing some neat and simple a priori schema on the stubborn "phenomena" of reality. He must be honest and take each case as it comes, responding to each as seems appropriate.

This hermeneutic of reality keeps him open to change as reality itself is changing, and if this leads him to take positions uncongenial to those of the left, right, or middle, this does not much matter.

Pinnock is always willing to set forth his case.

NOTES

1. Clark H. Pinnock's testimony included in "I Was a Teenage Fundamentalist," *Wittenburg Door* 70 (December 1982/January 1983): 18.

2. Clark H. Pinnock, *Evangelism and Truth* (Tigerville, SC: Jewel Books, 1969), pp. 18–19.

3. Ibid., pp. 28–29.

4. Clark H. Pinnock, *Set Forth Your Case* (Chicago: Moody Press, 1971), p. 67.

5. Ibid., p. 86.

6. Clark H. Pinnock, *Biblical Revelation: The Foundation of Christian Theology* (Chicago: Moody Press, 1976), p. 75.

7. Ibid., p. 178.

8. Pinnock, *Set Forth Your Case*, p. 66.

9. Pinnock, *Biblical Revelation*, p. 111. In *The Scripture Principle*,

Pinnock completely reverses this argument, rejecting strict inerrancy because it makes faith depend on the efforts of a priestly elite of scholarly inerrantist harmonists like Gleason Archer!

10. Clark H. Pinnock, *A Defense of Biblical Infallibility* (n.p.: Presbyterian and Reformed Publishing Company, 1975), p. 30. Again, in *The Scripture Principle* he reverses himself, having become convinced of this anti-inerrancy argument in the meantime.

11. Ibid., p. 23.

12. *Biblical Revelation*, p. 15; *Defense*, p. 15.

13. *Defense*, p. 13.

14. *Biblical Revelation*, p. 72.

15. In *A Defense of Biblical Infallibility*, Pinnock writes, "Infallibility is obviously restricted to the intended assertions of scripture as understood in an ordinary grammatical exegesis of the text" (p. 13). He seems to be referring to Warfield's dictum that before one presumes to charge the Bible with error, one had better make sure the supposed error was indeed the intended assertion of the writer. But Warfield simply meant that the critic should not set up a straw man, for example, some skeptics have said that Luke overestimated the distance between the Mount of Olives and Jerusalem when he said it took the whole Sabbath to make the trip (Acts 1:12), but this is fallacious exegesis. Luke refers to the rabbinic measurement of a "Sabbath day's journey," the short distance one could walk without reaking the Sabbath. It is the critic, not the Bible, who errs in this case. Warfield did not mean to draw Pinnock's line between an inerrant intended assertion and possibly errant statements made incidental to it. In fact, Warfield criticized this very view. Stranger still, so does Pinnock, in *A Defense of Biblical Infallibility*, p. 14, where he rightly attributes the distinction between the biblical writer's incidentally expressed opinion and his intended assertions to Charles Hodge. This is only one page after he embraces what seems to be the same view. In *Biblical Revelation* (p. 72), he seems to have realized the identity of Hodge's view with his own and now quotes Hodge on this point with approval.

16. *Biblical Revelation*, p. 76.

17. *Defense*, p. 21.

18. *Biblical Revelation*, p. 191.

19. *Defense*, p. 32.

20. *Set Forth Your Case*, p. 100.

21. *Biblical Revelation*, p. 135.

22. Ibid., p. 38.

23. *Set Forth Your Case*, p. 122, for example.

24. The parallel he sees between the loss of the divine Word in liberal theology and the loss of the gospel of grace in Galatian legalism occurs again and again throughout Pinnock's writing (for example, *Biblical Revelation*, p. 108). It also explains why his only volume of actual biblical exegesis is *Truth on Fire: The Message of Galatians*.

25. *Biblical Revelation*, pp. 195, 196.

26. Of course, such a move is now under way.

27. Ibid., p. 104.

28. Ibid., p. 12.

29. *Set Forth Your Case*, p. 28.

30. *Defense*, p. 80

31. *Biblical Revelation*, p. 104.

32. Ibid., p. 131.

33. *The Scripture Principle*, pp. 21–22.

34. Clark H. Pinnock, *The Untapped Power of Sheer Christianity* (Burlington, ON: Welch Publishing Company, Inc., 1985), p. 51. The author told me he intended to title the book simply *Sheer Christianity*, an obvious salute to C. S. Lewis's *Mere Christianity*. I don't know who persuaded him to change it (for the worse, I might add). I respect his original intent by henceforth referring to the book as *Sheer Christianity*.

35. Clark H. Pinnock, "Truce Proposals for the Tongues Controversy," *Christianity Today* 16, no. 1 (October 8, 1971): 609.

36. Mimeographed mailing to members of Theological Students Fellowship, May 1975.

37. *Set Forth Your Case*, p. 44.

38. *Biblical Revelation*, p. 132.

39. Clark H. Pinnock, "An Evangelical Theology of the Charismatic Movement" [TSF paper, see n. 36 above], p. 5.

40. Clark H. Pinnock, "A Call for the Liberation of North American Christians," in *Evangelicals and Liberation*, ed. Carl E. Armerding (Phillipsburg, NJ: Presbyterian and Reformed Publishing Company, 1979), p. 128.

41. Clark H. Pinnock, *Are There Any Answers?* (Minneapolis: Bethany Fellowship, Inc., 1976), pp. 17, 18.

42. *Set Forth Your Case*, pp. 58, 54–55.

43. Clark H. Pinnock, "An Evangelical Theology of Human Liberation," in *Sojourners*, supplement to the January 1977 issue, vol. 6, no. 1, p. 50.

44. *Sheer Christianity*, p. 64.

45. "A Call for the Liberation of North American Christians," p. 134.

46. Clark H. Pinnock, "Second Mile Lifestyle," *Sojourners* 6, no. 6 (June 1977): 31.

47. Clark H. Pinnock, "A Call for Triangular Christianity," an address given at the annual Pastors' Conference of the Baptist Convention of Ontario and Quebec, 1979, pp. 9, 11.

48. "An Evangelical Theology of Human Liberation," p. 49.

49. Ibid., p. 48.

50. Clark H. Pinnock, "Evangelicals and Inerrancy: The Current Debate," *Theology Today*, November 1978, p. 68.

51. "Evangelical Theology of Human Liberation," p. 49.

52. Ibid., p. 50.

53. Clark H. Pinnock, "Responsible Freedom and the Flow of Biblical History," in *Grace Unlimited*, ed. Clark H. Pinnock (Minneapolis: Bethany Fellowship, Inc., 1975), p. 104.

54. Schaeffer untiringly condemned neoorthodox "dialectical" theologians for denying "antithetical logic."

55. "Responsible Freedom and the Flow of Biblical History," pp. 96–97.

56. Clark H. Pinnock, "Introduction," *Grace Unlimited*, p. 15.

57. "Responsible Freedom and the Flow of Biblical History," p. 96.

58. "Introduction," p. 11.

59. Ibid., p. 12.

60. *Scripture Principle*, p. 102.

61. "Introduction," pp. 17–18.

62. Clark H. Pinnock, *Reason Enough: A Case for the Christian Faith* (Downers Grove, IL: InterVarsity Press, 1980), pp. 11, 18, 107.

63. *Set Forth Your Case*, p. 73.

64. Clark H. Pinnock, "Inspiration and Authority: A Truce Proposal," *Other Side* (May/June 1976): 63.

65. *Scripture Principle*, p. 58.

66. Clark H. Pinnock, Foreword to Stephen T. Davis, *The Debate about the Bible* (Philadelphia: Westminster Press, 1977), p. 12.

67. Clark H. Pinnock, "Limited Inerrancy: A Critical Appraisal and

Constructive Alternative," in *God's Inerrant Word*, ed. John Warwick Montgomery (Minneapolis: Bethany Fellowship, 1975), p. 148; contrast *Defense*, p. 23.

68. "Inspiration and Authority: A Truce Proposal," p. 62.

69. Clark H. Pinnock, "The Inerrancy Debate among the Evangelicals," in *Theology, News, and Notes*, Fuller Seminary, 1976, p. 13.

70. *Biblical Revelation*, pp. 195–96.

71. "Inspiration and Authority: A Truce Proposal," p. 64.

72. "Limited Inerrancy," pp. 148–49.

73. "Inerrancy Debate among the Evangelicals," p. 13.

74. "Inspiration and Authority: A Truce Proposal," p. 65.

75. "Evangelicals and Inerrancy: The Current Debate," p. 68.

76. Clark H. Pinnock, "Unforgiving Critic," *Sojourners* 8, no. 1 (January 1979): 31.

77. Clark H. Pinnock, "An Evangelical Theology: Conservative and Contemporary," *Christianity Today*, January 1979, pp. 72–73.

78. Clark H. Pinnock, "The Study of Theology: A Guide for Evangelicals," *TSF News and Reviews* 3, no. 4 (March 1980): 1–2.

79. *Sheer Christianity*, p. 91.

80. "Inerrancy Debate among the Evangelicals," p. 11.

81. Clark H. Pinnock, "Prospects for Systematic Theology," in *Toward a Theology for the Future*, ed. Clark H. Pinnock and David F. Wells (Carol Stream, IL: Creation House, 1971), p. 96.

82. "Evangelical Theology: Conservative and Contemporary," p. 24.

83. Clark H. Pinnock, "The Nature and Extent of the Modernist Impulse at McMaster University, 1887–1927," a paper given at An International Symposium on Baptists in Canada, 1979, p. 3.

84. "Study of Theology: A Guide for Evangelicals," p. 3.

85. *Scripture Principle*, p. 94.

86. Ibid., p. 86.

87. The parallel with then-recent attempts by Küng, Schillebeeckx, Berkhof, et al., to do "Christology from below" is intentional. *Scripture Principle*, p. 87.

88. Ibid., p. 59

89. Ibid., p. 34.

90. Ibid., p. 39.

91. Ibid., p. 47.

92. Ibid., p. 55.

93. Ibid.

94. Ibid., p. 54.

95. *Scripture Principle*, p. 104.

96. "An Interview with Clark H. Pinnock," *Faith and Thought* 2, no. 2 (Fall 1984): 56.

97. James T. Burtchaell, *Catholic Theories of Biblical Inspiration Since 1810* (Cambridge: Cambridge University Press, 1969), p. 47. Leonhard Leys called the model "divine assistance." Richard Simon called it "special direction." "Concomitant inspiration" was the nomenclature suggested by Jacques Bonfriere, and I have adopted it here. Pinnock himself has often made reference to this book to point up the parallels between the current evangelical rethinking of inspiration and the earlier Roman Catholic discussion of the same issues. It is hard to imagine he does not see, or intend, the parallel.

98. Ibid., p. 55.

99. *Scripture Principle*, p. 78.

100. Even here Pinnock does not mean we must refuse by an act of will to admit that pious frauds might occur in the Bible, but only to admit that their presence would falsify any doctrine of the inspiration of such works. If we found ourselves convinced by scholarship that 2 Peter was a forgery, we ought to admit it and then pick up the pieces, for example, perhaps ejecting it from the canon. Cf. *Scripture Principle*, p. 70, where Pinnock notes that when Luther judged that James contradicted Paul, he concluded quite properly that James did not belong in the canon.

101. *Scripture Principle*, p. 121.

102. Ibid., p. 104

103. Ibid., p. 73.

104. Ibid., p. 147.

105. Ibid., pp. 185–86

106. Ibid., p. 186.

107. *Biblical Revelation*, p. 67.

108. *Scripture Principle*, p. 195.

109. Ibid., pp. 101, 102.

110. Ibid., p. 58.

111. Ibid., pp. 128–29.

112. Ibid., p. 97.

113. *Reason Enough*, p. 16.

114. *Scripture Principle*, p. 166.

115. Ibid., p. xix.

116. Ibid., p. 228, n. 30.

117. Lecture at New College, Berkeley, July 23, 1979.

118. *Scripture Principle*, p. xix.

119. Clark H. Pinnock, "Between Classical and Process Theism," draft for inclusion in Ronald Nash, ed., *Process Theology*, p. 12.

120. *Sheer Christianity*, pp. 57–79.

121. *Scripture Principle*, pp. 113–15.

122. *Set Forth Your Case*, p. 30.

123. Ibid., pp. 113–14

124. H. Richard Niebuhr, *Christ and Culture* (NewYork: Harper Torchbooks, 1951), chapter 6, "Christ the Transformer of Culture," pp. 190–229.

125. *Sheer Christianity*, pp. 59, 104, n. 2.

126. Clark H. Pinnock, "This Treasure in Earthen Vessels," mimeographed manuscript, 1981, p. 196.

127. *Scripture Principle*, pp. 24–25, 27.

128. Clark H. Pinnock, "Baptists and Confessions of Faith," mimeographed paper, p. 1.

129. Ibid., p. 8.

130. *Sheer Christianity*, pp. 31–33.

131. "The Nature and Extent of the Modernist Impulse," p. 14.

Appendix 2

PARADIGM SHIFTING AND THE APOLOGETICS DEBATE

*O*f late, a new piece of jargon has intruded itself into discussions of theological and religious language. The newcomer is the "paradigm." One may find this concept, borrowed from the philosophy of science, in theological works as far removed from each other as Thomas Torrance's *Theological Science* and Charles Kraft's *Christianity in Culture*. It seems safe to suggest that the recent currency of this term and its attendant concept is in large part due to the efforts of Thomas S. Kuhn. Though Kuhn himself is a philosopher of science, the relevance of his work for other fields such as theology has become apparent. We would like to suggest the utility of his theory for the field of evangelical apologetics. More specifically, his schema of "paradigm shifting" will be shown to provide the key for grasping the differences in the evidentialist vs. presuppositionalist debate in apologetics.

In his *The Structure of Scientific Revolutions*, Kuhn takes issue with the common conception that scientific advancement has proceeded mainly by way of "new discoveries." In fact, really new data is relatively seldom discovered. Scientific progress has more to do with scientists coming to formulate new ways of construing the same old information, new keys to solve the puzzles presented by the data. One such paradigm will be accepted by scientists as long as it seems to make plausible sense of most of the evidence. Only when the paradigm starts to appear inadequate to the task of explaining this or that phenomenon do scientists begin looking for an alternative *gestalt*. The new paradigm will seek to incorporate much of the explicative power of the old, yet starting from at least a slightly different point, so as to deal plausibly with more of the hitherto-troublesome data. When the cogency and comprehensiveness of a new proffered paradigm becomes evident, a "paradigm shift" occurs. The new model for construing the data becomes the basis for the next stage of theorizing and research. Of course the likelihood is that it, too, will be superseded in time.

To give a famous example seen through the lenses provided by Kuhn, we will look at the contest between the geocentric paradigm of Ptolemy and the heliocentric paradigm of Copernicus. Ptolemy's model of the planetary system functioned well enough to predict the motion of the (apparently earth-orbiting) planets, but it ran into trouble when it came to the mysterious retrograde motion of the planets. In order for the geocentric model to predict accurately these erratic movements (hitherto considered to be the "free will" of the planets), Ptolemaic astronomers had to postulate myriad series of "epicycles," or wheels within hypothetical wheels on which the planets turned. Copernicus found that the whole system might be simplified by postulating that the sun, not the earth, was the center of planetary orbit. This way all the epicycles disappeared.

Eventually Copernicus's view became dominant. It wasn't that Copernicus had somehow "discovered" the earth to be orbiting the sun instead of the other way around. Such a thing would have been (and probably still is) incapable of observation. Rather, he merely formulated a new *gestalt* for the data that made its explanation less problematic, more natural, than before. And this is basically the way all scientific progress comes about, by a "conversion"[1] from one paradigm to another.

But there is an important tension, often unnoticed, in Kuhn's schema. Are paradigms self-sealing? That is, do they carry their own criteria of plausibility of explanation? Mustn't they, if they are truly comprehensive systems for understanding data (so that only in light of them are the data "data for" anything)? But if they do, then how is any shift from one paradigm to another ever possible? In terms of our example, why should Ptolemaists have felt ashamed of all those epicycles? Given the fundamental postulate, geocentricity, there could be nothing embarrassing or implausible about the resulting complexities. Why should not things be complex? If the paradigm itself carries its own criteria of plausibility, then any explanation assigned to "problematic" (or "anomalous") data must ipso facto be plausible.

But of course, the shift did occur. This implies that paradigms do not contain within themselves their own criteria of plausibility. And if they do not, they must be seen as subparadigms, or subsets of a larger, all-comprehensive paradigm. This superparadigm will be the field of presuppositions in which scientific thought occurs. It will include criteria by which given subparadigms (geocentricity or heliocentricity, Einsteinian or Newtonian physics, Big Bang or steady-state cosmologies) can be preferred to one another. Included among these criteria would probably be something like "economy and inductivness of explicability of the data." Such criteria will be the arbiters of which paradigm makes "better sense" of the evidence. They will tell which sense is the "better" sense.

This issue, merely implicit in Kuhn's discussion, is raised explicitly (albeit in different terminology) in the long-standing debate between "evidentialist" apologists (Clark Pinnock, John Warwick Montgomery, Josh McDowell, and so on) on the one hand, and their "presuppositionalist" rivals (Cornelius Van Til, Gordon Clark, and so on) on the other. In this context, the issue is that of "common ground," that is, does any exist between believers and nonbelievers? Evidentialists build their whole enterprise on a positive answer to this question. Indeed, they say, there can properly be no apologetics at all unless some commonly acknowledged criteria exist, whereby the evangelical position may be rendered probable or compelling to the fair-minded nonbeliever. Before examining the presuppositionalist objection to this belief, let us analyze the evidentialist position further in the light of Kuhn's categories. In effect, the evidentialists assume that they and their imagined non-Christian partners in dialogue both assent to a "superparadigm" of criteria for plausibility and explicability. The same kinds of grounds will determine which is the "better" sense made of the evidence. By their amassing of evidence, what McDowell, Montgomery, Pinnock, et al. seek to do is to show that the secular naturalists' paradigm cannot adequately (plausibly) explain "anomalous data" like, for example, the empty tomb. This is the point of the stock rehearsals of how "no explanation fits the facts of Easter Morning as well as the Resurrection does." The naturalists' explanations "demand more faith than the Resurrection itself" (Montgomery).[2] That is, the "Swoon theory," the "wrong tomb theory," and so on, are like epicycles. They are implausible. What makes them implausible? A common set of criteria including the notion that eyewitness reporting is valid, that crucified but surviving men are not likely to be able to roll away stones and stagger into Jerusalem, and so on. So no matter how much the skeptic cherishes his naturalistic paradigm, he really should admit its inadequacy to explain the evidence of Easter Morning. He should co nvert his paradigm (and with it, in this case, his eternal destiny).

Presuppositionalists, of whom we may take Van Til as the paramount example, repudiate this whole approach. There can be no common ground, he insists, because of the "noetic effects of the fall." It is a fundamental mistake to imagine that (Christ-rejecting) unregenerate persons can perceive enough of the facts correctly to be led from them (the common ground) to faith in Christ.[3] No, "all things hold together in Him" (Colossians 1:17). Since every single fact is to be properly construed only in the light of faith in Christ, then *any* perception by a Christ-rejecting (or Christ-blind) person is a misapprehension, even a delusion. Leaving aside the fact that this is pretty much the same rationale that has led historically to the branding and treatment of religious dissidents as insane, we will proceed to develop our interpretation of this view in Kuhn's terms. Van Til is essentially arguing that paradigms are self-sealing. They must carry their own criteria for plausibility within themselves, so that whatever explanation assigned to a datum is ipso facto plausible and natural. The apologetical/epistemological meaning of this is that religious certainty may be achieved only if it is defined into the system from the start. One can never reason his way to certain faith in Christ; he may only have certainty if he begins by defining Christ (the Logos) as the ground of reason. Then *by definition* faith in Christ is not only "a reasonable option," it becomes *the only rational option.* The evidentialist approach is unsatisfactory at least partially because it makes the Christ-Logos posterior rather than anterior to the reasoning process. In Kuhn's terms, evidential apologetics makes the evangelical Christian subparadigm subordinate to the larger paradigm of neutral, common criteria. And if it does this, then the same bridge from one subparadigm to the evangelical one, could as easily one day be the bridge to still a third subparadigm. The facts might lead the Christian elsewhere. Theoretically, this possibility must be left open. And what kind of faith-certitude would this be?

Evidentialists like Pinnock reply that such absolute theoretical certainty is neither available nor necessary to live any other area of life, so why here? We can have practical certainty. As Gordon J. Allport observes:

> The believer is often closer to the agnostic than we think. Both, with equal candor, may concede that the nature of Being cannot be known [with absolute certainty]; but the believer, banking on a probability . . . finds that the energy engendered and the values conserved prove the superiority of affirmation over indecisiveness.[4]

However, as full of common sense as the evidentialist position seems to be, the presuppositionalist critique is still a good one. Acquaintance with the literature of evidentialist apologetics makes it clear that their religious faith is more certain than is allowed by their common-ground approach with its inherent provisionality. For instance, John Warwick Montgomery writes of the doctrine of the Trinity, "I believe it with all my heart. I believe it because . . . it offers the best available 'construct' or 'model' for interpreting the biblical descriptions of God as Creator, Redeemer, and Sanctifier."[5]

Can one appropriately cling to a (mere) "model" or paradigm with "all one's heart"? Or to put it another way, can anyone reading such a statement really envision any rival interpretation of the evidence changing Montgomery's mind? Along the same lines, it is clear from a reading of much evidentialist literature that facts have been amassed to buttress beliefs already held on other grounds, and by willpower.[6] A subtle shifting of ground occurs. The apologist's faith causes him to deem "best" the reading of the data most in accord with his beliefs, even if it must be harmonized. But he proceeds to offer this reading to the nonbeliever as if it were the best reading of the facts *in and of themselves*. He claims to appeal to "common ground" (for example, "economy and inductiveness of explanation") but actually appeals to partisan criteria (for example, "which reading of biblical criticism conforms to evangelical beliefs?"). This results in what James Barr has called "maximal conservatism," the serving of a hidden dogmatic agenda.[7] The presuppositionalists, on the other hand, are quite open about their dogmatic agenda. They drop the pretense of a "common ground" and admit that the paradigm is self-sealing.

We have just suggested that, like their presuppositionalist rivals, the evidentialists actually seem to place their faith anterior to argumentation, though their principles call for the placing of it posterior to argumentation. (Both then are really in effect "presuppositionalists," though one side doesn't realize it.) And this inconsistency is no accident. Indeed if one thinks to use a truly evidentialist approach, he is dooming his apologetics from the start. There is something inherent in the common-criteria approach that makes its use in apologetics fundamentally wrongheaded.

Basically the trouble is that the only common ground is contemporary human experience of the world. (In terms of our discussion of paradigms, this is the same as "economic and inductive explanation" of the data at hand, without recourse to extraneous hypotheses.) Historical critics have a term for this: "the principle of analogy," as formulated by Ernst Troeltsch.[8] This principle, the basis of the historical-critical method's "denial of the miraculous," is a red flag to evangelicals. Yet they use exactly the same principle, only with a different name and applied to different cases. This is the common "empirical fit" argument used by Francis Schaeffer and Os Guiness to write off Eastern religions as failing to ring true to the depths of human experience.[9] In both cases, the idea is that, though theoretically anything (ancient miracle stories or modern philosophical worldviews) is quite *possibly* true, there is no available criterion for *plausibility* except present, shared human experience. This is why users of electric lights and radio may have trouble accepting the miracles of the New Testament. This is why those who know suffering or love may find it difficult to accept the Eastern denial of the reality of these things. If the "common ground" or "empirical fit" argument works at all, it works too well. Consistently pursued, such an inductive approach could of course lead only to some kind of natural theology, not to a "revealed religion" like evangelical Christianity.

Now if "common ground" is a chimera for apologetics, on what basis may the outsider opt for revealed religion? The evangelistic appeal of a consistent presuppositionalist must seem (from the human side) as a "leap of faith." And what the prospective convert sees, that the apologist-evangelist may not, is that this is only one of several invitations to leap in several directions. And the leap is "known" (felt) to be the right one *after* the choice has been made ("I once was blind, but now I see"). Before the fact, how is he to decide which faith to leap into? Walter Kaufmann said it well:

> They say their doctrine is infallible and true, but ignore the fact that there is no dearth whatsoever of pretenders to infallibility and truth. . . . Scores of other doctrines, scriptures, and apostles, sects and parties, cranks and sages make the same claim. . . . Those who have no such exalted notion of themselves have no way of deciding between dozens of pretenders if reason is proscribed [i.e., if common-ground criteria are disallowed because of the "noetic effects of the fall"].[10]

Quite a dilemma! The common-ground approach can never lead to conviction, but the presuppositionalist "leap of faith" could lead to Jim Jones as easily as to Jesus Christ! How could one decide? "Revolutionary suicide" in a Guyana rainforest is quite reasonable once one accepts the proper presuppositions. If one flinches because "obviously that's pathological," isn't he holding out on his piece of common ground, just like the unbelieving skeptic who judges the cross to be foolishness? If we cast away everyday experience as our standard of judgment, there can be no standard of judgment until after we make the leap of faith. But we could make that leap in any direction. And after we made it, it would seem right. The paradigm would carry with it its own criteria.

The upshot of all this is that the evidentialist apologetic with its common-ground approach finally backfires. A really inductive approach to this-worldly evidence can lead one only to this-worldly (that is, nonrevealed) religion. The presuppositionalist apologetic is consistent but not at all compelling, since the immunity from doubt that it wins for those inside the circle of faith simultaneously cancels its attraction to those outside. It can look neither more nor less plausible since there is no standard with which it may be compared. And the same approach is amenable to every sect. But the evangelical Christian (or believer in any sect) does not need to trouble himself about this. If he is safely within the circle of the truth himself, he can simply dismiss the other sects. And as for the outsider, doesn't the believer trust in the Spirit's conviction—if not actual predestination, then at least prevenient grace?[11] Then why worry about common ground, or for that matter about apologetics at all? Believers may plant the seed, but isn't it up to God to give the harvest (1 Corinthians 3:6–7)? Shouldn't faith rest on God's Spirit, not the persuasive words of man's wisdom (1 Corinthians 2:4)? Shouldn't it be revealed by the Father in heaven, not by flesh and blood (Matthew 16:17)?

And, finally, seen from the outsider's perspective, it would have to be said that the way to certain faith is an overwhelming "final experience," an enlightenment. Though the question of rational certitude is not theoretically *solved*, it is psychologically *settled*, since the new believer will no longer care to ask it. Now he *knows*.

By raising the question of the structure of paradigm shifts and how they are possible, Thomas S. Kuhn has provided a set of categories with which better to understand the long-standing apologetics debate. When seen in terms of his theory, the two apologetical strategies presently dominant in evangelical circles, the evidentialist and the pre-suppositionalist, seem to be beset with surprising difficulties. In fact, these difficulties run so deep as to indicate that the only consistent apologetic is fideistic presuppositionalism, which is in a sense no apologetic at all, since on principle it removes any external standards by which its faith might be "vindicated" or "defended."

NOTES

1. Thomas S. Kuhn, *The Structure of Scientific Revolutions* (Chicago: University of Chicago Press, 1969), p. 150.

2. John Warwick Montgomery, *The Suicide of Christian Theology* (Minneapolis: Bethany Fellowship, 1975), p. 39. This line of reasoning is to be found in a large number of books, and with very little variation. See, for example, John Stott's *Basic Christianity*; J. N. D. Anderson's *The Evidence for the Resurrection*; Michael Green's *Man Alive!*; Josh McDowell's *Evidence That Demands a Verdict*; Clark Pinnock's *Set Forth Your Case*.

3. Among Van Til's many works, see, for example, *The Protestant Doctrine of Scripture* ([n.p.]: Den Dulk Christian Foundation, 1967), p. 11: "One must be a believing Christian to study nature in the proper frame of mind and with proper procedure."

4. Gordon J. Allport, *The Individual and His Religion* (New York: Macmillan Publishing Company, 1974), p. 83.

5. Montgomery in *Spectrum of Protestant Beliefs*, ed. Robert Campbell (Milwaukee: Bruce Publishing Company, 1968), p. 20.

6. This assertion, I realize, invites a full-scale demonstration for which there is no space here. Basically, let me say that much apologetic argumentation for, for example, the total reliability of the gospels as historical records, and for the historicity of the Resurrection, are totally out of date and do not come to grips realistically with modern biblical criticism. This is true even of such recent works as Josh McDowell's *More Evidence That Demands*

a Verdict and Buell and Hyder's *Jesus: God, Ghost or Guru?* The interested reader may find a full-scale treatment of these questions in my *Beyond Born Again*.

7. See his incisive work *Fundamentalism* (Philadelphia: Westminster Press, 1978).

8. For two clear and sympathetic treatments of the principle of analogy, see Van A. Harvey, *The Historian and the Believer* (New York: Macmillan Company, 1972); and F. H. Bradley, *The Presuppositions of Critical History* (Chicago: Quadrange Books, 1968).

9. See, for example, Francis Schaeffer's *The God Who Is There* (Downer's Grove, IL: InterVarsity Press, 1968); *Escape from Reason* (Downer's Grove, IL: InterVarsity Press, 1968); and Os Guiness, *The Dust of Death* (Downer's Grove, IL: InterVarsity Press; 1973). Shaeffer's and Guiness's use of this argument, incidentally, shows them to be less consistently presuppositionalist than Van Til.

10. Walter Kaufmann, *The Faith of a Heretic* (Garden City, NY: Doubleday & Company, 1963), p. 86.

11. Van Til certainly does: "And it is only when the Holy Spirit gives man a new heart that he will accept the evidence of scripture about itself and about nature for what it really is. The Holy Spirit's regenerating power enables man to place all things in true perspective" (*Protestant Doctrine of Scripture*, pp. 10–11).

Appendix 3

THE CENTRALITY AND SCOPE OF CONVERSION

*T*he recent controversies over cult "brainwashing" and deprogramming have brought the question of "conversion" once again to people's minds. Just what is involved in such a sudden and unexpected turnabout? Is it the work of the Holy Spirit, or mere brainwashing? In the light of this questioning, perhaps the time is ripe for a reconsideration of conversion and its role in evangelical Christianity. This article will argue that conversion understood as the miraculous work of the Holy Spirit is not merely the entry point to the Christian life. Rather, it is integral to the theological agenda and determines the shape of evangelical religious life from beginning to end. And when the understanding of conversion as supernatural is modified, the far-reaching implications are both surprising and ironic.

CONVERSION AND MIRACLES

Among evangelicals (Christians who would describe themselves as "born-again" or "Bible-believing"), conversion is commonly believed to be a miraculous operation of the Holy Spirit, an act of God discontinuous with the ordinary chain of worldly cause and effect. One often hears such phrases as: "God just reached down into my life." It would be hard to deny that most born-again Christians mean this in more than a metaphorical . . . sense; we might call them "hard-line supernatural-

275

ists." But in recent years, some of their psychologists have become willing to admit that conversion is quite admissible to naturalistic causal explanation, and that the supernatural aspect of conversion must be redefined. This shift results in part from the embracing of general psychological methodology, wherein immanent causation, not otherworldly intervention, is the only calculable factor in diagnosis and treatment.

But one suspects that these psychologists have also felt the force of the challenge of William Sargant and others, who claim to be able to show the purely psychological roots of conversion. For example, Sargant wrote, "When we find that the technique of 'saving' people at revival meetings follows the same pattern [as abreactive treatment of wartime patients] and depends on the same brain mechanisms, it is impossible not to wonder about the reality of the divine power supposedly responsible for the 'change.'"[1] Long ago, of course, William James had made essentially the same observation:

> Psychology and religion . . . both admit that there are forces seemingly outside of the conscious individual that bring redemption to his life. Nevertheless psychology, defining these forces as "subconscious" . . . implies that they do not transcend the individual's personality; and herein she diverges from Christian theology, which insists that they are direct supernatural operations of the Deity.[2]

But James adds, "I do not see why Methodists need object to such a view."[3] That is, perhaps evangelicals might find acceptable some model of conversion that did not demand a miraculous intervention of God in the psychological process.

Now it seems that some psychologists have taken the bait, compelled to make some peace between their professional methodology on the one hand and their faith on the other. Malcolm Jeeves, responding to William Sargant, is certain that theological truth is of quite a different order than that of the facts of psychological causation. Thus even if Sargant is right, one need not doubt that the supernatural is still involved, at least in some sense. Jeeves writes:

Neither is the psychological account [of conversion] a competitor with the account which the person converted gives in his own personal and religious language. . . . The point is that within its own language system and at its own level, each account may be regarded as, at least in principle, *exhaustive* . . . but [not] *exclusive*. . . . Thus the personal account which refers to a personal encounter with God does not have to be "fitted in" to . . . the psychological . . . account. . . . In general, we find that the personal account of the event is much more concerned with the personal significance of the event than with the particular psychological . . . mechanism which may have been operative at the time.[4]

Thus conversion requires no miraculous intervention into the normal psychological process.

We find a similar approach to the mechanics of conversion in Keith Miller. After accepting James's basic outline of the psychological process of conversion, Miller goes on to explain conversion in terms borrowed from Abraham Maslow:

The experience of "Christian conversion" seemed very similar in some ways to Maslow's "peak experiences" in the lives of self-actualizers. . . . There may be a real correlation between what happens to a person through becoming a Christian and the meeting of different clusters of needs in Maslow's hierarchy. . . . What may have happened is that through a significant conversion experience some Christians have had *several* of their basic clusters of need met by God and the church.[5]

Indeed Maslow himself is hardly disinclined to see conversion experiences ("personal revelations") in such terms. But again he sees a significant implication that Miller does not see.

The big lesson that must be learned here, not only by the nontheists and liberal religionists, but also by the supernaturalists . . . is that mystery, ambiguity, illogic, contradiction, mystic and transcendent experiences may now be considered to lie well within the realm of nature. These phenomena need not drive us to postulate additional supernatural variables and determinants.[6]

Miller wants to facilitate our understanding of conversion for good pastoral reasons, but, as Maslow observes, the more explicable conversion becomes in immanent psychological terms, the less room is left for divine causation from without. The less mysterious it becomes, the less miraculous. And Maslow warns against simply redefining terms like "miraculous":

> I am myself uneasy, even jittery, over the semantic confusion which lies in store for us—indeed which is already here—as all the concepts which have been traditionally "religious" are redefined and then used in a very different way.[7]

Just such a redefinition seems to be implied in the writings of psychologists and counselors like Jeeves and Miller. The influence of the Holy Spirit is still supposed to underlie the process of conversion in a general but rather unclear way. It is striking to realize the continuity between the "soft-line supernaturalist" redefinition of the miraculous aspect of conversion, and the understanding of miracles in Liberal theology:

> In fact . . . a miracle in the sense of an action of God cannot be thought of as an event which happens on the level of secular (worldly) events. It is not visible, not capable of objective, scientific proof. . . . The thought of the action of God as [a] . . . transcendent action can be protected from misunderstanding, only if it is not thought of as an action which happens between worldly actions or events, but as happening within them. . . . The action of God is hidden from every eye except the eye of faith.[8]

In events like the Exodus or the Resurrection, Liberals say, no extraordinary events occurred, but God may still be said to have "acted" in the significance of events. Divine action did not interrupt or preempt the ordinary sequence of cause and effect. In Bultmann's terms, God did not actually vivify the corpse of Jesus, but he did "raise Jesus into the kerygma" in *Geschichte* (suprahistory).[9] Or as Gordon Kaufman puts it, God's acts take place in the "history of meaning," not in the history of events.[10]

The same tendency is apparent in the writings of Charles Martin. He also seeks to reply to the charge of Sargant, which he first summarizes:

> The mechanism by which [Christian conversion] is produced is akin to psychological brainwashing. Billy Graham and his fellow mass-evangelists are seen as expert mindbenders. . . . Thus becoming a Christian can be reduced to molecule-talk (mass psychology).[11]

Molecule-talk is one of three language-games enumerated by Martin. "Molecule-talk assumes a real world, cause and effect, and the significance of rational thought."[12] By contrast, the second and third language games are those of personal subjective freedom, and of ethical "oughtness" and obligation. Each is irreducible to the others:

> [N]ow "God" cannot be fitted in among these. . . . Yet God-talk gives accounts of things that can be accounted for in the other fields. . . . Certainly "God" cannot be fitted into any of these three frameworks nor can he go into a fourth area on the same level.[13]

Once again, God is the transcendent cause lying behind the whole works, not a "ghost in the machine" that interferes with its workings at opportune moments:

> The realm of nature, the molecule-talk area, is seen to depend upon God as creator in setting it going, and God as sustainer in keeping it going. It is regular and open to rational investigation because it is the work of a reliable, rational God.[14]

Not only has Martin repeated Jeeves's (and Bultmann's) sealing off of the historical/scientific and the theological levels of reality; he has (no doubt unwittingly) even recapitulated the assumptions of

Schleiermacher's polemic against miracles! Schleiermacher wrote in his magnum opus, *The Christian Faith*:

> Now some have represented miracle [as intervention in the cause and-effect process] as essential to the perfect manifestation of divine omnipotence. But it is difficult to conceiv . . . how omnipotence is shown to be greater in the suspension of the interdependence of nature than in its original immutable course which was no less divinely ordered. For, indeed, the capacity to make a change in what has been ordained is only a merit in the ordainer, if a change is necessary, which . . . can only be the result of some imperfection in him or in his work.[15]

Schleiermacher, like Martin, hails the Newtonian regularity of God's creation and attributes it to God's sovereign transcendence that he is *not* one more cause-among-causes. What Schleiermacher sees that Martin does not is that this observation demands the redefinition of "miracle" in a noninterventionist sense:

> Miracle [should be understood as] simply the religious name for event. Every event, even the most natural and usual, becomes a miracle, as soon as the religious view of it can be the dominant [view]. To me all is miracle.[16]

Literal miracles, or miracles as traditionally conceived, would require God to be one more finite causal agent within the realm of "molecule-talk," since it is God and no natural process which vivifies corpses and parts the sea.

Another way to approach this question would be to apply Francis Schaeffer's "line of despair" schema.[17] According to this theory, modern theology (as all modern culture) has opted for an explanation of mundane reality in terms of a closed system of cause and effect. Experienced reality is explicable naturalistically, without penetration by divine causation, that is, no miracles or miraculously revelatory scripture. If this is true, concludes Schaeffer, reality functions mechanistically. It is then nothing short of an arbitrary "upper-story leap" above the "line of despair" to postulate any noumenal realm of transcendent, divine reality.[18] If the rise of Easter faith can truly be accounted for without a literal resurrection, what besides religious nostalgia could lead Bultmann to postulate a "suprahistorical" act of God? The important thing to see is that by declaring theological explanation different in kind from psychological explanation, and parallel to it, Jeeves and the others have made God's alleged action in conversion "suprahistorical." Divine causation does not penetrate the continuum of worldly events; it runs parallel "above" it. Jeeves writes:

> It is not that the descriptions in terms of the various restricted categories [i.e., of psychology and theology] of the same events have gaps in them. Such descriptions might be in theory complete and perfectly valid as description on the scientific level. The point is that there are other levels.[19]

Jeeves, like Bultmann, has made an "upper-story leap." And if this kind of understanding of God's acting can be admitted at this point, shouldn't soft-line supernaturalists be willing to adjust theology across the board? In fact, the burden of proof would be on anyone who would hesitate at such consistency.

The same link between conversion and the biblical miracles is reflected in sort of a mirror-image fashion in the work of apologists like Carl F. H. Henry and Clark Pinnock. They have warned that Liberal theology dissolves the availability of the Gospel's answer for existential dilemmas of modern man."[20] What they have in mind is of course "born-again" faith. If one opted for a liberal *"heilsgeschichte"* understanding of God's activity, the possibility of real personal regeneration would be compromised a few steps down the line. If theologians deny that God intervenes miraculously in history, they cannot then affirm that he may intervene miraculously to regenerate individual lives today. Thus, apologists warn us, Liberalism is to be shunned. But now, ironically, some "soft-line" psychologists are beginning to erode the whole enterprise from the other end! If conversion is not literally miraculous, why must any other "act of God" be? Now such an implicit, wide-ranging theological readjustment might be a good thing. But if one is unwilling to make it, one might better push the camel's nose out of the tent. Evangelical psychologists should stick to their hard-line supernaturalist guns and try to refute Sargent and others, if they think they can.

CONVERSION AND THE CHRISTIAN LIFE

Having indicated the oft-unsuspected theological centrality of conversion, understood as supernatural, the discussion will show how miraculous conversion shapes the religious life from start to finish. A brief consideration of three aspects of "the born-again experience" will serve this purpose.

First, conversion produces what might fairly be labeled "a short circuited process of growth of the personal identity. It can be understood in Helfaer's terms as "precocious ego-identity formation."[21]

> In the case of the conservative Protestant subculture, the social identity around which the ego-identity is formed is that of the "Christian," or "follower of Christ." The identity is a relatively simple one, and it represents the internalization of the mutually recognized values and symbols of the community.[22]

If conversion occurs in late childhood, the born-again Christian will apparently have a head start over his secular friends: "Adolescence is not a time for major reorganization of the personality."[23] Why should it be? The evangelical youth has been given the answers, even before he or she becomes aware of the questions.

James Marcia has investigated what he calls the "foreclosed" personality among college students. The resulting portrait strikingly matches that of many fundamentalist college students and, we would argue, of other born-again Christians as well. According to Marcia:

A foreclosure subject is distinguished by not having had experienced a crisis [of identity formation] yet expressing commitment [to set values and beliefs]. It is difficult to tell where his parents' goals for him leave off and where his begin. He is becoming what others have prepared or intended him to become as a child. . . . College experiences serve only as a confirmation of childhood beliefs. A certain rigidity characterizes his personality; one feels that if he were faced with a situation in which parental values were nonfunctional, he would feel extremely threatened.[24]

Though Marcia shows that religious dogmatism is part of this personality package, "foreclosure" refers in general to the subject's attitudes toward vocation, politics, and other areas. Such a student has definite ideas on all these topics, yet without having wrestled with the questions on his or her own. By contrast, Marcia also dealt with "identity diffusion" subjects, sort of "good-time Charlie" students who drift through college years with neither settled goals nor definite convictions. They have also "successfully" avoided a crisis period, but have no firm commitment either. Then there were "identity moratorium" subjects who, at the time of testing, were in the throes of the identity crisis. For them everything was "up for grabs." Answers were not clear, but the hope was that they eventually would be. The last group, "identity achieved" subjects, were those who had completed the "moratorium" or crisis period, with the result that they had solid opinions and goals, integrated into their personalities, and wholly their own.

Returning to the "foreclosure" category, we may easily expand Marcia's references to "parents" to include the "significant others" of the individual's religious peer group, especially those responsible for his or her conversion if born-again faith has not been simply inherited from the family. The aptness of this sketch may be attested by anyone who has had much experience with campus Christian groups like Inter-Varsity Christian Fellowship, Navigators, Chi Alpha, and so on. Adopting Marcia's categories, Henry and Renaud describe the college experience of "foreclosed" students: "A good majority never consider any other path, and any question of alternative life styles rarely comes up for discussion."[25] Just so, the evangelical student may attend discussions where moral alternatives (say, premarital sex) are raised only to be refuted with proof-texts.

> Awareness of options or the possibility of change tends to precipitate anxiety in such young people, and left to themselves they skirt the unfamiliar. . . . Thus they effectively insulate themselves from meeting new people and being exposed to new ideas.[26]

Accordingly, Campus Crusade and Inter-Varsity "action groups" establish a cozy support group where the student's "plausibility structure."[27] is maintained against the pressures of the secular environment. The student is to venture forth to meet the "unsaved" only on covert missions of "friendship evangelism." Contact with those of different opinions is initiated for the purpose not of interaction but of proselytizing:

> One of the implications of such a mode of operation for the college experience is that these students, already largely closed down to new experiences and ideas when they enter college, usually continue to avoid faculty whose views might challenge theirs.[28]

This observation accounts for the frequent avoidance of religion or Bible courses by fundamentalist students on secular campuses. Of course there are exceptions that prove the rule; nowadays one finds more fundamentalists taking such courses specifically in order to "defend the faith" against unbelieving professors. For this purpose, the student is armed by the evangelical staff worker with apologetics literature such as Josh McDowell's *Evidence That Demands a Verdict.*[29] The InterVarsity Press, probably the most sophisticated arm of that organization, seems largely dedicated to providing an extensive range of apologetics material dealing with every issue from biblical criticism to comparative religion, from Behavioristic psychology to Marxism. The student is led to believe that he or she just happens to be heir to the most cogent interpretation of the facts in virtually every field. And this of course is just what these students want to believe anyway. Why bother to evaluate the alternatives for themselves? The apologists have saved them the trouble.

Besides falling short of liberal-arts academic ideals, do such "foreclosed" students, whether born-again Christians or otherwise, really suffer ill effects from their "foreclosure"? Yes, it seems as if they do. Marcia found that such individuals' self-esteem was more easily threatened by negative feedback than those who had "achieved" identity through struggle. They also seemed inclined to set unrealistic goals for themselves. And, not surprisingly, they tended toward authoritarian thinking. The relevance of this last observation is only too clear relative to those students who are taught to settle all questions by biblical proof-texting instead of inductive reasoning. Chesen summed up the problem well: "Rigid, confined, and stereotyped religious thinking patterns can be directly contributory to emotional instability."[30] It would certainly seem to be in the interests of the campus evangelism groups themselves to encourage a more flexible and inductive approach to college experience among their members. Evangelical students might then arrive at a faith better integrated and more balanced, though obviously the dangers of assimilation and secularization would also be increased. Yet this risk is the price of trusting students to think for themselves. Certainly more might drift away from faith and into the secular mainstream. But others would no longer be driven from faith by the narrow limits of it defined by their campus groups. And graduates from these groups might be more capable and valuable members of the evangelical movement.

We have been concentrating on young people and students, but it would seem that basically the same dynamics are in play no matter at what age conversion occurs, since much evangelical rhetoric tends to make the goal of all personal ("spiritual") growth the ideal of "conformity to the image of Christ," characteristically interpreted as being *religiously* mature. Other facets of life tend to be ignored. The effect of this adoption of a relatively simple, and basically religious, ego-identity has two important, superficially positive, results. First, it accounts in large measure for the much-vaunted "sense of purpose" and of "having the answers." Born-again Christians seem to "have peace" in a troubled world because they do not have to work out the answers for themselves. Second, this sudden "ego-identity formation" explains the ideological "party-line" approach to moral issues present among most rank-and-file evangelicals. For example, the minions of Jerry Falwell and Anita Bryant *know* homosexuality is evil, perhaps without ever sensing the need to reason it out.

FORTRESS MENTALITY

A second area in which the importance of conversion is manifest, is that of "witnessing" and apologetics. Conversion provides a bond of emotional tenacity that no reasoning is likely to affect.

Leuba wrote, "As the ground of assurance here is not rational, argumentation is irrelevant. . . . It is a gross error to imagine that the chief practical value of the faith-state is its power to stamp with the seal of validity certain particular conceptions."[31] He means to disallow emotive nonsequitors like "You ask me how I know he lives? He lives within my heart."

But can anyone deny that born-again believers constantly confuse emotional fervency and rational convincement in this manner? This can be seen most readily in the quasi-rational approach taken in trying to deal with objections of a nonbeliever whom one is trying to convert. The lay evangelist has taken the trouble to master the answers to "questions non-Christians most commonly ask," but if he is stumped, he has been coached to reply, "Say, that's a good question! I don't have an answer, but I'll try to get one for you." The irony of this reply should be, but may not be, obvious. The whole appeal to the skeptic is an allegedly rational one, seeking to satisfy rational objections, but the last statement makes it clear that the believer himself holds his view on the strength of sheer will power!

Otherwise, how could a "good" (that is, genuinely cogent) objection not phase him? This common practice is depicted in cartoon form in a recent flyer distributed by the International Council on Biblical

Inerrancy, advertising a "Lay Seminar on the Authority of Scripture." In the drawing, a smirking skeptic challenges a (literally) wide-eyed believer carrying a huge Bible: "Don't you believe the Bible is full of errors?" The believer answers "No, the Bible is inerrant." The skeptic barrages the inerrantist with questions about textual contradictions, evolution, and so on, to which the believer replies variously "Well . . . ," "Ahh . . . ," "Well ahh. . . . " The skeptic: "Doesn't anyone have answers to my questions?" Not the believer! For he answers, "Funny you should mention that. There is this seminar. . . . "[32] Since born-again faith was probably accepted because of emotional-existential factors, not intellectual factors, the latter have little to do with the maintenance of faith.

Apologetics is only a strategy, and often a subtly dishonest one.

INSTANT SANCTIFICATION

Third, conversion can be seen to be determinative of the whole shape of "the Christian life" because of the "get-saved-quick" scheme it proffers. It cannot really be disputed that most evangelistic rhetoric offers virtually instant solutions to all problems through conversion. For example, take the "Four Spiritual Laws" booklet[33] used extensively by Campus Crusade for Christ, their "Here's Life America" campaign, and many local churches. A diagram characterizes the "carnal" life as chaotic and troubled as long as "self" is on the throne. By contrast, the "spiritual" life has all interests in order, orbiting serenely about the enthroned Jesus Christ. And the difference is as simple as praying the standard prayer that follows. However, this promise is seldom completely fulfilled.

A second Campus Crusade booklet, "Have You Made the Wonderful Discovery of the Spirit-Filled Life?" reveals the hitherto-unsuspected existence of a *third* classification, the "carnal Christian." One's life is again a shambles, even with Christ as savior, but again the remedy is simple. "Spiritual breathing" (confessing sins and appropriating the Spirit's fullness) will rectify things.[34] Note that all of life's problems are here reducible to sin. And one need seek no further for a solution than religious repentance. Let no one think that Bill Bright (founder of Campus Crusade) is unique in this perception of things. In slightly different idioms this "hard religious line" (to modify our earlier terminology) is common to evangelicals ranging from Jay Adams with his "nouthetic counseling"[35] to Don Basham and his "deliverance ministry,"[36] with several stages in between: for example, Vernon Grounds,[37] Tim La Haye.[38]

All this implies what might bluntly be called the "Shazam model of sanctification." If regeneration is to be accomplished in an essentially miraculous manner without the effort of the convert himself, why not the subsequent process of growth? That is, whenever the born-again Christian encounters some personal obstacle or deficiency, he must "lay it on the altar," "give it to the Lord." It would be positively impious to try to struggle through it oneself, and so act "in the flesh." But isn't such struggling, fortunately or unfortunately, the only path to personal maturity? And isn't this model of growth an attempt to leapfrog one's way miraculously into maturity, as when youngster Bill Batson said the magic word "Shazam" and suddenly became the adult Captain Marvel?[39] It is not likely to work; immaturity will be protracted as long as one takes Malcolm Smith'sadvice to "turn your back on the problem."[40]

THE "SOFT RELIGIOUS LINE"

Eventually, growing numbers of evangelicals (including Bruce Larson, Keith Miller, O. Quentin Hyder, Cecil Osborne, and Gary Collins) have some to see the lack of psychological realism in this "hard religious line." They seek to substitute a more humanistic approach, whereby all problems are not simply spiritual in origin or solution, and whereby the only goal is *not* "spiritual growth."

Sentiments like these are representative: "If my faith is in God, then my job is not to build a successful, untainted religious life; it is to live a joyful and creative human life."[41] "[It] is absolutely untrue that Christians cannot or should not become mentally ill. We are just as vulnerable as pagans."[42] We might call this a shift to a "soft religious line."

Interestingly, the same sort of modification of initially absolutist claims has been observed among Meher Baba sectarians by Anthony, Robbins, Doucas, and Curtis:

> The early stages of involvement in a mystical movement may also involve unrealistic expectations of rapid spiritual apotheosis, e.g., Nirvana, Satori, God Realization. Such decisive realization could be expected to obviate all emotional difficulties. . . . The press of worldly experience tends to result eventually in the diminution of the unrealistic character of such expectations. Over time, converts realize that conversion to a mystical perspective does not result in the early transcendence of all earthly burdens.[43]

Renouncing the repression and perfectionism they see in the hard religious line, such soft-line writers announce a new freedom for born-again Christians, a new possibility of "being human." The irony is that the "burdens" being shed according to this new gospel are precisely the "blessings" promised by the old! Hard-liners like Bright, LaHaye, and Adams offer spiritual-psychological miracles that are supposed to give relief from the burdens of worldly existence. Soft-liners like Larson, Miller, and Osborne recognize such promises as incapable of delivery. Thus the latter group's "good news" is that tired and frustrated Christians can have relief from their burdens by being more like everyone else! It would seem that insofar as evangelicals move toward this soft religious line, they ought to be prepared to rethink their evangelistic claims about spectacular benefits available only through Christ. The whole situation comes to look somewhat more ambiguous.

A POSSIBLE SOLUTION

Up to this point, this article has argued that miraculous conversion is not merely the beginning of the "born-again experience," but is instead integral to evangelicalism's theological program, as well as to the shape of its religious life. But this far-reaching significance of conversion, *understood as miraculous*, is often unsuspected. Thus many soft-line psychologists in seeking to tone down and redefine the supernatural side of conversion have set in motion changes that are far more significant than they intended. In seeking just a bit more psychological realism, they turn out to alter implicitly but radically both the theological and the experiential claims of evangelical Christianity. It is proving to be more difficult than they had imagined to hold onto humanistic psychology with one hand, and traditional evangelicalism with the other.

Is there, then, any solution, or are the difficulties exposed here insurmountable embarrassments to the notion of conversion? What sort of salvage operation might a psychologist or theologian attempt? One might acknowledge a more liberal approach to the nature of revelation and religious language and try accommodating theology to it.[44] The implied changes would be far reaching indeed. And though various factors (for example, biblical criticism) may yet force such a change, the solution to our particular problem seems less drastic.

One need not revise or weaken the concept of "miracle." One only need alter its *application* to the concept of "conversion." It would go most of the way toward solving the problem if soft-liners shifted the focus of the "miraculous" from the subjective pole (conversion *per se*) to the objective pole—that *to* which one is converted. Evangelicals need only maintain the supernatural character of the truths of faith to which one converts. They are the "saving truths," that is, one's life is affected by the implications of the divine facts themselves, whether or not there is any magic in the believing *of* them.

Though by-and-large a hard-liner in approach, Bill Gothard's view of scripture meditation is, in isolation, a perfect example of what we are suggesting. Gothard's idea is that God has ordered human life according to certain unchanging structures that can be disregarded only at the cost of the inevitable "reproofs of life." The person converted to the study of scripture will be at a distinct advantage in life because the Bible tells him or her all about those built-in "structures." Thus if one continually meditates on God's Word, one is assured of "successful living." The process is one of simple common sense. Certainly the divine truths involved are supernaturally ordained and revealed.

But so little "miraculous" is either the process of observing these truths or the gaining of results that Gothard admits even nonbelievers will have success when they follow them. All that is necessary is that one reform one's "thought-structures" by the prolonged and repeated rehearsing of those biblical truths. The doing of it is not supernatural at all, and this is no embarrassment.

Another example would be Bruce Larson's observation that the born-again Christian's faith in Christ's love provides a head start in the process of learning to love others, a process that in itself is quite natural, however difficult. Similarly, one's faith in eternal life will surely provide a sense of direction in this life that a nonbeliever will lack. And one who believes in God's loving providence will take adversity with more resilience than one who is resigned to the blows of blind fate."[45] The point in all this is that certain notions cannot help but have positive psychological effects when believed. So the believer in Christ's love, eternal life, and divine providence can certainly expect the benefits of peace, assurance, and purpose. *But there need be nothing supernatural in the believing of these things* for these benefits to accrue. Is there anything miraculous in one's joy at hearing a confession of love from his or her spouse? No, it simply follows "naturally." Even so here.

It would be useless to pretend that nothing would be different on this understanding. There could be promised no supernatural shortcuts to mature self-identity, no easy answers to questions of personal ethics, no automatic freedom from depression. (On the other hand, believers would be freed, as soft-liners want to free them, from the guilt of believing that they should be miraculously free of problems and confusion when they are not.) Such an awakening to reality, however rude for some, should be welcomed since it ends the illusion that Christian faith is to be embraced for the sake of the benefits one stands to gain. And this is undeniably the approach of much evangelism today, wherein the Gospel is hawked as a miraculous panacea, a happiness elixir. (Witness the amazing bumper sticker: "Make life a little easier with Jesus.") Any sober reading of New Testament statements like "Anyone who does not carry his cross and follow me cannot be my disciple" (Luke 14:27) suggests that Christian discipleship may actually be more of a liability than an asset for life in this world. The spectacular (and unrealistic) promises of the hard-liners tend to obscure this fact.

So soft-line "supernaturalists," on the present understanding, do not need to trouble themselves about redefining and compromising the miraculous quality of conversion. They would be well advised instead to leave the meaning of "miracle" intact and deny that conversion is miraculous *at all*! Surely the whole point is the supernatural miracle *to* which one is converted, namely Christ. The decision to believe the Gospel message is "merely" a decision like any other decision. But the message is like no other message. Revivalist Charles Finney knew that there was nothing particularly mysterious about the decision to embrace Christianity. The important thing was how to persuade people to make it.

And this observation raises an apparent difficulty with the present proposal. Though nothing inherent in the concept of conversion implies a supernatural character, conversion might be required to be miraculous because of the other tenets of one's theology. For example, Calvinists might be more reluctant to accept this solution than Arminians, since Reformed theology seems to require Calvinists to make conversion other than human in origin. But all that need be said in a Calvinist framework is that while the conversion decision is preordained by God, it comes about by no special act of God, but rather as a result of his general providence, just like other, more mundane, events. That is, the causation involved in conversion is more analogous to that operating in a common auto accident or the winning of a contest, than to that at work in the parting of the Red Sea or the resurrection of Jesus Christ.

In conclusion, it can be observed that, as often happens, a problem has been created by a misleading delineation of the issues, in this case by evangelical writers and counselors themselves. And the solution is as simple as putting the issues into better perspective. When this is done, the need to weaken the concept "miracle," with the ensuing theological implications, vanishes. And though the evangelist will still be justified in promising experiential benefits arising from faith, these promises will be more realistic both biblically and psychologically. In fact, it becomes superfluous to promise that God will "miraculously" cause peace and joy to spring up in the convert's life. Anyone who has come to believe that he or she has eternal life with a loving God will need no help in feeling peace and joy.

NOTES

1. William Sargant, *The Mind Possessed* (New York: Penguin, 1975), p. 194.

2. William James, *Varieties of Religious Experience* (New York: New American Library, 1958), p. 173.

3. Ibid., p. 191.

4. Malcolm A. Jeeves, *Psychology and Christianity: The View both Ways* (Downers Grove, IL: InterVarsity Press, 1976), p. 141.

5. Keith Miller, *The Becomers* (Waco, TX: Word Books, 1978), pp. 78–79.

6. Abraham H. Maslow, *Religions, Values, and Peak-Experiences* (New York: Viking, 1974), p. 45.

7. Ibid.

8. Rudolf Bultmann, *Jesus Christ and Mythology* (New York: Scribner's, 1958), pp. 61–62.

9. Rudolf Bultmann, "New Testament and Mythology," in *Kerygma*

and Myth, ed. Hans Werner Bartsch (New York: Harper & Row, 1961), pp. 41–42.

10. Gordon D. Kaufman, *Systematic Theology: A Historicist Perspective* (New York: Scribner's, 1968), p. 433.

11. Charles Martin, *How Human Can You Get?* (Downers Grove, IL: InterVarsity Press, 1973), p. 114.

12. Ibid., p. 110.

13. Ibid.

14. Ibid., p. 111.

15. Friedrich Schleiermacher, *The Christian Faith* (New York: Harper & Row, 1963), p. 179.

16. Friedrich Schleiermacher, *On Religion: Speeches to Its Cultured Despisers* (New York: Harper & Row, 1958), p. 88.

17. Francis A. Schaeffer, *The God Who Is There* (Downer's Grove, IL: InterVarsity Press, 1976), p. 22.

18. Ibid., p. 58.

19. Malcom A. Jeeves, *Scientific Psychology and Christian Belief* (London: InterVarsity, 1967), p. 13.

20. Clark H. Pinnock, *Biblical Revelation* (Chicago: Moody Press, 1976), p. 14; Carl F. H. Henry, *Frontiers in Modern Theology* (Chicago: Moody Press, 1968), pp. 152–53.

21. Philip M. Helfaer, *The Psychology of Religious Doubt* (Boston: Beacon Press, 1972), p. 5.

22. Ibid., p. 65.

23. Ibid.

24. James E. Marcia, "Development and Validation of Ego-Identity States," *Journal of Personality and Social Psychology* 2, no. 5 (1966): 552.

25. Mildred Henry with Harriet Renaud, "Examined and Unexamined Lives," *Research Reporter* 7, no. 1 (1972): 5.

26. Ibid.

27. Peter L. Berger, *A Rumor of Angels* (Garden City, NY: Doubleday, 1970).

28. Henry and Renaud, "Examined and Unexamined Lives," p. 5.

29. Josh McDowell, *Evidence That Demands a Verdict* (San Bernardino, CA: Campus Crusade for Christ International, 1973).

30. Eli S. Chesen, *Religion May Be Hazardous to Your Health* (New York: Collier, 1974), p. 27.

31. James H. Leuba, *Studies in Psychology of Religious Phenomena: The Religious Motive, Conversion, Facts and Doctrines* (Worcester, MA: J. H. Orpha), quoted in James, *Varieties of Religious Experience*, p. 198.

32. "Lay Seminar on the Authority of Scripture" (Philadelphia: International Council on Biblical Inerrancy, 1980), p. 1.

33. "Have You Heard of the Four Spiritual Laws?" (San Bernardino, CA: Campus Crusade for Christ International, 1972).

34. "Have You Made the Wonderful Discovery of the Spirit-Filled Life?" (San Bernardino, CA: Campus Crusade for Christ International, 1972).

35. Jay E. Adams, *Christ and Your Problems* (Nutley, NJ: P & R Publishing, 1971); Adams, *What Do You Do When You Become Depressed?* (Nutley, NJ: P & R Publishing, 1975); Adams, *The Use of the Scriptures in Counseling* (Grand Rapids, MI: Baker, 1976).

36. Don Basham, *Deliver Us from Evil* (New York: Bantam, 1977).

37. Vernon Grounds, *Emotional Problems and the Gospel* (Grand Rapids, MI: Zondervan, 1976).

38. Tim LaHaye, *Ten Steps to Victory over Depression* (Grand Rapids, MI: Zondervan, 1974).

39. Jim Steranko, *History of the Comics* (New York: Supergraphics, 1970).

40. Malcolm Smith, *Turn Your Back on the Problem* (Plainfield, NJ: Logos, 1972).

41. Miller, *The Becomers*, p. 190.

42. O. Quentin Hyder, *The Christian's Handbook of Psychiatry* (Old Tappan, NJ: Revell, 1974), p. 153.

43. Dick Anthony, Thomas Robbins, Madeline Doucas, and Thomas E. Curtis, "Patients and Pilgrims: Changing Attitudes toward Psychotherapy of Converts to Eastern Mysticism," *American Behavioral Scientist* 20, no. 6 (1977): 873.

44. Charles Kraft, *Christianity in Culture* (Maryknoll, NY: Orbis Books, 1979).

45. Bruce Larson, *No Longer Strangers* (Waco, TX: Word, 1974).

BIBLIOGRAPHY

Achtemaier, Paul J. *The Inspiration of Scripture*. Philadelphia: Westminster Press, 1980.

———. *An Introduction to the New Hermeneutic*. Philadelphia: Westminster Press, 1969.

Adams, Jay E. *The Use of the Scriptures in Counseling*. Grand Rapids: Baker Book House, 1976.

Aiken, David W. "What Is an 'Evangelical'?" 1979. (Mimeographed.)

Alexander, William Menzies. *Demonic Possession in the New Testament*. Grand Rapids: Baker Book House, 1980.

Alley, Robert S. *Revolt against the Faithful: A Biblical Case for Inspiration as Encounter*. New York: J. B. Lippincott Co., 1970.

Barr, James. *The Bible in the Modern World*. New York: Harper & Row, 1973.

———. *Fundamentalism*. Philadelphia: Westminster Press, 1978

Basham, Don. *Deliver Us from Evil*. New York: Bantam Books, 1977.

Bauer, Walter. *Orthodoxy and Heresy in Earliest Christianity*. Philadelphia: Fortress Press, 1971.

Beegle, Dewey M. *The Inspiration of Scripture*. Philadelphia: Westminster Press, 1963.

———. *Scripture, Tradition, and Infallibility*. Grand Rapids: William B. Eerdmans Publishing Co., 1973.

Benoit, Pierre. *Aspects of Biblical Inspiration*. Chicago: Priory Press, 1965.

Berger, Peter L. *A Rumor of Angels: Modern Society and the Rediscovery of the Supernatural*. Garden City, NY: Doubleday, 1970.

Berk, Stephen E. "The Radical Christianity of the Sojourners Community." *Agora* 3 (Spring 1980):12–15.

Berkouwer, G. C. *Holy Scripture*. Translated by Jack Rogers. Grand Rapids: William B. Eerdmans Publishing Co., 1975.

Bloesch, Donald G. *Essentials of Evangelical Theology*. 2 vols. New York: Harper & Row, 1978–1979.

———. *The Evangelical Renaissance*. Grand Rapids: William B. Eerdmans Publishing Co., 1973.

Boardman, William W., Jr., Robert F. Koontz, and Henry M. Morris. *Science and Creation*. San Diego: Creation Science Research Center, 1973.

Boer, Harry R. *Above the Battle? The Bible and Its Critics*. Grand Rapids: William B. Eerdmans Publishing Co., 1977.

Boice, James Montgomery. *Does Inerrancy Matter?* Oakland, CA: International Council on Biblical Inerrancy, 1979.

———, ed. *The Foundation of Biblical Authority*. Grand Rapids: Zondervan Publishing House, 1978.

———. Fundraising letter. n.p.: International Council on Biblical Inerrancy, n.d.

Bolich, Gregory G. *Karl Barth & Evangelicalism*. Downers Grove, IL: InterVarsity Press, 1980.

Boraker, Robert C. "The Holy Bible—Is It Reliable?" *Plain Truth*, September 1980, pp. 18–19, 45.

Boswell, John. *Christianity, Social Tolerance, and Homosexuality*. Chicago: University of Chicago Press, 1980.

Boudreau, Albert H. *The Born-Again Catholic*. Locust Valley, NY: Living Flame Press, 1980.

"The Bout for the Bible." *Wittenburg Door*, February–March 1980, pp. 10–15.

Brake, Donald L. "The Preservation of the Scriptures." In *Counterfeit or Genuine?* ed. David Otis Fuller, 175–217. Grand Rapids: Grand Rapids International Publications, 1975.

Briggs, Charles Augustus. *The Authority of Holy Scripture: An Inaugural Address*. New York: Charles Scribner's Sons, 1891.

———. *Whither? A Theological Question for the Times*. New York: Charles Scribner's Sons, 1890.

Bright, John. *The Authority of the Old Testament*. Grand Rapids: Baker Book House, 1975.

Brown, Raymond E. "The History and Development of the Theory of a *Sensus Plenior*." *Catholic Biblical Quarterly* 15 (April 1953): 141–62.

Bryan, William Jennings. *The Bible or Evolution?* Murfreesboro, TN: Sword of the Lord Publishers, n.d.

———. *The Modern Arena*. Upland, IN: Taylor University, n.d.

Bultmann, Rudolf. "Is Exegesis without Presuppositions Possible?" In *Existence and Faith: The Shorter Writings of Rudolf Bultmann*, ed. Schubert Ogden, 289–96. New York: World Publishing Co., 1964.

———. *Jesus Christ and Mythology*. New York: Charles Scribner's Sons, 1958.

———. "New Testament and Mythology." In *Kerygma and Myth*, pp. 1–44.

edited by Hans Werner Bartsch, translated by Reginald H. Fuller. New York: Harper & Row, 1961.

Burtchaell, James T. *Catholic Theories of Biblical Inspiration Since 1810.* Cambridge: Cambridge University Press, 1969.

Carey, George. *God Incarnate.* Downers Grove, IL: InterVarsity Press, 1978.

Carnell, E. J. *The Case for Orthodox Theology.* Philadelphia: Westminster Press, 1959.

Charlot, John. *New Testament Disunity.* New York: E. P. Dutton, 1970.

"The Chicago Statement on Biblical Inerrancy." n.p.: International Council on Biblical Inerrancy, 1978.

Clark, Gordon H. *The Concept of Biblical Authority,* Phillipsburg, NJ: Presbyterian and Reformed Publishing, 1980.

Cobb, John B., Jr. *Christ in a Pluralistic Age.* Philadelphia: Westminster Press, 1975.

Cole, Stewart G. *The History of Fundamentalism.* New York: Richard R. Smith, 1931 .

Coleman, Richard J. "Another View: The Battle for the Bible." *Journal of the American Scientific Affiliation* (June 1979): 74–78.

———. "Biblical Inerrancy: Are We Going Anywhere?" *Theology Today* (January 1975): 295–303.

———. *Issues of Theological Warfare, Evangelicals and Liberals.* Grand Rapids: William B. Eerdmans Publishing Co., 1972.

Conzelmann, Hans. *The Theology of St. Luke.* Translated by Geoffrey Buswell. New York: Harper & Row, 1961.

Counts, Bill. *The Evangelical Orthodox Church and the New Covenant Apostolic Order.* Berkeley, CA: Spiritual Counterfeits Project, 1979.

Davis, Stephen T. *The Debate about the Bible.* Philadelphia: Westminster Press, 1977.

Dayton, Donald W. "The Battle Rages On: Emerging Issues in the Evangelical 'Battle for the Bible.'" *Theology Today* (April 1980): 18 (in prepublication MS).

———. "Evangelicalism without Fundamentalism." *Christian Century,* July 19–26, 1978, pp. 710–13.

———. "Where Now Young Evangelicals?" *Other Side* (March–April 1975): 30–37.

———. "Wrong Front." *Other Side* (May–June 1976): 36–37.

De Wolf, L. Harold. *The Case for Theology in a Liberal Perspective.*

Philadelphia: Westminster Press, 1959.

———. *Present Trends in Christian Theology*. New York: Association Press, 1960.

Dodd, C. H. *The Authority of the Bible*. New York: Harper & Bros., 1958.

Doulos, Bill Lane. "Mere Orthodoxy." *Sojourners*, December 1976, pp. 24–25.

Drury, John. *Tradition and Design in Luke's Gospel*. Atlanta: John Knox Press, 1977.

Dunn, James D. G. "Demythologizing—The Problem of Myth in the New Testament." In *New Testament Interpretation*, ed. I. Howard Marshall, 285–307. Grand Rapids: William B. Eerdmans Publishing Co., 1977.

———. *Unity and Diversity in the New Testament*. Philadelphia: Westminster Press, 1977.

Ebeling, Gerhard. "Significance of the Critical Historical Method." In *Word and Faith*, translated by James W. Leitch. Philadelphia: Fortress Press, 1963.

Erickson, Millard. *The New Evangelical Theology*. Westwood, NJ: Fleming H. Revell Co., 1968.

Evans, Llewelyn J., and Henry Preserved Smith. *Biblical Scholarship and Inspiration*. Cincinnati: Robert Clarke & Co., 1891.

Fee, Gordon D. *The Disease of the Health and Wealth Gospels*. Costa Mesa, CA: Word for Today, 1979.

———. "Hermeneutics and Common Sense." In *Inerrancy and Common Sense*, ed. Roger R. Nicole and J. Ramsey Michaels, 161–86. Grand Rapids: Baker Book House, 1980.

———. "Hermeneutics and Historical Precedent—A Major Problem in Pentecostal Hermeneutics." In *Perspectives on the New Pentecostalism*, ed. Russell P. Spittler, 118–33. Grand Rapids: Baker Book House, 1976.

Fichter, Joseph. *The Catholic Cult of the Paraclete*. New York: Sheed & Ward, 1975.

Ford, J. Massyngbaerde. *Which Way for Catholic Pentecostals?* New York: Harper & Row, 1976.

Forestall, J. Terence. "The Limitation of Inerrancy." *Catholic Biblical Quarterly* 20 (January 1958): 9–18.

Forster, Roger T., and V. Paul Marston. *God's Strategy in Human History*. Wheaton, IL: Tyndale House Publishers, 1974.

Fosdick, Harry Emerson. *The Modern Use of the Bible*. New York: Macmillan Publishing Co., 1961.

France, R. T. "Inerrancy and New Testament Exegesis." *Themelios* 1 (Autumn 1975): 12–18.

Frei, Hans. *The Eclipse of Biblical Narrative*. New Haven: Yale University Press, 1977.

Frey, John D. *Is the Bible Inerrant?* Prairie Village, KS: John D. Frey, 1976.

Fuller, Daniel P. "Benjamin B. Warfield's View of Faith and History." *Bulletin of the Evangelical Theological Society* 11 (Spring 1968): 75–83.

————. "Biblical Theology and the Analogy of Faith." In *Unity and Diversity in New Testament Theology*, edited by Robert A. Guelich, 195–213. Grand Rapids: William B. Eerdmans Publishing Co., 1978.

————. *Easter Faith and History*. Grand Rapids: William B. Eerdmans Publishing Co., 1965.

————. "Inspiration and Authority of the Bible." *Decision*, April 1966.

————. "The Nature of Biblical Inerrancy." *Journal of the American Scientific Affiliation* (June 1972): 47–50.

————. "On Revelation and Biblical Authority." Quoted in Davis, *Debate about the Bible*, p. 42.

Furniss, Norman F. *The Fundamentalist Controversy, 1918–1931*. Hamden, CT: Archon Books, 1963.

Gaebelein, Frank L., ed., *New Scofield Reference Bible*. New York: Oxford University Press, 1967.

Gardner, Martin. *Fads and Fallacies in the Name of Science*. New York: Dover Publications, 1957.

Geisler, Norman L., ed. *Inerrancy*. Minneapolis: Bethany Fellowship, 1980.

Ginger, Ray. *Six Days or Forever? Tennessee vs. Scopes*. New York: Quadrangle Books, 1969.

Gish, Duane T. *Evidence against Evolution*. Wheaton, IL: Tyndale House Publishers, 1972.

————. *Evolution? The Fossils Say No!* San Diego: Creation-Life Publishers, 1979.

Goldingay, John M. "Inspiration, Infallibility and Criticism." *Churchman*, January–March 1976, pp. 6–23.

Goulder, Michael D. *Midrash and Lection in Matthew*. London: SPCK, 1974.

Greene, John C. *Darwin and the Modern World View*. New York: New American Library, 1963.

Greidanus, Sidney. *Sola Scriptura: Problems and Principles in Preaching Historical Texts*. Toronto: Wedge Publishing Foundation, 1970.

Griffin, David R. *A Process Christology*. Philadelphia: Westminster Press, 1973.

Grimstead, Jay. "The Inerrancy Debate among Evangelicals." n.p.: International Council on Biblical Inerrancy, February 1977. (Mimeographed.)

Grollenberg, Lucas. *Bible Study for the 21st Century*. n.p.: Consortium, 1976.

Gundry, Robert F. *The Church and the Tribulation*. Grand Rapids: Zondervan Publishing House, 1979.

Hamaan, Henry P. *The Bible Between Fundamentalism and Philosophy*. Minneapolis: Augsburg Publishing House, 1980.

Hammond, Frank, and Ida Mae Hammond. *Pigs in the Parlor: A Practical Guide to Deliverance*. Kirkwood, MO: Impact Books, 1973.

Handy, Robert T. *A Christian America: Protestant Hopes and Historical Realities*. New York: Oxford University Press, 1971.

Harrison, Everett F. "Criteria of Biblical Inerrancy." In *A Christianity Today Reader*, edited by Frank E. Gaebelein, 62–67. New York: Meredith Press, 1966.

Held, Heinz Joachim. "Matthew as Interpreter of the Miracle Stories." In Günther Bornkamm, Gerhard Barth, and Heinz Joachim Held, *Tradition and Interpretation in Matthew*, translated by Percy Scott, 165–300. New Testament Library. Philadelphia: Westminster Press, 1976.

Henry, Carl F. H. *Frontiers in Modern Theology*. Chicago: Moody Press, 1968.

———. *God, Revelation, and Authority*, 4 vols. Waco: Word Books Publishers, 1976–1979.

"Heresies to Be Expected." n.p.: International Council on Biblical Inerrancy, June 1977. (Mimeographed.)

Hick, John, ed. *The Myth of God Incarnate*. Philadelphia: Westminster Press, 1977.

Hodge, Archibald A., and Benjamin B. Warfield. *Inspiration*. Grand Rapids: Baker Book House, 1979.

Hordern, William F. *The Case for a New Reformation Theology*. Philadelphia: Westminster Press, 1959.

———. *A Layman's Guide to Protestant Theology*. New York: Macmillan Co., 1975.

Houlden, J. Leslie. *Patterns of Faith*. Philadelphia: Fortress Press, 1977.

Hunter, A. M. *The Message of the New Testament*. Philadelphia: Westminster Press, 1944.

ICBI? n.p.: International Council on Biblical Inerrancy, n.d.

ICBI Update. n.p.: International Council on Biblical Inerrancy, Fall 1979.

ICBI Update. n.p.: International Council on Biblical Inerrancy, Winter 1980.

"Input Sheet Response." n.p.: International Council on Biblical Inerrancy, n.d. (Mimeographed.)

"The International Council on Biblical Inerrancy Statement of Purpose." n.p.: International Council on Biblical Inerrancy, n.d. (Mimeographed.)

Is the Bible Really the Word of God? New York: Watchtower Bible and Tract Society of New York, 1969.

Jeeves, Malcolm A. *Christianity and Psychology: The View Both Ways.* Downers Grove, IL: InterVarsity Press, 1976.

————. *Scientific Psychology and Christian Belief.* London: InterVarsity Press, 1967.

Jeremias, Joachim. *The Central Message of the New Testament.* New York: Charles Scribner's Sons, 1965.

Jewett, Paul K. *Man as Male and Female.* Grand Rapids: William B. Eerdmans Publishing Co., 1975.

Johnston, Robert King. *Evangelicals at an Impasse.* Atlanta: John Knox Press, 1979.

Kantzer, Kenneth S. "The Communication of Revelation." In *The Bible, the Living Word of Revelation*, edited by Merrill Tenney, 53–82. Grand Rapids: Zondervan Publishing House, 1976.

Käsemann, Ernst. "The Canon of the New Testament and the Unity of the Church." In *Essays on New Testament Themes*, translated by W. J. Montague, 95–107. London: SCM Press, 1964.

Kaufmann, Walter. *The Faith of a Heretic.* Garden City: Doubleday, 1963.

Kraft, Charles H. *Christianity in Culture: A Study in Dynamic Biblical Theologizing in Cross-Cultural Perspective.* Maryknoll: Orbis Books, 1979.

Kümmel, Werner Georg. *The Theology of the New Testament.* Translated by John E. Steely. New York: Abingdon Press, 1973.

Küng, Hans. *The Church.* Garden City: Doubleday, 1976.

————. *On Being a Christian.* Translated by Edward Quinn. New York: Pocket Books, 1978.

Ladd, George Eldon. *The New Testament and Criticism.* Grand Rapids: William B. Eerdmans Publishing Co., 1967.

————. *The Pattern of New Testament Truth.* Grand Rapids: William B. Eerdmans Publishing Co., 1968.

————. "The Saving Acts of God." In *Basic Christian Doctrines*, edited by Carl F. H. Henry, 7–13. Grand Rapids: Baker Book House, 1973.

————. *A Theology of the New Testament*. Grand Rapids: William B. Eerdmans Publishing Co., 1974.

Lawrence, Jerome, and Robert E. Lee. *Inherit the Wind*. New York: Bantam Books, 1976.

Levie, Jean. *The Word of God in Words of Men*. New York: P. J. Kenedy & Sons, 1961.

Lewis, Gordon R. *Decide for Yourself*. Downers Grove, IL: InterVarsity Press, 1973.

Lightner, Robert P. *Neoevangelicalism Today*. Schaumburg, IL: Regular Baptist Press, 1978.

Lincoln, Andrew T. "A Report on Attendance at Tyndale Fellowship Study Conference, Cambridge, July 3–8, 1978." (Mimeographed.)

Lindsell, Harold. *The Battle for the Bible*. Grand Rapids: Zondervan Publishing House, 1976.

Longenecker, Richard N. *Biblical Exegesis in the Apostolic Period*. Grand Rapids: William B. Eerdmans Publishing Co., 1974.

Machen, J. Gresham. *Christianity and Liberalism*. Grand Rapids: William B. Eerdmans Publishing Co., 1923.

————, ed. *The American Evangelicals, 1800–1900*. New York: Harper & Row, 1968.

Maier, Gerhard. *The End of the Historical-Critical Method*. St. Louis, MO: Concordia Publishing House, 1977.

Marrow, Stanley B. *The Words of Jesus in Our Gospels: A Catholic Response to Fundamentalism*. New York: Paulist Press. 1979.

Marsden, George M. *Fundamentalism and American Culture*. New York: Oxford University Press, 1980.

Marshall, I. Howard. *Biblical Inspiration*. Grand Rapids: William B. Eerdmans Publishing Company, 1982.

Marty, Martin E. *Righteous Empire: The Protestant Experience in America*. New York: Dial Press, 1970.

Mattill, A. J., Jr. "The Bible and the Battle of Faith." Auberry, CA: Cedar Springs Library, 1977.

Mbiti, John S. "Theological Impotence and the Universality of the Church." In *Mission Trends No. 3, Third World Theologies*, edited by Gerald H.

Anderson and Thomas F. Stransky, 6–18. New York: Paulist Press, 1976; Grand Rapids: William B. Eerdmans Publishing Co., 1976.

McGarry, Michael B. *Christology after Auschwitz*. New York: Paulist Press, 1977.

McLoughlin, William G. *Revivals, Awakenings, and Reform*. Chicago: University of Chicago Press, 1978.

Michaels, J. Ramsey. "Inerrancy or Verbal Inspiration? An Evangelical Dilemma." In *Inerrancy and Common Sense*, edited by Roger R. Nicole and J. Ramsey Michaels, 49–70. Grand Rapids: Baker Book House, 1980.

———. "Scripture, Tradition, and Biblical Interpretation." *Reformed Journal* (May–June 1970): 14–17.

Michaelson, Wes. "What Nurtures Us." *Sojourners*, May 1978, pp. 16–19.

Miller, Zane L. *Boss Cox's Cincinnati: Urban Politics in the Progressive Era*. New York: Oxford University Press, 1968.

Mollenkott, Virginia Ramey. *Women, Men, and the Bible*. New York: Abingdon Press, 1977.

Mollenkott, Virginia Ramey, and Letha Scanzoni. *Is the Homosexual My Neighbor?* New York: Harper & Row, 1978.

Montgomery, John Warwick, ed. *Demon Possession*. Minneapolis: Bethany Fellowship, 1976.

———. *Faith Founded on Fact*. New York: Thomas Nelson, 1978.

———. *History and Christianity*. Downers Grove, IL: InterVarsity Press, 1974.

———. *Principalities and Power: A New Look at the World of the Occult*, 2nd ed., Minneapolis: Bethany Fellowship, 1975.

———. *The Suicide of Christian Theology*. Minneapolis: Bethany Fellowship, 1975.

Mouw, Richard J. "Evangelicals in Search of Maturity." *Theology Today* (November 1978): 42–51.

———. "New Alignments: Hartford and the Future of Evangelicalism," In *Against the World for the World*, edited by Peter L. Berger and Richard John Neuhaus, 99–125. New York: Seabury, 1976.

Nash, Ronald H. *The New Evangelicalism*. Grand Rapids: Zondervan Publishing House, 1963.

———. *The Word of God and the Mind of Man: The Crisis of Revealed Truth in Contemporary Theology*. Grand Rapids: Zondervan Publishing House, 1982.

"New Group Combines Evangelism and Orthodoxy." *New York Times*, March 11, 1979, p. 25.

Newport, John P., and William Cannon. *Why Christians Fight over the Bible*. New York: Thomas Nelson, 1974

Nicholls, Bruce J. *Contextualization: A Theology of Gospel and Culture*. Downers Grove, IL: InterVarsity Press, 1979.

Ockenga, Harold John. "Resurgent Evangelical Leadership." In *A Christianity Today Reader*, edited by Frank E. Gaebelein, 133–39. New York: Meredith Press, 1966.

O'Laughlin, Michael. "Scripture and Tradition." *Again* 2 (July–September 1979): 14–15.

Packer, J. I. *Evangelism and the Sovereignty of God*. Downers Grove, IL: InterVarsity Press, 1973.

———. *'Fundamentalism' and the Word of God*. Grand Rapids: William B. Eerdmans Publishing Co., 1960.

———. "Hermeneutics and Biblical Authority." *Themelios* 1 (Autumn 1975): 3–12.

Padilla, Rene C. "The Contextualization of the Gospel." n.p., n.d. (Mimeographed.)

Pawlikowski, John T. *What Are They Saying about Christian-Jewish Relations?* New York: Paulist Press, 1980.

Payne, J. Barton. "Hermeneutics as a Cloak for the Denial of Scripture." *Evangelical Theological Society Bulletin* 3 (Fall 1960): 93–100.

Pickthall, Mohammed Marmaduke, trans. *The Meaning of the Glorious Koran*. New York: New American Library, n.d.

Pierce, Kenneth M. "Putting Darwin Back in the Dock." *Time*, March 16, 1981, p. 80.

Pinnock, Clark H. *Biblical Revelation: The Foundation of Christian Theology*. Chicago: Moody Press, 1976.

———. "Can We Dispense with Chalcedon?" n.p., 1980. (Mimeographed.)

———. *A Defense of Biblical Infallibility*. Nutley, NJ: Presbyterian & Reformed Publishing, 1975.

———. "Evangelicals and Inerrancy: The Recent Debate." *Theology Today* (November 1978): 65–69.

———. "Evangelical Theology: Conservative and Contemporary." *Christianity Today*, January 5, 1979, pp. 23–29.

———. "The Inerrancy Debate among the Evangelicals." n.p., n.d. (Mimeographed.)

———. "Inspiration and Authority: A Truce Proposal." [Theological Students Fellowship.] n.d. (Mimeographed.)

———. "Limited Inerrancy: A Critical Appraisal and Constructive Alternative." In *God's Inerrant Word*, edited by John Warwick Montgomery, 143–58. Minneapolis: Bethany Fellowship, 1974.

———. "The Ongoing Struggle over Biblical Inerrancy." *Journal of the American Scientific Affiliation* (June 1979): 69–73.

———. "Review of James Barr, *Fundamentalism*." *Agora* 12 (Fall 1978): 6–27.

Plato. *The Republic*. Translated by Desmond Lee. Baltimore: Penguin Books, 1974.

Preus, Robert D. "Biblical Hermeneutics and the Lutheran Church Today," In *Crisis in Lutheran Theology*, edited John Warwick Montgomery, 143–58. Grand Rapids: Baker Book House, 1967.

Punt, Neal. *Unconditional Good News*. Grand Rapids: William B. Eerdmans Publishing Co., 1980.

Quebedeaux Richard. *The Young Evangelicals*. New York: Harper & Row, 1974.

Radmacher, Earl, ed. *Can We Trust the Bible?* Wheaton, IL: Tyndale House Publishers, 1980.

Ramm, Bernard. *The Christian View of Science and Scripture*. Grand Rapids: William B. Eerdmans Publishing Co., 1974.

———. *The Pattern of Religious Authority*. Grand Rapids: William B. Eerdmans Publishing Co., 1965.

———. *Special Revelation and the Word of God*. Grand Rapids: William B. Eerdmans Publishing Co., 1968.

Rauschenbusch, Walter. *A Theology for the Social Gospel*. New York: Abingdon Press, 1945.

Reed, David. "Aspects of the Origins of Oneness Pentecostalism." In *Aspects of Pentecostal-Charismatic Origins*, edited by H. Vinson Synan, 143–68. Plainfield, NJ: Logos International, 1975.

"Reformation Study Center Statement [on the Meaning of Biblical Infallibility]." n.p.: International Council on Biblical Inerrancy, June 1977, n.p. (Mimeographed.)

Rice, John R. *Our Perfect Book the Bible*. Murfreesboro, TN: Sword of the Lord, 1958.

Ridderbos, Herman. *Paul: An Outline of His Theology.* Grand Rapids: William B. Eerdmans Publishing Co., 1974.

————. *Studies in Scripture and Its Authority.* Grand Rapids: William B. Eerdmans Publishing Co., 1978.

Roberts, Oral. *The Call.* New York: Avon Books, 1973.

Robinson, John A. T. *The Human Face of God* Philadelphia: Westminster Press, 1973.

Rogers, Jack [B.], ed. *Biblical Authority.* Waco: Word Books, 1977.

————. *Confessions of a Conservative Evangelical.* Philadelphia: Westminster Press, 1974.

Rogers, Jack B., and Donald McKim. *The Authority and Interpretation of the Bible.* New York: Harper & Row, 1979.

Russell, C. Allyn. *Voices of American Fundamentalism.* Philadelphia: Westminster Press, 1976.

Ryrie, Charles Caldwell. *What You Should Know about Inerrancy.* Chicago: Moody Press, 1981.

Sandeen, Ernest R. *The Roots of Fundamentalism.* Grand Rapids: Baker Book House, 1978.

Sanders, J. Oswald. *How Lost Are the Heathen?* Chicago: Moody Press, 1972.

Sargant, William. *The Mind Possessed.* Baltimore: Penguin Books, 1975.

Scanzoni, John. "Resurgent Fundamentalism: Marching Backward into the 80s?" *Christian Century*, September 10–18, 1980, pp. 847–49.

Schadewald, Robert J. "Equal Time for Flat-Earth Science." *Creation/ Evolution* (Winter 1981): 37–40.

Schaeffer, Francis A. *The God Who Is There.* Downers Grove, IL: Inter-Varsity Press, 1974.

————. *He Is There and He Is Not Silent.* Wheaton, IL: Tyndale House Publishers, 1973.

————. *No Final Conflict, the Bible without Error in All That It Affirms.* Downers Grove, IL: InterVarsity Press, 1977.

Schokel, Luis-Alonso. *The Inspired Word.* New York: Herder & Herder, 1965.

Scholer, David M. "The Authority and Character of Scripture, A Brief Statement of Position." n.p., 1978. (Mimeographed.)

————. "Cultural Relativity and Trans-cultural Normative Authority in the New Testament." n.p., 1979. (Mimeographed.)

————. "Women's Adornment—a Biblical Study." *Daughters of Sarah* 6 (January–February 1980): 3–6.

Scott, E. F. *The Varieties of New Testament Religion*. New York: Charles Scribner's Sons, 1946.

Scroggs, Robin. "Tradition, Freedom, and the Abyss." In *New Theology No. 8*, edited by Martin E. Marty and Dean G. Peerman, 84–103. New York: Macmillan Co., 1971.

Settle, Mary Lee. *The Scopes Trial*. New York: Franklin Watts, 1972.

Sheppard, Gerald T. "Biblical Hermeneutics: The Academic Language of Evangelical Identity." *Union Seminary Quarterly Review* (Winter 1977): 81–94.

Smith, Timothy L. *Revivalism and Social Reform: American Protestantism on the Eve of the Civil War*. New York: Harper & Row, 1965.

Stevens, George W. *Indonesia Revival: Focus on Timor*. Grand Rapids: Zondervan Publishing House, 1973.

Stevick, Daniel B. *Beyond Fundamentalism*. Richmond: John Knox Press, 1964.

Stone, Irving. *Clarence Darrow for the Defense*. New York: Bantam Books, 1961.

Stott, John R. W. *The Lausanne Covenant*. Minneapolis: World Wide Publications, 1975.

Stringfellow, William. "The Bible and Ideology." *Sojourners*, January 1977, pp. 92–93.

Tertullian. "Prescriptions against Heretics." In *Early Latin Theology*, edited by S. L. Greenslade, 21–64. Philadelphia: Westminster Press, 1956.

Tillich, Paul. *Christianity and the Encounter of the World Religions*. New York: Columbia University Press, 1964.

———. *Dynamics of Faith*. New York: Harper & Row, 1958.

———. *Theology of Culture*. New York: Oxford University Press, 1977.

Toon, Peter. *The Development of Doctrine in the Church*. Grand Rapids: William B. Eerdmans Publishing Co., 1979.

Torrey, R. A., and A. G. Dixon, eds. *The Fundamentals*. 4 vols. Grand Rapids: Baker Book House, 1980.

The Trial of C. A. Briggs before the General Assembly: A calm Review of the Case by a Stranger who attended all the sessions of the court. New York: Anson D. F. Randolph and Co., 1893.

Vawter, Bruce. *Biblical Interpretation*. Philadelphia: Westminster Press, 1972; London: Hutchinson, 1972.

Von Allmen, Daniel. "The Birth of Theology, Contextualization as the Dynamic Element in the Formation of New Testament Theology." *International Review of Missions* 44 (1975): 37–55.

Wallis, Jim. *Agenda for Biblical People*. New York: Harper & Row, 1976.

———. Peoples Christian Coalition, Chicago. Interviewed by Robert M. Price. November 1974.

———. "What Is Conversion?" *Sojourners*, May 1978, pp. 10–14.

Walvoord, John F. *The Blessed Hope and the Tribulation*. Grand Rapids: Zondervan Publishing House, 1979.

Warfield, Benjamin B. *Counterfeit Miracles*. London: Banner of Truth Trust, 1972.

———. *The Inspiration and Authority of the Bible*. Phillipsburg, NJ: Presbyterian and Reformed Publishing, 1979.

———. *Limited Inspiration*. Philadelphia: Presbyterian and Reformed Publishing, 1974.

Webber, Robert E. *Common Roots: A Call to Evangelical Maturity*. Grand Rapids: Zondervan Publishing House, 1979.

———. *Evangelicals on the Canterbury Trail: Why Evangelicals Are Attracted to the Liturgical Church*. Waco: Word Books, 1985.

———. "Historic Models of Social Responsibility." Paper delivered to the Evangelicals for Social Concern Workshop, September 1975. (Mimeographed.)

———. "On the Implications of the Incarnation: A Critique of Popular Evangelicalism." *New Oxford Review*, October 1979, pp. 6–10.

Webber, Robert E., and Donald G. Bloesch, eds. *The Orthodox Evangelicals*. New York: Thomas Nelson, 1978.

Wenger, John C. *Basic Issues in Nonconformity*. Scottdale, PA: Mennonite Publishing House, 1951.

Wierwille, Victor Paul. *Jesus Christ Is Not God*. New Knoxville, OH: American Christian Press, 1975.

Wilken, Robert L. *The Myth of Christian Beginnings*. Garden City, NY: Doubleday, 1972.

Willis, David S. *Origins and Change: Selected Readings from the Journal of the American Scientific Affiliation*. Elgin, IL: American Scientific Affiliation, 1978.

Wink, Walter. *The Bible in Human Transformation*. Philadelphia: Fortress Press, 1977.

Wolff, Richard. *The Final Destiny of the Heathen*. Lincoln, NE: Back to the Bible Publishers, 1961.

Wollenberg, Bruce. "The Evangelical Orthodox Church: A Preliminary Appraisal," paper presented to American Academy of Religion, Western

Regional Meeting, Berkeley, CA, March 27–29, 1980.

Woodbridge, Charles. *The New Evangelicalism*. Greenville, SC: Bob Jones University Press, 1970.

Woodward, Kenneth L. "Today's Oxford Movement." *Newsweek*, January 12, 1981, p. 80.

Wright, G. Ernest. *God Who Acts*. London: SCM Press, 1966.

Wright, G. Ernest, and Reginald H. Fuller, *The Book of the Acts of God*. Garden City, NY: Doubleday, 1960.

GENERAL INDEX

AUTHORS

SUBJECTS

SCRIPTURE INDEX